teach yourself®

**improve your
italian**

D0307682

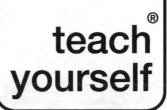

**improve your
italian**
sylvia lymbery

For over 60 years, more than
40 million people have learnt over
750 subjects the **teach yourself**
way, with impressive results.

be where you want to be
with **teach yourself**

For UK order enquiries: please contact Bookpoint Ltd, 130 Milton Park, Abingdon, Oxon OX14 4SB. Telephone: +44 (0) 1235 827720. Fax: +44 (0) 1235 400454. Lines are open 09.00–18.00, Monday to Saturday, with a 24-hour message answering service. Details about our titles and how to order are available at www.teachyourself.co.uk

For USA order enquiries: please contact McGraw-Hill Customer Services, PO Box 545, Blacklick, OH 43004-0545, USA. Telephone: 1-800-722-4726. Fax: 1-614-755-5645.

For Canada order enquiries: please contact McGraw-Hill Ryerson Ltd, 300 Water St, Whitby, Ontario L1N 9B6, Canada. Telephone: 905 430 5000. Fax: 905 430 5020.

Long renowned as the authoritative source for self-guided learning – with more than 40 million copies sold worldwide – the **teach yourself** series includes over 300 titles in the fields of languages, crafts, hobbies, business, computing and education.

British Library Cataloguing in Publication Data: a catalogue record for this title is available from the British Library.

Library of Congress Catalog Card Number: on file.

First published in UK 1999 by Hodder Arnold, 338 Euston Road, London, NW1 3BH.

First published in US 1999 by Contemporary Books, a Division of the McGraw-Hill Companies, 1 Prudential Plaza, 130 East Randolph Street, Chicago, IL 60601 USA.

This edition published 2004.

The **teach yourself** name is a registered trade mark of Hodder Headline Ltd.

Copyright © 1999, 2004 Sylvia Lymbery.

Typeset by Transet Limited, Coventry, Warwickshire.
Printed in Great Britain for Hodder Arnold, a division of Hodder Headline, 338 Euston Road, London NW1 3BH, by Cox & Wyman Ltd, Reading, Berkshire.

Hodder Headline's policy is to use papers that are natural, renewable and recyclable products and made from wood grown in sustainable forests. The logging and manufacturing processes are expected to conform to the environmental regulations of the country of origin.

Impression number   10 9 8 7 6 5 4 3 2
Year   2010 2009 2008 2007 2006 2005 2004

contents

acknowledgements

I should like to thank Marina Bastianello, Emanuela Beltrami, Gabriella Bertone, Cinzia Buono, Silvia Lena, Paolo and Piera Ravarino, Annalisa Romizi, Mario and Nicola Rotondale, Renata Savio, Carlo Sigliano, Felicità Torrielli, Angioletta Viviani, three members of the Gruppo Mio and three members of the Moncalieri Branch of the Club Alpino Italiano for so kindly finding time to be interviewed, thus giving me the basis for this book. At the time of the interviews, it was not my intention to use the material verbatim, but it soon became clear that to do so would produce a more lively and stimulating book. I am therefore also grateful to those I have quoted for allowing me to do so and to attribute their words to them by name. Some people also helped in other ways, notably Cinzia Buono and Angioletta Viviani who made further recordings for me. I was unable to use more than a fraction of the material gathered but it has all proved valuable. I should also like to thank Sandra Silipo for reading the text as it was being written, acting as language adviser and writing a number of exercises; and Antonio Ravarino for drawing the two maps. Thanks also to everyone else who has helped me.

In addition I am grateful to: *La Stampa* for permission to reproduce various articles; *Repubblica* for permission to reproduce articles from their website; Ermete Realacci, National President of Legambiente, for permission to reproduce his article in *Legambiente Notizie*, October 1996; Giulio Einaudi Editore for permission to reproduce extracts from *Le piccole virtù* by Natalia Ginzburg, Copyright © 1962 Giulio Einaudi editore s.p.a., Torino; Zanichelli Editore, Bologna, for permission to quote definitions from *lo Zingarelli 2004, Vocabolario della lingua italiana di Nicola Zingarelli*; Little Brown and Company, London and New York, for permission to quote a sentence from *Long Walk to Freedom* by Nelson Mandela; and Macmillan Children's Books for permission to reproduce *Jabberwocky* from Lewis Carroll's *Through the Looking-Glass: and what Alice found there* (London, 1948).

Without language, one cannot talk to people and understand them, one cannot share their hopes and aspirations, grasp their history, appreciate their poetry or savour their songs.

Nelson Mandela, *Long Walk to Freedom*
(Little, Brown and Company, 1994)

Symbols used

▶ Material on recording
ⓘ Information about Italy, the people and language

Improve Your Italian is for you if you have learned some Italian and would like to widen and improve your knowledge of the language. If you are already following a course aiming to do that, you will find it offers valuable supplementary material. Teachers also will find much that they can exploit in the classroom in post-beginners classes.

Learning a language is best done by contact with the language. And you can always understand more than you can say. *Improve Your Italian* gives you rich experience of spoken Italian through interviews with Italians talking about the sort of topics people discuss everywhere. There is plenty of help with understanding what they say and the interviews have been recorded so that you can listen to them as often as you wish. In this way, you become really familiar with them, almost learning them by heart. This can be done while you are doing other things: washing up, waiting for a bus, travelling, so that you are using your precious time twice over. Gradually you will find you too can say the sort of things our speakers say. All the time, Italian will get easier!

Of course you also need to develop your understanding of the way the language works. To help you, we look at various aspects of the structure of Italian; this is followed by practice in using the language.

The conversations are organized into units around a single theme. The intention is that you should work through the text as you would any book. We have tried to make the style friendly and accessible, as if we were talking to you. To make the sections manageable, since you may not have long periods of time to devote to your Italian, each unit is subdivided into sessions which we hope are small enough for a single sitting.

They vary in length as will your available time and the pace you work at. However, if you cannot manage to complete a 'session' in one go, don't worry. Go back to the beginning of that part when you next sit down to study and go through it again. Indeed you should consider going back over earlier units from time to time too. It will help you retain what you have learnt.

Improve Your Italian will give you other suggestions about the best way to go about learning a language. Different people learn in different ways and you need to try to find what works best for you. Language learning is not easy, for most people at least, so it is important not to be discouraged by the amount of time it seems to take. You will also probably find you have good patches and bad ones. Sometimes the language seems to flow, other days it just won't come. Don't worry! This is normal. But do try to persevere. And there is no doubt that regular sessions pay dividends. They need not be very long. Little and often is not a bad recipe. Three hours in six half-hour sessions during a week may well be more productive than one three-hour session. But you must do what fits in with your lifestyle.

At this point however we should like to stress just one thing: speaking a language is about saying what you want to say, about communication. You do not have to get it absolutely right to communicate. Mostly, your meaning will come over even if there are mistakes in what you say. Just think of all the non-native speakers of English you know who get by perfectly well speaking an English which you know is not what an English native speaker would use. So the most important rule of all is to try. Don't worry about making mistakes. If the listener understands, that is what matters. Many students of Italian report that when they try their Italian, native speakers are delighted. They are generally tolerant, patient and encouraging. So there's no need to worry! The worst you can do is make everyone laugh and that's no bad thing, anyway. Gradually, as you get more and more practice, you will get more and more right.

Good luck! **Buona fortuna! In bocca al lupo!**

Italy: the twenty regions and the regional capitals

01

i piaceri della vita

In this unit we shall
- talk about what we like doing and things we like or dislike
- remind ourselves about Italian verbs: the infinitive
- say what we have to do
- revise the use of subject personal pronouns
- say what we should like to do: the conditional
- think about learning strategies

SESSION 1

▶ Interview 1

We asked Angioletta Viviani, a teacher of English, to tell us what she enjoyed doing in her spare time; we also sought her advice on learning a foreign language (see Interview 2).

Read the interview which follows, listening to the recording at the same time if possible. If you need help understanding individual words, there is an Italian–English word list at the back of the book to help you. At the end of the passage, you will find comprehension questions which are designed to help you focus on the meaning of the passage.

Prof.ssa Angioletta Viviani is a high school teacher. She lives near Arezzo in a house with views over the Val di Chiana, a broad valley in southern Tuscany, between Arezzo and Siena.

Interviewer	Angioletta, che cosa ti piace fare nel tuo tempo libero?
Angioletta	Nel mio tempo libero? Eh, direi la cosa che mi piace forse più di tutte è leggere. E leggo tanto in maniera molto disordinata nel senso che leggo tante cose di vario genere ... e poi leggo molta narrativa contemporanea e se l'autore è un autore di lingua inglese lo devo leggere assolutamente in inglese. Mi rifiuto di comprare traduzioni e anzi devo dire che l'estate scorsa avevo comprato anche un romanzo in spagnolo, uno in francese perché volevo anche riprendere queste due lingue. E ... poi mi piace camminare e ... andare in giro, nei dintorni, mi piace.
Interviewer	In campagna?
Angioletta	In campagna, sì. Poi andare in bicicletta, sempre più o meno nella Val di Chiana. Poi mi piace cucinare ... Soprattutto mi piace cucinare pasta e dolci. Se devo scegliere ... La carne, non credo neanche di essere molto brava a cucinare la carne. Insomma non è una mia passione, infatti mi piace anche più mangiare i primi.
Interviewer	Sì?
Angioletta	Sì, sì, più della carne. E poi che mi piace fare? Eh, mi piace chiacchierare ... Non so se è un pregio o un difetto comunque insomma ... stare con amiche e parlare ... Mi piace andare al cinema e ...
Interviewer	Vai spesso?
Angioletta	Sì, andiamo con mio marito e con una coppia di amici

che anche loro amano andare al cinema ... più o meno l'inverno una volta alla settimana. Forse ogni dieci giorni, facendo la media. E poi mi piace andare in giro a visitare posti ... nuovi ... e pure rivedere vecchi posti dove sono stata. Mi piacerebbe conoscere di più la Toscana perché, sembra strano, ma ci sono ancora tanti piccoli paesi che non ho mai visto ... e specialmente, per esempio, non so, nella parte nord della Toscana, Garfagnana, Lunigiana ... Sono posti che non conosco.

Interviewer	Sei stata a Barga?
Angioletta	No.
Interviewer	E' molto pittoresca.
Angioletta	Infatti. E poi che mi piace anche fare? Ah, mi piace leggere i giornali anche, leggere quotidiani; m'interessa proprio la politica e voglio essere sempre aggiornata, sapere le notizie. La prima cosa che faccio la mattina è accendere la radio o la televisione perché credo di essere anche un po' fanatica, cioè .... non posso resistere se non so che cosa è successo.

facendo la media	*on average* (literally: *making an average*)
Garfagnana, Lunigiana	areas in north-west Tuscany. Lunigiana also covers part of eastern Liguria.
Barga	a small hill town in the Garfagnana, in the province of Lucca, well worth a visit.

Comprehension 1

These questions are designed to help you check you have understood the main points. Your answers should be in English.

1 What does Angioletta like doing most of all?
2 How does she organize her reading?
3 What sort of books in particular does she appear to enjoy?
4 What does she refuse to buy?
5 Why did she buy books in Spanish and French last summer?
6 Can you list two forms of physical exercise Angioletta says she enjoys?
7 Angioletta says she enjoys cooking, particularly preparing ... what?
8 What sort of food does she prefer eating and which does she enjoy less?
9 Angioletta is a very sociable person. How might you guess this from what she says?

10 What do she and her husband regularly enjoy, along with another couple, friends of theirs?
11 Angioletta lives in an area of Italy popular with tourists, Tuscany. She enjoys visiting places. What does she says she would like to do?
12 Finally, what does she need to start her day off properly?

Check your answers in the Key at the back of the book. This is important and you will also find the Key contains information to help you with possible difficulties.

SESSION 2

One of the aims of *Improve Your Italian* is to help you to a better understanding of the structure of Italian. Yes, the grammar. Some language learners go into a state approaching panic when they hear the word grammar but it is just another way of saying 'structure'. No language can work without structure; it would be just a jumble of sounds. To convey meaning, especially the subtleties human language is capable of, there has to be a structure. And when you study a foreign language, you need to develop an understanding of the structure so that you can make it work for you. If you are one of those who worry about grammar, your problem is probably that you are unfamiliar with the technical jargon used to talk about it. There is help for you at the back of the book in the section entitled **Grammar – the technical jargon explained.**

Saying you like doing something: *piacere* + infinitive
Angioletta said:

	leggere	reading
	camminare	walking
Mi piace	andare in giro	I like walking around the area
	andare in bicicletta	cycling
	cucinare	cooking

and so on. What was the question the interviewer asked her at the beginning?

Che cosa ti piace fare?   *What do you like doing?*

The interviewer was an old friend of Angioletta's and therefore used the familiar form **ti piace**. The question using the formal form is:

Che cosa Le piace fare?   *What do you like doing?*

You will probably use the formal phrase more than the familiar one at first. The verb is the same in both cases, however, it is the pronoun (the word for *you*) which changes. What is going on? It helps if you understand precisely how the structure works. **Piace** is part of the verb **piacere** which means *to please, to be pleasing*. So the structure for expressing the idea *I like reading* is not the same as when you say **mi piace leggere**. You are in fact saying: *reading is pleasing to me*. Here is the whole picture:

Mi		**leggere**	Reading		me
Ti		**andare in bicicletta**	Cycling		you (fam.)
Le		**cucinare**	Cooking		you (form.)
Gli	**piace**	**stare con le amiche**	Being with friends	is pleasing to	him
Le		**parlare con le amiche**	Talking to friends		her
Ci		**chiacchierare**	Chatting		us
Vi		**andare al cinema**	Going to the cinema		you (pl.)
Gli		**camminare**	Walking		them

Note that **Le piace** can mean *You* (formal) *like* or *She likes*. It usually becomes clear in context.

If you name the person who likes doing something you get:

A Giovanni piace cucinare. *John likes cooking.*
Ai nostri amici piace andare *Our friends like going to*
al cinema. *the cinema.*

If you have already named them:

A lui piace cucinare, a loro *He likes cooking, they like*
piace andare al cinema, ma a *going to the cinema, but*
me piace leggere in tranquillità. *I like reading in peace and quiet.*

Here you are using 'strong pronouns', which are needed after a preposition.

Activity 1

Say you like doing the following things. To help you we have put the Italian equivalents in a list, but not in the same order. So, using your previous knowledge, guesswork, elimination and, if necessary, a dictionary, pick the correct Italian verb from the list.

Example: reading   **Mi piace leggere.**

1. dancing   guardare la televisione

2. going to the theatre   parlare italiano
3. travelling   ballare
4. surfing the Net   guidare la mia nuova macchina
5. gardening   andare a teatro
6. watching television   andare in discoteca
7. listening to classical music   viaggiare
8. going to the disco   lavorare in giardino
9. driving my new car   ascoltare la musica classica
10. speaking Italian   navigare su Internet

Activity 2

Here are some things for you to say. Use the formal form **Lei** (**Le piace**) when speaking to the person you have just met and the familiar **tu** (**ti piace**) when speaking to your friend and her husband.

1 You are practising your Italian on a fellow-traveller in the aeroplane. How would you ask him: Do you like going to the cinema?
2 Ask him if he likes travelling by car.
3 You are having supper with an Italian friend. Ask her if she likes cooking.
4 Ask her what she likes cooking.
5 Ask her husband if he likes gardening.

Saying you like something

Have you checked your answers to Activities 1 and 2 in the Key at the back of the book? So far, we have looked at how you say you like *doing something*. You probably also know how to say you like *something*:

Mi piace la pizza.   *I like pizza.*
Mi piace il cinema.   *I like the cinema.*
Le piace il giardinaggio?   *Do you like gardening?*
Ti piace la carne?   *Do you like meat?*

Do you remember what happens when whatever is liked is plural? Think back to what **piace** actually means. You will realize, of course, it is singular, so that when what is liked is plural, you need to say:

Mi **piacciono** i libri di   *Antonio Tabucchi's books*
Antonio Tabucchi.   *are pleasing to me* or
       I like Tabucchi's books.

| Ti piacciono di più i primi o i dolci? | *Do you prefer pasta dishes or puddings?* |
| Le piacciono i film italiani? | *Do you* (formal) *like Italian films?* |

Saying you don't like something or doing something

Non mi piace la carne.	*I don't like meat.*
Non mi piacciono i gatti.	*I don't like cats.*
Non mi piace lavorare in giardino.	*I don't like gardening.*

There is another verb you can use to say what you like, perhaps with slightly more force. Angioletta uses it once, when talking about the friends they go to the cinema with. Can you find it?

| una coppia di amici che anche loro amano andare al cinema | *a couple, friends, who also like going to the cinema* |

Amare, *to love,* works as in English, i.e. as regards the structure of who likes what. **Amo la musica** = *I love music.* The difference in meaning between **mi piace** and **amo** is much the same as between *I like* and *I love.* And *to hate* is **odiare.**

SESSION 3

Verbs – infinitives

The infinitive is the part of the verb the dictionary gives you. The meaning will be given as *to read, to buy,* etc. But that is not always the most satisfactory translation. For instance, if you speak American English you probably say *I like to read*; if you speak British English you are likely to say *I like reading.* Either is fine, but remember that literal translations are not always right.

Activity 3

When Angioletta talked about what she likes doing, she used **mi piace** + the infinitive of the verb. Regular Italian verbs fall into three different types. Group 1 have an infinitive ending in **-are;** Group 2 have infinitives ending in **-ere** and Group 3 in **-ire.** Look back to what Angioletta said and list all the infinitives she used, putting the infinitives into their respective groups. Make a group for any irregular verbs you find. Look up any words you do not know.

Example: Group 2: **rivedere**

Check your answer in the Key.

Saying you must/have to do something:
dovere + infinitive

In Italian, the infinitive is used after **piacere**. It is also used after a number of other verbs. Angioletta uses a very common one, more than once. Can you pick it out?

devo leggere	*I must/have to read*
devo dire	*I must/have to say*
se devo scegliere	*if I must/have to choose*

Other verbs followed by the infinitive in this text include **volere** (**volevo riprendere** *I wanted to pick up ... again*) and others which, in addition, require **di** before the infinitive (**mi rifiuto di comprare** *I refuse to buy*; **non credo di essere molto brava a** *I don't think I am very good at*). Note that **potere**, not in the text, also works like **dovere** and **volere** (e.g. **Posso aiutare?** *Can I help?*). Indeed, they make up a most useful trio. For the moment we will not investigate this point further. Let's get back to the infinitive itself.

Group 2 verbs – stress in the infinitive

You need to be aware which group a verb falls into in order to know how it will behave, i.e. what its form will be in its various parts. One small point: in the second group, some verbs are stressed on the ending -**ere** (**rivedere**), others (more) on the preceding syllable: **leggere**, **riprendere**, **scegliere**, **accendere**, **resistere**. Learners sometimes wonder about this. The way the stress falls has no relation to the way the verb works. And the only way to find out where the stress falls is to consult a dictionary – or check with an Italian.

The infinitive for polite instructions

The infinitive is often used for instructions, for instance on doors:

spingere	*push*	tirare	*pull*

or other written instructions destined to be read by many people, e.g. cookery recipes:

Spuntare e tagliare a pezzetti le zucchine, lavarle, scolarle e gettarle in un tegame con cipolla tagliata sottilmente e olio.	*Cut the ends off the courgettes and cut them into small pieces, wash and drain them and put them into a frying pan with finely chopped onion and oil.*

LANGUAGE LEARNING TIP If you are unsure of a verb form, particularly for giving instructions, telling people to do something, use the infinitive. You may even find Italians do this to you with all verbs, thinking they are making themselves clearer – like the sort of pidgin some English speakers reserve for addressing non-English speakers. But you should gradually try to master the verb forms and this book will help you do so.

Subject personal pronouns – use

How often does Angioletta use the subject personal pronouns, **io**, **noi**, **loro** which are the ones we might expect when she is talking about herself, her husband and friends? Correct! She uses just one, once. Italians use subject personal pronouns for emphasis or contrast, that is when they are necessary to the meaning or add something. The rest of the time the verb alone is adequate. The ending is enough to indicate the subject in most contexts. Try to cut out inessential use of subject pronouns; this will give your Italian a more Italian flavour. Here is an activity which shows you the pronouns in action.

Reading

Read this extract from an essay by Natalia Ginzburg entitled 'Lui e io'. She is writing about her husband – and herself. At the end there are some activities for you.

Lui ama il teatro, la pittura, e la musica: soprattutto la musica. Io non capisco niente di musica, m'importa molto poco della pittura, e m'annoio a teatro. Amo e capisco una cosa sola al mondo, ed è la poesia.

Lui ama i musei, e io ci vado con sforzo, con uno spiacevole senso di dovere e fatica. Lui ama le biblioteche, e io le odio.

Lui ama i viaggi, le città straniere e sconosciute, i ristoranti. Io resterei sempre a casa, non mi muoverei mai.

Lo seguo, tuttavia, in molti viaggi. Lo seguo nei musei, nelle chiese, all'opera. Lo seguo anche ai concerti, e mi addormento.

Siccome conosce dei direttori d'orchestra, dei cantanti, gli piace andare, dopo lo spettacolo, a congratularsi con loro. Lo seguo per i lunghi corridoi, che portano ai camerini dei cantanti, lo ascolto parlare con persone vestite da cardinali e da re.

...

A lui piacciono le tagliatelle, l'abbacchio, le ciliege, il vino rosso. A me piace il minestrone, il pancotto, la frittata, gli erbaggi.

'Lui e io' (written in 1962) in Natalia Ginzburg,
Le piccole virtù, Einaudi 1962

senso di dovere	**dovere** can be used as a noun, *duty*.
pancotto	a simple soup containing bread
erbaggi	*vegetables, salads*

Activity 4

1 Pick out the subject pronouns in the passage above.

2 What do you notice about Natalia Ginzburg's use of **amare** and **piacere**?

3 Pretend to be her husband and say some of the things you like. You probably think your wife also likes all your activities but you know what she likes in the way of food. Say what she likes to eat. You don't like these things; say so.

See the **Reference Grammar** for a table of the personal pronouns.

Activity 5

You've been asked by an Italian acquaintance about your leisure time activities back home. Here is what you want to say. How might you say it in Italian?

1 The children love swimming.

2 We like walking in the country round about.

3 My husband likes cooking and each of us (**ognuno**) prepares part of the meal.

4 He prefers to cook meat.

5 I am good at puddings.

6 My husband likes reading. I prefer to play (**suonare**) the piano.

7 My daughter likes singing. She is very good.

8 We love visiting museums, going to the cinema and sometimes concerts.

9 We don't like television.

SESSION 4

Saying what you would like to do

Reread what Angioletta says and pick out how she says she'd like to know Tuscany better:

Mi piacerebbe conoscere di più la Toscana …	*I'd like to know Tuscany better…*

She is using the form of the verb which is the equivalent of the English *would like*. Literally, *knowing Tuscany more would be pleasing to me*. Elsewhere she says:

Direi la cosa che mi piace forse più di tutte è leggere.	*I would say the thing I like most of all is reading.*

This is the 'I', first person singular, form. The tense is the conditional. The use of **direi** is common in spoken Italian where in English one might say: *I think* … Natalia Ginzburg also uses the conditional in the extract above to say what she would do, implying if it were not for her husband.

Io **resterei** sempre a casa.	*I would always stay at home.*
Non mi **muoverei** mai.	*I wouldn't ever move (go out).*

You will find you often want to say what you would do if … The first and third persons singular are probably the forms you will use most often, with the endings **-ei** (1st person) and **-ebbe** (3rd person).

Most verbs add these ending to the infinitive minus the final **-e**.

direi	*I would say*
mi piacerebbe	*I would like*
non mi muoverei	*I wouldn't move*
finirei	*I would finish*
capirei	*I would understand*
partirei	*I would leave*
conoscerebbe	*He/she would know / be acquainted with*
deciderebbe	*He/she would decide*

Group 1 verbs change the **a** of the infinitive to **e**.

comprerei	*I would buy*
cucinerei	*I would cook*
parlerei	*I would speak*
rifiuterebbe	*he would refuse*
mangerebbe	*he would eat*

Irregular verbs often have a bigger change to the root. You almost certainly know:

vorrei *I'd like*

from **volere**. Others which also substitute double **rr** for **l** or **n** plus **r** are:

venire: verrei	*I would come*
rimanere: rimarrei	*I would stay, remain*

Other irregular verbs simply have a contracted form of the infinitive:

andare: andrei	*I would go*
avere: avrei	*I would have*
cadere: cadrei	*I would fall*
dovere: dovrei	*I would have to, I should, I ought to*
potere: potrei	*I would be able to, I could*
sapere: saprei	*I would know*
vedere: vedrei	*I would see*
vivere: vivrei	*I would live*

Essere is more irregular: **sarei** *I would be*

Note also:

fare: farei	*I would do/make*
dare: darei	*I would give*
stare: starei	*I would be/stay*

Activity 6

How would you say the following in Italian?

1 Your partner (**compagno/a**) likes going to the gym (**la palestra**) in the evenings. You would prefer to stay at home. You'd read, or watch TV, or perhaps listen to a little music.
2 Your partner would spend his/her holidays at home. He/she would go for walks in the surrounding area, play tennis and go to the cinema. You would prefer to go abroad. You like travelling. You would like to visit America. You would visit New York. You would see the Metropolitan Museum of Art, you would go to the Met and it would be interesting to visit the museum about immigration on Ellis Island. You are interested in Italian emigration to the USA.

Note: As well as **compagno/a** Italians also use the word **partner** (e.g. **il mio/la mia partner**).

SESSION 5

Getting your meaning across – communication

Language learning is about learning to communicate, to make yourself understood – and to understand the person speaking to you. Eventually, you will want to get things right, but when you are learning, it is more important to get the word out, even if incorrectly, than to be accurate. Accuracy will come gradually as you learn more. If in the heat of the moment, you use the infinitive of all verbs, or say *he reads* when you mean *I read*, because you are in a real-life situation, you will probably be understood. So don't worry too much about always getting it right. Try to learn the forms, but when you are trying to talk Italian, speak and forget about the mistakes. Think of all the foreign speakers of English you know who you understand even when they say things in a way which you never would and you know is not good English. They communicate – and that must be your primary aim.

Words – how to consolidate and extend your stock

To get your meaning over, what you need most of all is **words** (**vocabulary** is the technical word often used for a stock or list of words), lots of them, as many as you can muster. There are various aspects to this.

1 Learning the words you meet

This is one of the areas where you need to develop your own personal learning style. Were there any words you didn't know in what Angioletta said? What did you do about it? Assuming you looked them up, what did you then do? Many people find it helps to write new words down in a systematic way. Try dividing your page in half vertically and writing the Italian in one column and the English in the other. You can then cover up one half and test yourself on the other. Or you can make cards, initially perhaps one word per card, with Italian on one side and English on the other. You can also test yourself with these by putting the cards out on a table. And you can turn any card over when you can't remember the meaning. You can play a game: put a number of cards out, study them, and then cover them up and see how many you can remember. Try again a few days later and see if you have improved. And ... even if you write the words down and then don't look at them again – in a busy life, these things can happen – just the act of writing the word down will help fix some of them. And they will be there for you to use when you go over the passage again – another important language-learning tool.

Another ploy is to group words: you might for instance group words connected with reading. From Angioletta you might take: **leggere, narrativa contemporanea, romanzo, giornale, quotidiano, traduzione, autore.**

You might follow this with some research of your own into words which in your mind relate to reading e.g. *reader* **lettore, lettrice;** *bookshop* **libreria;** *library* **biblioteca;** and you can probably guess the meaning of **storia; biografia; autobiografia; poesia; lettera; scrivere; scrittore, scrittrice; novella** – careful: you have had the word for *novel* in the interview with Angioletta – **novella** means *short story*. **Storia** means *history* as well as *story*.

A basic understanding of memory may be helpful: memory fades. Resign yourself to the fact that you will probably forget some words and have to re-learn them. But you can increase your chances of remembering if you have a follow-up learning session soon after the original one, say next day. Forgetting will not have set in to any great extent and re-learning slows down the forgetting process. If for some reason you are unable to work at your Italian for a long period, you will probably be upset at how much you have forgotten. Most speakers of foreign languages, even those who have achieved quite a high degree of fluency, find that a gap without using the language sets them back. So if you can work regularly it will help. But if you do have a gap and forget, don't despair. It will come back to you when you start working at it again.

Memory can also be helped by working out associations. Link the word in your mind with an image, another word, a context, something that will help you remember it. Many learners will find that becoming familiar with the Italian presented in a book like this is a possible way to extend their vocabulary, learning the words in a context. There is no need to learn by heart, but, over time, re-read, listen again and again to the recording, and you will get to know the material. Later you will find you can use the words in another context.

2 Understanding words you don't know, which you meet when you can't look them up or ask anyone

You need to develop strategies for coping. In Activity 1, we suggested you use **guesswork** and **elimination.** Elimination won't work outside a limited context, like the list you had. Guesswork can however be refined:

a   Is the word like any other Italian word you know? For instance, perhaps you didn't know **dintorni.** But you do know **intorno** = *around*. Maybe, looking at the context: **mi piace camminare e andare in giro, nei dintorni ...** you can guess that **dintorni** means *surroundings, surrounding area*.

b Is the word like an English word you know? For instance, **tempo libero**. Possibly you haven't met **libero**. But you do know *liberate* meaning *set free*. And of course, **libero** goes with **tempo**. Could the pair mean *free time, leisure*?

c Sometimes you may be thrown back on just guessing from the context. **Chiacchierare** doesn't look like any English or Italian word, you probably agree. But its context is: **mi piace chiacchierare ... Non so se è un pregio o un difetto comunque insomma ... stare con amiche e parlare**. What do friends do when they get together? *Talk* (**parlare**), or another word for that? Yes, *chat* (**chiacchierare**). Nicely onomatopaeic. But be a bit careful. Guessing can lead you horribly astray!

3 Increasing your vocabulary (stock of words) generally

Words are best learned in a context. It is unlikely to be profitable to learn lists of words, although if they are linked around a topic, it may work for you. Most people find words in use easier to grasp. This really means making efforts to 'meet' as much Italian language as possible. See the last part of this unit.

Activity 7

We are assuming you don't know the words in bold type taken from what Angioletta said in Session 1. How might you work out what they mean without using a dictionary?

1 cose di vario **genere**
2 **Mi rifiuto** di comprare traduzioni
3 Non so se è un **pregio** o un **difetto**
4 una **coppia** di amici
5 visitare **posti** nuovi ... rivedere vecchi posti
6 voglio sempre essere **aggiornata**
7 non posso resistere se non so che cosa è **successo**

The spoken language

When we speak, the language we use is not the same as the written form. When we write, we have time to think and therefore we structure more carefully, correct, try to be concise, etc. In speech, we change direction in mid-sentence, we leave sentences unfinished and we include words that are not necessary, but which perhaps give us time to think or make it easier for the listener to follow. In English, you will be aware of the way some people use *sort of, I mean, anyway* and other expressions which when written down seem to be adding little to the meaning, but which we do not always even notice as we listen – or indeed when we use them ourselves. Angioletta uses some of the common equivalents in Italian, for instance:

direi, anzi, comunque, insomma, non so

Look back at how she uses these words.

Note also her use of **infatti**. It means *indeed, yes*. It is used to express agreement. The interviewer asked her whether she had been to Barga and she said she hadn't. When the interviewer followed up by saying how lovely Barga is, Angioletta felt that this provided support for what she had said about wanting to explore northern Tuscany which she doesn't know well. **Infatti** is very widely used in everyday Italian and it does not mean *in fact*. It is what is sometimes called a 'false friend', a word which sounds like an English word but which does not mean the same as the English word. You have met others in this unit, for instance: **libreria, novella**. We shall return to the question of 'false friends'.

SESSION 6

▶ Interview 2

Imparare una lingua alla maniera di Angioletta Viviani

Angioletta was asked whether she, as a language teacher, had any advice to offer a student learning a foreign language. Here is what she said. Her answer showed, perhaps more than the interview at the beginning of the unit, some of the characteristics of the spoken language.

Angioletta Mah, io potrei dire quello che dico di solito ai miei studenti, che s'impara a scuola, ma s'impara anche tanto volendo … cercare l'occasione, no? per imparare. E io dico sempre, per esempio, guardate gli ingredienti dei biscotti quando fate colazione la mattina, per la lingua che volete imparare, per esempio, e lì sicuramente imparerete magari una o due parole nuove. Cercate le occasioni anche … se sentite … Io mi ricordo quando andavo all'università, viaggiando in treno da Arezzo a Pisa, se sentivo qualcuno che parlava l'inglese mi sedevo di sicuro vicino e tentavo di attaccare discorso per fare un po' di pratica. E poi ascoltare cose registrate, cercare di parlare a sé stessi ad alta voce nella lingua che si vuole imparare; io dico anche pensare dentro di sé ma aspettate l'occasione. Se siete in autobus e vedete un signore strano, pensate come lo descrivereste nella lingua che state studiando, no? E poi, che altro? Ecco: cercate di trovare delle cose, dei sistemi di memorizzazione che voi sapete funzionano per voi. Poi … È certo che per l'inglese è tutto più facile, voglio dire … non che l'inglese sia facile ma le occasioni sono moltissime. Trovi canzoni, trovi riviste, molto di più che non probabilmente, non so, per l'italiano oppure altre lingue. Però dev'essere un atteggiamento mentale, quello di volere imparare e effettivamente se faccio delle interviste ai ragazzi più bravi, scopro sempre che fanno tutte queste cose, soprattutto che parlano ad alta voce, si raccontano le cose quando sono soli e questo, secondo me, serve tantissimo perché si diventa più sciolti, più sicuri. Io facevo così e vedo che funziona.

volendo	literally: *wanting to*. Frequently used to mean: *if you want to.*
gli ingredienti dei biscotti	Angioletta is thinking of packets of biscuits which show the ingredients in several languages since they are sold in several countries. An equivalent for English people might be reading the labels on sauce bottles. Note also: many Italians breakfast on biscuits!
se sentite …	A very obvious moment when Angioletta changes direction. She was clearly

	planning to say: *If you hear someone speaking the language ...*
descrivereste	*you* (plural) *would describe*. The **voi** form of the conditional.

Activity 8

Reread Angioletta's advice and look for unfinished sentences using expressions of the same type as the English: *you know*, *well*, etc. Make a list of them and check your answer in the Key.

Comprehension 2

Make a list of the various suggestions Angioletta makes to students to help them learn a foreign language.

Further language learning suggestions

We would endorse everything that Angioletta said and add:

Reading is also very valuable. It doesn't really matter what you read. If you can find newspapers or magazines, you may enjoy them. Following Italian politics is difficult for the uninitiated, but you can read about world events that you already know of. The *Cronaca* section which contains news of crime, accidents, etc. can be fascinating! Sometimes just going through the headlines concerning the latest natural disaster or world crisis provides plenty of new vocabulary. If there is a particular subject you are very keen on, try reading about it. Maybe you follow Italian football, for instance. You will find that your enthusiasm carries you along because you want so much to know.

Editions of Italian texts prepared by English-language publishers for students can be a good starting point for the more ambitious reader, since they often have notes and help with vocabulary. There are editions with parallel texts: the Italian on one page and on the facing page the translation. Natalia Ginzburg is a possible author to try since she writes in a style rather different to the flowery one once favoured by Italian writers. *Le voci della sera*, might be an enjoyable starting point although the humour is rather black. Or another essay in *Le piccole virtù*: 'Elogio e compianto dell'Inghilterra' perhaps. This was written when Natalia came to London where her husband had become Director of the Italian Cultural Institute. She was suffering from writer's block at the time and the cultural shock was so great that she wrote *Le voci della sera* in a very short time. But be warned, in the essay she is expressing her homesickness.

The Internet: Try the sites mentioned on page 208 – newspapers, evironmental groups, 'Slow Food' supporters ...

Music: It is true there is not much opportunity to hear Italian pop songs in the English-speaking world; if your taste lies in that direction, opera may offer you some practice – though the Italian may be a little old-fashioned.

Meeting Italians, hearing Italian: Seize every opportunity you can find for contact with the Italian language. In many towns an evening out at an Italian restaurant is a real possibility and if you are lucky some of the staff will speak Italian with you. Try Italian films, subtitled perhaps. When they are shown on television, record them so that you can watch at leisure, perhaps more than once, rewind to hear something again, etc. See if there is an Italian circle near you. Many towns have an organization where people interested in Italy and Italians living locally meet for talks and social events. If you live within a reasonable distance of a capital city or any other very important city, contact the Italian Cultural Institute for their programme.

Coraggio e ... buona fortuna!

Activity 9

Talking to yourself

Before you leave this unit, re-read the texts in which people say what they like. Then think out how you would tell an Italian about what you *like* and *don't like*, what you *would like*, etc. During the next few days, come back to your thoughts, refine them, add to them. Then pretend to be someone you know and think out what they might say. Give yourself as much practice as you can on likes and dislikes. There is no entry in the Key for this activity since everyone will have a different answer.

Remember Angioletta's advice about talking to yourself and try it! It really does help. Throughout the book we shall suggest topics and you will doubtless have your own. It is an excellent use of time which might otherwise be quite wasted: time spent in traffic jams, in the bath, doing boring chores, waiting for a visitor to arrive. Just try saying out loud what you are doing, a kind of running commentary, it is all good practice.

Eccomi qui in questo ingorgo. Davanti a me c'è una Cinquecento gialla. Non riesco neanche a vedere il semaforo. Sono qui da cinque minuti ...

Here I am in this traffic jam. In front of me there is a yellow Cinquecento. I can't even see the traffic lights. I've been here for five minutes ...

If you are working with a friend or family member, or if you are learning in a group or class, you can of course also have real discussions.

02 mi presento

In this unit we shall
- meet a number of different Italians
- examine how to talk about ourselves and others including descriptions of appearance and character
- review the present tense
- say how long we have been doing something
- revise vocabulary for talking about the family
- review the possessives: *my, your, his* etc.

SESSION 1

▶ Interview 1

Assuming you have the recording, listen to the interviews which follow. Try not to look at the text. If you do not have the recording, you will of course only be able to read the interviews.

First we meet three young people who belong to a group called **Il Gruppo Mio**. *(You will learn what this group does in another unit.)*

Antonella Allora, io sono Antonella, ho 25 anni, sono studentessa all'università e studio scienze dell'educazione.

Riccardo Io sono Riccardo, ho 31 anni e lavoro, faccio il rappresentante di farmaci e faccio parte del Gruppo Mio da parecchio tempo.

Monica Io mi chiamo Monica, ho 24 anni e mi sono laureata da poco in magistero delle scienze religiose, e ... sono insegnante di religione ... e niente. Sono nel Gruppo Mio dall'87.

Now a young man who manages a sports centre:

Mario Mi chiamo Mario Rotondale. Ho trent'anni, o quasi. Li compierò ad agosto di quest'anno, il 17 agosto. Sono nato a Torino.

And now someone else with the same surname as Mario:

Interviewer Si chiama?
Man Nicola.
Interviewer Nicola Rotondale?
Man Sì. Figlio di Mario Rotondale.
Interviewer Un altro Mario Rotondale?
Man Quello lì era mio padre.

And two women:

Silvia Mi chiamo Silvia Lena. Abito a Bologna da circa vent'anni, però ho studiato a Milano. Sono laureata in lingue e letterature straniere. Ho insegnato nella scuola media per parecchi anni.

Renata Sono Renata Savio. Sono neuropsichiatra infantile come preparazione, come prima specializzazione, anzi naturalmente sono medico, sono laureata in medicina, sono specializzata in neuropsichiatria infantile, sono anche specializzata in igiene e medicina preventiva.

io	The three speakers from the **Gruppo Mio** use the personal pronoun **io** as they start to introduce themselves. This is because they are aware of representing a group but each is introducing him/herself rather than the group. In English speakers in the same circumstances would stress the word 'I' with their voice. None of the three uses the pronoun with subsequent verbs. Notice that the other speakers, who are being interviewed alone, do not do this. (See Unit 1.)
niente	It usually means *nothing* but as used here by Monica it doesn't have much meaning at all. It is commonly used in this way in spoken Italian, when the speaker comes to the end of her/his thoughts. It would not be used in written Italian in this throwaway usage.
da parecchio tempo	for quite a long time
per parecchi anni	for several years

Comprehension 1

Read the questions, then listen to the speakers again and answer the questions.

1 What is the name of the person who

   a is still a student?
   b trained as a doctor?
   c passes himself off as older (by a few months) than he actually is?
   d sells pharmaceuticals?
   e taught in middle schools for some years?
   f lives in Bologna?
   g teaches religion?

2 Two of the people mentioned are father and son. Can you work out which is the father, which the son?

Check your answers in the Key. Don't forget that the Key often contains useful explanations as well as straight answers.

Activity 1

To encourage you to listen to how people say things as well as what they say, listen to the interviews again and try to pick out:

1 two ways of saying: *my name is ...*
2 two ways of saying: *I am a* + a job or profession.
3 how to say: *I have a degree in ...*
4 the usual way of saying *how old you are.*
5 how to say *I was born in* + place ...
6 how you say *you have been doing something for a certain amount of time*, with the implication you still are doing it.
7 how to say *you did something for a certain amount of time* but implying you no longer do it.

Check your answers in the Key.

SESSION 2

Saying how long you have done/been doing something

In Activity 1, question 6, the point is the way the speakers say this. What tense do they use? Compare the Italian and the English. Italian is simpler. You use the present tense of the verb and then **da** before the words saying how long.

Faccio parte del Gruppo Mio da parecchio tempo.	*I have been in the Gruppo Mio for some time.*
Abito a Bologna da circa vent'anni.	*I have lived in Bologna for about twenty years.*

Sometimes in English we would say: *I have been ...ing*

Faccio questo lavoro da solo un mese.	*I've only been doing this job for one month.*
Mia sorella abita a Roma da un anno e mezzo.	*My sister has been living in Rome for a year and a half.*
Studio l'italiano da due anni.	*I have been studying Italian for two years.*

You can also indicate the time when you started doing whatever it is:

Sono qui da giovedì.	*I've been here since Thursday.*
Cerca alloggio da Natale.	*He/She has been looking for a place to live since Christmas.*

In Activity 1, question 7 draws attention to what you say when you did something for a while but no longer do it.

Ho insegnato nella scuola media per parecchi anni.	*I taught in middle schools for several years.*

> **LANGUAGE LEARNING TIP** It is helpful when learning a foreign language to focus particularly on points where the foreign language and English differ. Get that sort of thing right and you sound good.

In English too the tense is different. *I taught* not *I have taught* or *I have been teaching*.

Verbs – the present tense

Some learners may be very much at home with the present tense, others not very aware of how it works. It is not nearly as complicated as it might seem at first glance because verbs in the three groups differ only in certain parts. In Unit 1 we looked for infinitives and put them into groups. If you need to, remind youself about them. Group 3 subdivides in the present tense with verbs of the type we have called 3b adding an extra syllable in some parts.

Question

What do you think the underlining in the text indicates? Study the table and try to decide before you look at the answer below.

Group 1	Group 2	Group 3a	Group 3b
amare	**conoscere**	**partire**	**capire**
amo	conosco	parto	capisco
ami	conosci	parti	capisci
ama	conosce	parte	capisce
amiamo	conosciamo	partiamo	capiamo
amate	conoscete	partite	capite
amano	conoscono	partono	capiscono

Answer

The underlining draws attention to parts of the verb where the ending is a characteristic one for that group, where the groups differ. However, look again. You must agree overall the differences are small. Each group has a characteristic vowel which we use to classify the infinitive: Group 1: **a**, Group 2: **e**, Group 3: **i**. This vowel appears in the infinitive and the second person plural for all Groups; for Group 1 also in the third person singular and plural and for Group 2 also in the third person singular. Note that the third person plural of Group 2 and Group 3 verbs has the same ending. The same applies to their third person singular. Of course the Group 3b type of verb has an extra syllable but you will be familiar with that from common verbs such as **capire, capisco** ...

A point to remember is that the ending indicates the subject. **Amo** = *I love*; **amiamo** = *we love*. The subject pronoun is usually omitted (see Unit 1). This means that in the long term, in order to speak Italian well, you need to learn to use the correct verb ending. But in the relatively early stages of speaking Italian, if you are not sure, just have a go. Gradually, as your confidence in communicating grows, you will find it easier and you can aim to become more correct.

Spelling and sound changes in the present tense

You may have learned that there are spelling changes in certain verbs. These are verbs where the letters c and g occur before the verb ending. Essentially, what happens is this:

a   Group 1 verbs do not have a sound change and therefore have a spelling change.
b   Group 2 verbs do the opposite: the sound changes so the spelling does not.

You have probably learned how Italian spelling reflects the sounds represented in English by the letters *k, g, ch, j,* and *sh*. We are sure you say: **ciao** (*ch*) and **chianti** (*k*) correctly. If you need to remind yourself, look at the section **The sounds of Italian**, at the back of the book.

Group 1 verbs

In the present tense, where the verb has the letters **c, sc, g,** before the ending, the spelling changes to reflect the fact that the sound stays the same in all persons of the present tense:

cercare	**cerco, cerchi, cerca, cerchiamo, cercate, cercano** (hard *k* sound throughout)
pagare	**pago, paghi, paga, paghiamo, pagate, pagano** (hard *g* sound throughout)
mangiare	**mangio, mangi, mangia, mangiamo, mangiate, mangiano** (soft *j* throughout and only one **i** where the ending starts with an **i**, i.e. -i, -iamo)
schiacciare	**schiaccio, schiacci, schiaccia, schiacciamo, schiacciate, schiacciano** (English sound *ch* throughout. There are not many verbs of this type.)
lasciare	**lascio, lasci, lascia, lasciamo, lasciate, lasciano** (soft *sh* throughout)

Just in case we have not made this clear, we will give a precise example using **cercare**: if we were to write **cerco, cerci** we would pronounce these [cherko, cherchi]. But that is not the correct sound, so the hard *k* in [cherki] needs to be indicated by the insertion of **h** after the **c**. (The square brackets indicate a use of letters to represent Italian pronunciation.)

Group 2 verbs
These do the opposite, i.e. the spelling does not change because the sound does.

vincere	**vinco, vinci, vince, vinciamo, vincete, vincono** (hard *k* in 1st person singular and 3rd person plural, soft *ch* in the others)
leggere	**leggo, leggi, legge, leggiamo, leggete, leggono** (hard *g* in 1st person singular and 3rd person plural, soft *j* in the others)
conoscere	**conosco, conosci, conosce, conosciamo, conoscete, conoscono** (hard *k* sound in 1st person singular and 3rd person plural, soft *sh* in the others)
scegliere	**scelgo, scegli, sceglie, scegliamo, scegliete, scelgono** (hard *g* sound in 1st person singular and 3rd person plural, the soft sound in the others – similar to *lli* in *million*)

LANGUAGE LEARNING TIP Generally, the learner should not worry too much about these details. You need a balance between getting your meaning across without too much hesitation and aiming for accuracy. Some people will find it easier than others to develop a sense of what sounds right. Most will probably find the best way of learning these points is to listen to Italians and say what they say. But others, depending on their learning style and the availability of Italians to listen to, will perhaps want to try to learn them by chanting verbs to themselves. What you are trying to do is to develop a 'feel' for what sounds right.

Activity 2

Here and now, say the verbs above out loud to yourself once at least. If you think it will help you, always do this when learning a verb.

SESSION 3

▶ Interview 2

We meet Gabriella and Piera who were asked to introduce themselves.

Gabriella Mi chiamo Gabriella Bertone. Sono nata il 6 dicembre 1940 a Torino. Ho vissuto, potrei dire, un'infanzia meravigliosa in una famiglia molto semplice ma sempre allegra, questo mi ricordo. Mia madre era inglese, mio papà italiano. Mamma non ha mai bene imparato l'italiano per cui la prendevamo sempre in giro. Sono la terza figlia. Ho una sorella e un fratello maggiore. I miei genitori si sono sposati in Inghilterra ma hanno vissuto in Francia perché mio papà lavorava in Francia, infatti lì è nato mio fratello. Poi quando è scoppiata la guerra, papà è rientrato in Italia, logicamente si è portato la famiglia dietro, la mamma ... e per mamma sono stati tempi brutti, tempi duri.

Piera Dunque sono Piera Ravarino. Sono alta un metro e sessantotto e peso 63 chili e mezzo. Sono biondissima, ho gli occhi castani. Ho due figli, uno di 25 anni, l'altro di 30, ed ho anche un nipotino di un anno ... che vedo pochissimo e per questo mi dispiace tanto. Si chiama Thibaut e abita in Francia, in Bretagna, e vorrei tanto averlo più vicino e partecipare di più alla vita di questo bambino.

per cui	*so, therefore* (literally: *on account of/for which*)
prendere in giro	*to tease*
quando è scoppiata la guerra	*when the war broke out.* The subject (**la guerra**) coming after the verb shows it to be the important element in the phrase. Note also: **lì è nato mio fratello**.

Comprehension 2

Listen more than once. As you listen, think about this: both are married women of about the same age and neither works.

1 What did you think they focussed on to define themselves?
2 Work out the family trees of Gabriella and Piera from what you hear.

Vocabulary for talking about the family

Both Gabriella and Piera talk about their families. Do you have the vocabulary you need to talk about your family? It is probably sensible to learn the words in pairs. If there is a word here you don't remember, look it up in the Glossary at the back of the book and write it down in your vocabulary notes.

> bisnonno/bisnonna
> nonno/nonna
> padre/madre – genitori (sing: genitore)
> marito/moglie
> fratello/sorella
> figlio/figlia
> cognato/cognata
> suocero/suocera
> genero/nuora
> cugino/cugina
> zio/zia
> nipote (m or f)

Note that **nipote** can mean either *nephew/niece* or *grandson/granddaughter*. Often in the latter case, the diminutive **nipotino/a** is used. The context usually makes the relationship clear. Sometimes however the speaker clarifies by saying: '**nipote di zio**' or '**nipote di nonno**'. The article (**il nipote/la nipote**) or the possessive (**mio/mia**) normally indicate the sex.

Note the following:

papà	*daddy*. Affectionate, informal, also usually used when addressing one's father, e.g.: **Papà, c'è qualcuno al telefono per te.** Not to be confused with **il Papa** *the Pope*. The correct stress is important. The capital letter is usual in **Papa**.
babbo	*daddy*. Mainly in Tuscany but note: **Babbo Natale** *Father Christmas*.
mamma	*mummy*. As with **papà**, used when addressing one's mother and talking about her affectionately or informally.

Expressing possession

Below is a table of the possessive adjectives, the words for *my*, *your* etc. You will certainly have met some or all of these. Now you need to check you understand their correct use, so that you can aim to get it right.

Masc. Sing. noun	Fem. Sing. noun	Masc. Pl. noun	Fem. Pl. noun
il mio lavoro	la mia famiglia	i miei amici	le mie amiche
il tuo lavoro	la tua famiglia	i tuoi amici	le tue amiche
il suo lavoro	la sua famiglia	i suoi amici	le sue amiche
il nostro lavoro	la nostra famiglia	i nostri amici	le nostre amiche
il vostro lavoro	la vostra famiglia	i vostri amici	le vostre amiche
il loro lavoro	la loro famiglia	i loro amici	le loro amiche

Ti piace il tuo lavoro?   *Do you like your work/job?*
Il nostro itinerario comprende   *Our itinerary includes*
    Siena e Orvieto.   *Siena and Orvieto.*

1 Don't forget that **suo, sua** etc. mean *his, her, your* (formal form). In other words you can't convey the gender of the possessor or owner as you can in English. This confuses Italians speaking English; listen to them. And you may remember the convention which uses the capital letter for the formal **Lei**, the possessives **Suo, Sua** etc. This helps reduce confusion in the written word.

Conosci Piero? Conosci anche   *Do you know Piero? Do*
    sua madre?   *you know his mother*
                          as well?

Conosci Anna? Conosci anche   *Do you know Anna? Do*
    sua madre?   *you know her mother*
                          as well?

Mi scusi, signor Rossi. Non   *Forgive me, Mr. Rossi.*
    conosco Sua madre, me la   *I don't know your mother,*
    presenta, per piacere?   *will you introduce her to*
                          me, please?

2 Note the need for the definite article as well as the possessive adjective. There is an exception. Look for it in what Gabriella says. She talks about: **mia madre, mio papà, mio fratello**. The exception is singular words expressing family relationship. They have the possessive without the definite article. Unless the noun is qualified (i.e. has an adjective describing it) or is a modified form (e.g. a diminutive etc.): **il mio giovane cugino, il mio fratellino, la mia mamma**. Note Gabriella makes (technically) a mistake by saying: **mio papà**. You would expect her to say: **il mio papà** as **papà** counts as a modified form. The way she says it is very common in the north. Similarly: **mia mamma, mio nonno** instead of **la mia mamma, il mio nonno**. In fact, you will meet either **il mio papà** or **mio papà**.

3 Loro always has the definite article: **il loro figlio.**

4 Un mio amico *a friend of mine*. **Questo mio amico** *this friend of mine*. After **questo, quello** and numerals, there is no definite article.

5 Il mio, il nostro, etc. are used as, in English, *mine, ours*, etc. that is to say, as the possessive pronoun.

'Piove e non ho un ombrello.'   *'It's raining and I don't have an umbrella.'*

'Prego, prendi il mio.'   *'Please take mine.'*

Abbiamo offerto un passaggio   *We offered Paolo and*
nella nostra macchina a Paolo e   *Marianna a lift in our car*
Marianna ma preferiscono   *but they prefer to come*
venire con la loro.   *in theirs.*

6 Note the following expressions:

i miei, i suoi, ecc.   are often used to mean *my family, his family,* etc.

la mamma   is very frequently used (i.e. without the possessive) to mean *my mother.* Similarly: **il papà, il babbo, il nonno, la nonna, lo zio, la zia.** For other family members, **mio cugino, mia sorella,** etc.

a casa mia, a casa tua ...   *at my house, at your house, at home ...*

dire la sua   *to have his/her say*
a ciascuno il suo   *to each his own*

Activity 3

Say in Italian:

1 My friends.   6 Their brothers.
2 Our family.   7 My friend.
3 His book.   8 His (female) friend
4 Her book.   9 Her (female) friend.
5 Their brother.   10 Our mother.

Activity 4

How would you say the following in Italian? If you don't know some of the words you need, try guessing, or even cheat and look at the Key. What is more important is that you should think out the various ways of expressing ideas such as saying what a person does, how old he/she is, how long they have been doing something etc.

1 My name is Jonathan. I am a teacher of foreign languages. I have been teaching for three years.
2 My sister's name is Olimpia. She is a doctor. She works in a hospital. She has worked in the hospital for 6 years.
3 George is 32 year old and works for a large company. They make accessories for the motor industry. George has worked for the company for 18 months.
4 My son is studying medicine. He is a student at the University of Southampton. He has been studying medicine for two years.
5 My brother is a psychiatrist. He works in Boston. He loves Boston. He was born in Cambridge, England, and now he lives in Cambridge, Massachusetts. He has lived in Cambridge for 8 years.
6 My wife is called Jane. She is a writer. Her mother is a famous actress. Her father is American. We have three children. Our eldest son is 8, our daughter is 6 and our second son is 4.
7 I've been learning Italian for nine months.
8 We understand Welsh. We lived in Wales for 24 years. (in Wales: **nel Galles**). Now we live in London.
9 I've spoken French for twenty years.
10 I often read an Italian magazine which is called *Panorama*.

SESSION 4

▶ Interview 3

In Session 3, Interview 2 Piera was asked to describe herself. Reread what she said. How did she describe herself? She didn't find it easy and gave very basic information: **Sono alta un metro e sessantotto e peso 63 chili e mezzo. Sono biondissima, ho gli occhi castani.** Note that Piera says: **Sono alta 1m. 68.** *I am 1m.68 tall.* Spot the difference with English and imitate it!

Now listen to her husband.

Paolo   Allora, io mi chiamo Gianpaolo Ravarino. Sono nato a Torino nel gennaio del '45, appena finita la guerra. Sono una persona … mi ritengo normalissimo, alto di statura, longilineo, abbastanza longilineo, sono ingegnere. Ho avuto problemi nella vita che tutti hanno avuto, mi ritengo proprio perfettamente normale. Non sono un bell'uomo, sono una persona normale, come l'ho detto. Non ho niente di particolarmente sgraziato ma penso di non aver niente neanche di particolarmente aggraziato. Per quello che riguarda la testa, la testa è di una persona normale. Le capacità rientrano nell'ordinaria media delle persone. Non sono né deficiente né troppo intelligente. Forse sono un po' bonaccione ...

bonaccione	easy-going, good-natured

Comprehension 3

1 What do you learn about Paolo's physical appearance?
2 About his character?
3 What do you think he means when he uses the word **testa**?

Activity 5

Describing yourself – and other people – is not easy. And it is not something you often need to do. At most, you sometimes need to give a few obvious characteristics so that someone can recognize you or a friend at the airport, for instance. So on paper pull together what you know how to say. Do you remember the names of the parts of the body, or other words relating to physique? Then look at the Key and compare your list with ours.

LANGUAGE LEARNING TIP This last activity probably sent you to your dictionary. As your knowledge increases, you should consider buying an Italian–Italian dictionary. It won't help when you do not know the Italian expression for an idea you want to put in words, of course. But if you use it when reading and working on texts you will find it will be a valuable tool. Thinking constantly from Italian to English and back again isn't always helpful. Nor are there always precise word-for-word equivalents between the two languages. And it can be instructive to see how the meaning is defined for Italians. In the Key for Activity 5 for instance, the differences between **snello** and **svelto** or **tarchiato** and **tozzo**, which are perhaps slight and subtle, become a little clearer. An Italian–Italian dictionary – a good one, fairly bulky, not a pocket one – will give you examples of how the word is used, what contexts it can be used in. And simply keeping your mind working in Italian helps. How much you enjoy the dictionary activity will depend upon how much you enjoy words, i.e. it's a question of taste.

For all the definitions in *Improve Your Italian*, we have used *Lo Zingarelli 2004, Vocabolario della lingua italiana di Nicola Zingarelli*, published by Zanichelli, Bologna, with their very kind permission. It is a hefty tome, and the publishers update it annually. It is also available on CD-ROM.

Activity 6

You are flying to Milan next week to meet an Italian business associate. His secretary is coming to meet you at the airport. Send him an email describing your appearance. Include height, hair colour etc. It need not be more than two or three sentences.

Activity 7

Practise your descriptive skills by thinking through a brief physical description of two or three people: relations, friends, colleagues, to help anyone needing to identify them.

SESSION 5

▶ Interview 4

It is sometimes easier to sum up character, especially in other people. Listen to Gabriella describing her two grown-up daughters. Gianni, whom she mentions, is her husband.

Gabriella Ho avuto due figlie, Silvia e Barbara, molto vicine, infatti hanno solo due anni di differenza. Silvia assomiglia molto a Gianni, Barbara a mia mamma. E' rossa di capelli e ha un carattere, diciamo, più inglese che italiano. Molto allegra. Silvia è molto posata, molto seria, molto ligia al dovere, quello che deve fare, lo fa. Mentre la Barbara, no. E' più allegra, più spensierata, senza testa, molto disubbidiente. Adesso, Silvia è sposata, aspetta un bambino; mentre Barbara è andata a vivere per conto suo, ed è molto felice e contenta. Io ne ho fatto una grande malattia quando Barbara è andata via però adesso devo riconoscere che ha fatto bene. Sì, sì, ha fatto bene a lei e ha fatto bene a me. Il nostro rapporto è decisamente cambiato e lei è molto più vicina a noi adesso che è lontana e direi quasi che senz'altro capisce più tante cose lei che non Silvia. Alla quale abbiamo sempre attribuito doti insomma ...

la Barbara	In Tuscany and northern Italy, it is common to use the definite article before a female first name. It is also sometimes used before male first names.

Activity 8

Lots of useful words there for talking about people. Make a list. Where the word could have an opposite, do you know it? Compare your result with the one in the Key.

Activity 9

Think of some family members and work out character descriptions of. How would you describe your own character?

Reading

UN MANAGER SENZA COMPROMESSI

'Romiti ha una personalità e una professionalità sfaccettate e fuori dal comune ... L'elemento unificante della sua azione appare essere la sua fortissima volontà di vincere le battaglie che decide di affrontare e anche il vizio di volerle addirittura stravincere ... Non pare interessato, lui romano, all'arte tutta romana del compromesso e non si preoccupa troppo di piacere all'opinione pubblica.' (Mario Deaglio, in un articolo 'Un manager senza compromessi')

'Nei rapporti personali mi è parso meno feroce dell'immagine che se ne dà. Della sua durezza ho apprezzato l'esplicitezza, la chiarezza, la sincerità.' (Gianni Vattimo, filosofo)

'Un uomo pragmatico, concreto, dotato di una grande volontà. Una persona che non ha mai promesso a vanvera, che ha sempre realizzato.' (Enzo Ghigo, presidente della regione Piemonte)

'Ho un ricordo bellissimo. Appena arrivata nel '90 non avevo i soldi per pagare gli stipendi. Era il 250° anniversario del Teatro. Chiesi una sponsorizzazione alla Fiat. Romiti mi chiamò subito e mi disse che aveva firmato l'assegno di un miliardo. Era sensibile alla musica, ma anche al fatto che gli stipendi a chi lavora vanno pagati.' (Elda Tessore, ex-sovrintendente del Teatro Regio di Torino.)

'Lo descrivono come un burbero o un rude. Ma a tavola da noi con gli amici è sempre stato molto simpatico, aperto, semplice, colloquiale.' (Vittorio Urbani, titolare del ristorante preferito di Romiti)
(*La Stampa*, 22 giugno 1998)

In June 1998, Cesare Romiti left Fiat after nearly 25 years as Managing Director (**Amministratore Delegato**) and then, briefly, Chairman (**Presidente**). Such is the importance of Fiat in Italy that the event was given wide media coverage. Romiti had guided Fiat successfully through the effects of the oil crisis of the early 70s, the years of terrorism and a period of intense worker unrest. He used tough methods, notably with the trades unions, and won. He has a reputation for plain speaking and for determination to win battles. Although aged 75, he was leaving to take up an apppointment as Chairman of the publishing group *Rcs-Corriere della Sera*. Above, from *La Stampa*, are extracts from various people's descriptions of Romiti. It should be added *La Stampa* is published in Turin, Fiat is also based there, indeed Fiat stands for *Fabbrica Italiana Automobili Torino*. It is also the Latin for 'Let it be done/made'. Fiat also owns *La Stampa!*

sfaccettato	*multifaceted.* **Sfaccettato** is *faceted* – as a jewel is. It also has an idea of being cutting.
a vanvera	*to no effect,* i.e. Romiti never made promises he did not intend to keep.
realizzare	*to make real, to implement* (not: *realize* in the everyday English sense. Another false friend)
burbero	*gruff, grumpy, crusty*
rude	the English–Italian dictionary says *coarse*. The Italian dictionary explains that it is used to describe someone who is frank and determined, but not **grossolano** (*coarse*)! Note the value of an Italian monolingual dictionary!

Comprehension 4

1 What does Mario Deaglio consider the unifying element in the way Romiti behaves?
2 Romiti is from Rome. What Roman characteristic does he NOT possess? What is his attitude to public opinion?
3 How did Gianni Vattimo find Romiti in personal relationships?
4 From what Enzo Ghigo says, pick out the words which are the opposite of (a) **astratto**, (b) **teorico**.
5 What is the story which Elda Tessore, formerly in charge of the Turin Opera House (**Teatro Regio**) tells?
6 Vittorio Urbani whose restaurant Romiti patronized describes him as (a) **simpatico**, (b) **aperto**. What might be the opposites of these two words?

▶ Interview 5

*And finally, one more person introducing herself and clarifying
… well, what does she clarify? She is Emanuela and is married
to an American called John. They live in an apartment. It is
usual at the entrance to an apartment block to have a bell for
each apartment and usually there is space for two names beside
each bell.*

Emanuela Io mi chiamo Emanuela Beltrami e Beltrami è il mio
cognome da nubile perché in Italia anche sposandosi,
non si cambia cognome, si mantiene il cognome della
famiglia. Questo vale per il lavoro, vale per la sanità, vale
per tutto. Mentre è una cosa che ha lasciato un po'
sorpresa la famiglia di John. Credevano non fossimo
sposati quando hanno visto sopra il campanello della
porta due cognomi diversi. Fa ridere quella cosa!

Comprehension 5

1 What does Emanuela clarify?
2 What did John's family suspect when they saw the names
over the bell at the entrance to the building where John and
Emanuela live?

Activity 10

Talking to yourself

You remember we said that it has been shown that people who
are good at learning a foreign language tend to talk to
themselves in the foreign language they are learning. It really is
good practice. Here are some possible topics.

1 Stereotipi nazionali: Gabriella considera che sua figlia
Barbara, che è 'allegra, spensierata, senza testa, molto
disubbidiente,' ha un carattere più inglese che italiano. Invece la
figlia Silvia, che è 'molto posata, molto seria, molto ligia al
dovere,' è più italiana. Cosa ne pensa Lei? Come vede Lei il
carattere italiano, quello inglese, americano, ecc? Esiste il
fenomeno di un carattere nazionale?

2 L'età pensionabile: al momento dell'articolo, Cesare Romiti,
all'età di 75 anni, stava per cominciare un nuovo lavoro, come
presidente di un importante gruppo editoriale. Secondo Lei, era
troppo vecchio? In Italia, molte persone vanno in pensione il più
presto possibile, qualche volta a 55 anni. Invece, altri,
soprattutto in politica e nel mondo della finanza e degli affari,

continuano ben oltre i 70 anni. Che cosa ne pensa? Ci dovrebbe essere un'età oltre la quale non è permesso continuare a lavorare? Quando, secondo Lei, si è troppo vecchi per lavorare? Lei ha progetti per la pensione? Come vede la prospettiva degli anni della pensione?

3 In inglese esiste un detto: la vita comincia a 40 anni. Quali sono secondo Lei gli anni più belli della vita?

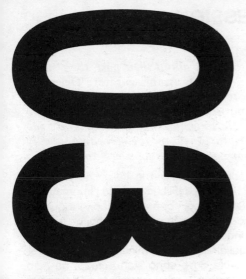

03

la mia storia

In this unit we shall
- look at the Italian education system
- look at aspects of spoken Italian
- review ways of talking about past events
- do more guessing at meanings

SESSION 1

▶ Interview 1

We asked various people to tell us about their past, their story. First Marina Bastianello. Marina is **Amministratore Delegato,** *Managing Director, of Ristoranti Brek, a chain of self-service restaurants, and she has an office in Milan. She first knew the interviewer many years ago in England, in the school where she was a student. Listen to the interview on the recording, ideally without the text. If necessary go through it several times.*

Marina Come sai, ho studiato, dapprima in Italia fino ai sedici anni, poi gli ultimi due anni del liceo ho fatto l'International Baccalaureate a Oxford, poi sono stata a Londra quattro anni, prima facendo la laurea in economia, poi un master, tutti e due alla London School of Economics, e poi sono tornata in Italia e qui a Milano ho cominciato a lavorare per una società finanziaria dove sono stata, credo, un paio d'anni. Dopo sono andata … mi sono trovata ad essere un po' forse impreparata al mercato italiano. Ero stata via parecchi anni, quindi mi trovavo un po' a disagio al mio ritorno. Quindi sono andata a fare un MBA, un Masters in Business Administration, alla Bocconi qua a Milano. E questo mi ha un po', diciamo, introdotto al mondo degli affari italiano. E quando sono uscita dalla Bocconi sono andata in una società della Fiat, una grossa impresa di costruzione, ho lavorato nella pianificazione strategica, anche lì per un anno e mezzo, due anni, e alla fine di questo iter sono arrivata in Brek, che è una società di ristorazione, quindi non c'entra assolutamente niente con quello che avevo fatto prima, però fa parte del gruppo di famiglia, è una società abbastanza piccola in un settore che mi diverte abbastanza perché mi piace mangiare, mi piace la cucina quindi la ristorazione è un settore, diciamo, più divertente dell'edilizia e quindi dall'89 circa lavoro qui.

un paio d'anni	*a couple of years* (literally: *a pair*)
a disagio	*uncomfortable, not at home* (opposite: **a mio/ tuo/suo** ecc. **agio**)
la Bocconi	**l'università Bocconi, Milano** – Founded by Ferdinando Bocconi, it is one of a small number of private

	universities in Italy; it specializes in economics, business administration, finance etc.
impresa	*enterprise, undertaking, business* (cf. **imprenditore** *entrepreneur*)
pianificazione	*planning* (**piano** *plan*. Don't forget your guessing strategies).
iter	the Latin word for *a journey*. Normally used for journeys through procedure, e.g. **un iter legislativo, un iter burocratico.**
non c'entra niente con	*it's nothing to do with*
fa parte del gruppo di famiglia	Marina's family own a group which also includes the **PAM** supermarkets.

▶ Interview 2

And now Mario Rotondale who runs **un circolo sportivo,** *a small leisure centre or club with tennis courts, a pitch for* **calcetto,** *five-a-side soccer, a gym* **una palestra** *and of course a bar for an after-match drink, with a terrace where you can also sit and watch others playing tennis.*

Mario   Ho fatto le scuole elementari e le medie inferiori a Poirino, in provincia di Torino. E poi sono passato a fare le scuole medie superiori a Chieri. Ho fatto ragioneria, dopodiché mi sono accorto di essere un pessimo ragioniere, di non ... che molto probabilmente non avrei mai potuto lavorare in una banca e allora ho proseguito facendo l'ISEF, l'Istituto Superiore di Educazione Fisica, qui a Torino. E' un corso di tre anni, è un diploma di grado universitario, non è riconosciuto – unico paese in Europa – come laurea.

Interviewer In che cosa consiste il corso?

Mario 28 esami più una tesi.

Interviewer Quanti di questi esami erano pratici?

Mario Contrariamente a quello che uno può pensare, una gran parte erano teorici. Spaziavano dalla medicina generale, la medicina dello sport, all'anatomia, alla fisiologia, alla endocrinologia, a tutte queste materie che … E una volta diplomato, ho – siccome qui in Italia non c'è possibilità alcuna di insegnare nella scuola, perché lo sbocco professionale principale è quello di insegnare nella scuola, nella scuola, di ogni ordine e grado …

Interviewer Perché non c'è possibilità?

Mario Non c'è possibilità perché c'è una situazione di cattedre sature da tanti anni, in poche parole non assumono e non fanno più concorsi e quindi mi sono lanciato nella … nelle attività private. Ho cominciato a lavorare in vari centri sportivi e poi mi si è presentata una … la possibilità di gestire questo centro. Mi sono, come si dice in italiano, mi sono tuffato, in gergo sportivo, e questo è successo nel novembre del '94 quando è iniziata questa gestione. Sotto questa gestione avevamo soltanto campi da tennis, e poi abbiamo aperto questa palestra. Abbiamo cominciato, o meglio ripreso, a fare attività giovanile, quindi sia per il tennis che per altre cose. E adesso il futuro è questa piscina, quest'ampliamento con nuove, con probabilmente anche nuove palestre con possibilità di fare un discorso completo anche per quanto riguarda la palestra.

concorsi	*competitive examinations* (see **i** section)
il futuro è questa piscina	at the time of the interview construction had just begun on a swimming pool for the club.
un discorso completo	Mario means *'have a full range of equipment, cover all needs'*: the original gym was small and therefore had limitations. **Discorso** usually means *speech, discourse*. Note: **cambiare discorso** to *change the subject, talk about something else.*

Comprehension 1 and 2

1 Marina's schooling was untypical. In what ways?
2 What was her reason for doing an MBA?
3 What link is there between the three areas of business she has worked in?
4 Why does she feel her present company is more fun that the construction company she worked for?
5 What made Mario decide to go to ISEF?
6 He appears to feel a little 'cheated' in respect of the status of his qualification. Why?
7 Why did he not take a job in a school?
8 How long has he been in his present job?
9 He mentions expansion of the facilities of the club. What sort of facilities will it have in the future?

SESSION 2

i La scuola italiana

Scuola materna (non obbligatoria) 3 anni
⇓
Scuola elementare (dell'obbligo) 5 anni (si entra a 6 anni)
⇓
Scuola media inferiore (dell'obbligo) 3 anni
⇓
Scuola media superiore
⇓
Università
Istituti superiori statali (p.es. ISEF)
Accademia Militare
Accademia di Belle Arti

(La scuola) dell'obbligo	compulsory schooling
Scuola media superiore	high school. There is a variety of types, both academic (**liceo classico, liceo scientifico, liceo linguistico** etc.) and vocational (**istituto tecnico, istituto professionale,** etc.). Whether the student attends an academic **liceo** or a vocational **istituto**, his/her course of studies will be broad.

The above schema was true of the Italian education system over a long period. For some time there has been talk of the need for change – which is slow to come. The **maturità**, the final school-leaving examination which also serves as a qualification for university entry and which had been 'temporary' for some thirty years, was reformed with effect from the 1999 parliamentary session. Also in 1999 the school-leaving age was raised from 14 to 15, making the length of compulsory schooling nine years.

Parliament approved a radical reform of the whole education system in 2001 but the part which affected the school system was never implemented. A new government, elected in May 2001, set it aside and proposed its own changes which became law in March 2003. They involve some new names and new programmes but the structure is not so very far fromthe schema given above:

Scuola dell'infanzia
(non obbligatoria) 3 anni, inizia dai 2½ anni
⇓
Scuola primaria (5 anni)
⇓
Scuola secondaria di 1° grado (dura 3 anni)
⇓
Liceo (dura 5 anni) o **Istruzione professionale**

The intention is tht there should be much greater flexibility at secondary level. The **Liceo** will as now be an academic high school/ **istruzione professionale** will take place partly in specialist schools as at present but students will be able to move between the workplace and school and one type of school and another. The reform involves much more than the structure of the system, and includes curricula, career counselling etc. For most families, important changes are that schooling can now start during the child's sixth year rather than in the year after the child's sixth birthday. A first foreign language is also now taught right from the first year of school. At the time of writing, however, much of this reform has yet to be implemented and the stated intention is to do so gradually.

Mario went to an **istituto commerciale** (i.e. one of the **istituti professionali** named in the first schema). There he learned the financial side of business and became a **ragioniere**. Other people you meet in this book who trained as **ragionieri** are Carlo and Emanuela.

Explaining the ISEF course, Mario said it consisted of **28 esami più una tesi**. Most university courses are not selective and a student with a **maturità** can enrol in the course of his choice. To get a degree the student has to take a number of modules and pass the end-of-course exam. The numbers of modules vary from course to course. Students also prepare a thesis. They usually start degree courses at the age of 19 and study for a minimum of four years. The drop-out rate is high. In recent years shorter courses (**laurea breve**) have been introduced. Holders of full degrees in Italy are called **dottore**. As Mario says, however, his course, although equivalent to a degree course, did not confer a degree.

Mario refers to **cattedre sature** and **concorsi**. New teachers are recruited centrally at national level by competitive exam (**concorso**) to a **cattedra**, a permanent post in the school system. At the time Mario graduated, no new recruits were being taken on since falling pupil numbers meant there were too many teachers. Access to many jobs in the public sector is by competitive examination.

Spoken language, written language

Note how Marina says: **poi … poi … poi …** She is talking off the cuff. Were she to write her life story she would avoid the repetition of **poi** (*then, next*) which in writing would be considered poor style. Other spoken language usages in what she says are: **quindi** (*so, then*), **diciamo** (*shall we say? let's say*), and the tendency to very long sentences of parallel clauses. Note the voice doesn't fall as it would if the speaker were intending to end the sentence. In writing, Marina would go for a more varied and perhaps more complex sentence structure.

Mario too was talking off the cuff. Note how his sentences change direction, as often happens in speech. As we think out what we are saying, our thoughts just one jump ahead of our words, we realize things would be clearer, more effective if we restructured. As we listen to a speaker do this, we are scarcely aware of it. The same applies to Marina's repetitive clauses. The listener's mind follows the speaker's thought processes and focuses on the content rather than the structure of his/her sentences. It is only when the words are transcribed for us to read that we notice it.

SESSION 3

Talking about the events in our lives: 'il passato prossimo', the perfect tense

Activity 1

One of our aims in this unit is to talk about our life story. Both Marina and Mario were asked to talk about how they came to be in their current jobs. When you do this, you tend to spell out the stages of your education and career: *first I did this, then I went to X, after that I ...* You are talking about what you did, i.e. you use verbs. First for Marina and then for Mario, pick out the steps in their careers, just the verbs, what they <u>did</u>, what Marina calls her **iter**.

Example: Marina: ho studiato, ho fatto (l'International Baccalaureate), ...

Now that you have done that and checked your answers in the Key, you will have two lists of verbs, all in the tense used for completed actions in the past. You have probably met it and called it, perhaps, the *perfect* or in Italian **il passato prossimo**. It is a tense which we use often. Let's try and understand it.

The two parts of the perfect

The perfect is a compound tense, that is a tense composed of two parts:

a   **an auxiliary verb**, i.e. a verb which helps form the tense, shedding its own meaning but not carrying the meaning of the main verb, (e.g. in English: *have* as in *I have seen*)

b   and **a past participle**. This comes from the verb with the main meaning and in English most of them end in *-ed* (*finished, received, wanted* etc). Some are irregular, such as *eaten, been, had, seeen* – even English has its complications.

The regular past participle

Let's look first at the past participle. We come back to our three verb groups and they work as follows:

Group 1	Group 2	Group 3
cantare	**ricevere**	**gestire**
cantato	**ricevuto**	**gestito**

Activity 2

Probably you are familiar with this but for practice and to refresh your mind, make a few past participles. Give the English past participle too.

> Example: **temere** to *fear*
> past participle: **temuto** *feared*

1 andare   *to go*
2 uscire   *to go out*
3 tornare   *to return, go back, come back*
4 lanciare   *to throw*
5 sapere   *to know* (fact, information)
6 conoscere   *to know* (person, place – i.e. be acquainted with)
7 capire   *to understand*
8 cadere   *to fall*

Activity 3

What about the irregular verbs? They are mostly verbs in Group 2 (**-ere** type) with also some in Group 3 (**-ire** type). Can you pick out any irregular past participles in the list of verbs you made in Activity 1 from what Marina and Mario said? Check the answer in the Key.

Irregular past participles: Group 2 verbs

The translations are a guide only. They will not necessarily work in all contexts.

chiesto	chiedere *to ask*	**discusso**	discutere *to discuss*
rimasto	rimanere *to remain*	**messo**	mettere *to put*
risposto	rispondere *to answer*	**successo**	succedere *to happen*
scelto	scegliere *to choose*	**letto**	leggere *to read*
vinto	vincere *to win*	**rotto**	rompere *to break*

chiuso	chiudere *to close*		scritto	scrivere *to write*
preso	prendere *to take*		nato	nascere *to be born*
deciso	decidere *to decide*		vissuto	vivere *to live*

As you might expect, **essere** *to be*, has an irregular past participle: **stato**.

You may notice we have grouped together verbs which work in a similar way. Some people find that helpful. It is important to realize that a verb made up of one of these verbs, preceded by a prefix, will also follow this model, e.g: **messo** (**mettere**) → **ammesso** (**ammettere** *to admit*); **preso** (**prendere**) → **sorpreso** (**sorprendere** *to surprise*). For a number of verbs in this group the form most commonly met is the past participle used as an adjective, e.g: **cotto** as in **prosciutto cotto**, **panna cotta**, from **cuocere**; **mosso** as in **mare mosso** *rough sea*, from **muovere**.

Verbs with more than one possible past participle

One or two verbs in this group have more than one possible past participle. The most common are: **perso/perduto** (**perdere** *to lose*) **visto/veduto** (**vedere** *to see*). It really doesn't matter which you use.

But don't despair! Many common verbs which are irregular in other ways have nice, regular past participles:

avuto	avere *to have*		dovuto	dovere *to have to*
potuto	potere *to be able*		seduto	sedere *to sit*
tenuto	tenere *to hold*		voluto	volere *to want*

And you have already seen **saputo** (**sapere** *to know*).

Verbs whose present-day infinitive is an abbreviated form

A small number of verbs can be classed as Group 2 because they have a present-day infinitive which is an abbreviated version of an earlier infinitive ending in **-ere**. They nearly all have irregular past participles:

| fatto | fare [facere] *to make, to do* | | detto | dire [dicere] *to say* |
| posto | porre [ponere] *to place* | | tradotto | tradurre [traducere] *to translate* |

The exception is **bevuto** (**bere** [**bevere**] *to drink*) which actually has the form of a regular Group 2 past participle.

Irregular past participles: Group 3 verbs

aperto	aprire *to open*
coperto	coprire *to cover*
sofferto	soffrire *to suffer*
morto	morire *to die*
venuto	venire *to come*

> **LANGUAGE LEARNING TIP**   As usual we would stress that when trying to get your meaning over, you should not worry too much about correctness. After all, small children using their own language often make things regular when they should be irregular, and we just laugh gently with them. But in the long run you will want to have the full picture and to aim at accuracy. As you listen to what Italians say, you will become familiar with these forms painlessly. Train yourself to listen – and then to imitate.

The auxiliary verb

But of course that is only half the story. We said it had two parts: they are the past participle and another verb, called an auxiliary verb. You have probably learned or noticed that there are two possible auxiliary verbs. How do you know which to use?

Activity 4

Look back at the list you made for Activity 1. Pick out the two auxiliary verbs. Reorganize your list so that verbs using each are grouped together.

Verbs which use *essere*

Let's start with the verbs which use **essere**. Did you see any pattern?

1 You should have noticed that reflexive verbs make their **passato prossimo** with essere: **mi sono trovata, mi sono lanciato, mi sono tuffato, mi si è presentata.** The past participle agrees with the subject of the verb. So Marina says: **mi sono trovata** while Mario says **mi sono lanciato**.

2 Then you hear Marina using: **sono andata, sono tornata, sono uscita, sono arrivata** and Mario: **sono passato.** You will probably have already learned that verbs whose meaning relates to coming and going, moving from one place to another, make their **passato prossimo** with essere.   Quite a large number of verbs make their perfect with essere. The essential point about

them is that they are intransitive, which means they cannot have a direct object. This is for some language learners a difficult point to grasp. The verb **passare** can be transitive or intransitive. Compare:

Intransitive

L'errore è passato inosservato.   *The mistake went unnoticed.*
Noi siamo passati per la strada   *We went by the road but*
ma Marco è passato per i   *Mario went across the*
campi. Così non ci siamo   *fields. So we didn't see*
visti.   *each other.*

Transitive

Ho passato il mio ombrello   *I passed my umbrella to*
a Giorgio.   *George/I let George have*
                                  my umbrella.

L'anno scorso abbiamo passato   *Last year we spent the*
le vacanze in montagna.   *holidays in the mountains.*

In the last two sentences **passare** has an object (**il mio ombrello, le vacanze**). It is used transitively. In the first two sentences there is no direct object nor is one possible with this meaning. So in the first two sentences, **essere** is used as auxiliary.

Verbs using **essere** include verbs of movement from one place to another, as we have said: **andare, venire, entrare, uscire, arrivare, partire, scendere, salire, tornare, fuggire** and others with similar meanings.

Also verbs of not moving, of state, use **essere: stare, rimanere, restare, essere.**

And verbs expressing change of state: **arrossire, impallidire, dimagrire, ingrassare, nascere, morire, diventare, divenire, invecchiare, guarire, iniziare,** etc.

Anna è impallidita quando ha   *Anna turned pale when she*
visto il professore.   *saw the teacher.*
Quanto sei dimagrito!   *You've lost a lot of weight!*

Again, some of these verbs can also be used transitively: **Ho iniziato un sistema nuovo per ...** *I've started a new system for ...*

Verbs related to weather phenomena, e.g. **piovere,** also form their past with **essere,** although in everyday spoken Italian many people use **avere.**

Verbs which use *avere*

Transitive verbs use **avere**, whether the object is expressed or not; also many intransitive verbs, e.g. **parlare**:

Ho parlato con Gianna.   *I talked/have talked to Gianna.*

A good dictionary will indicate which auxiliary is used with a given verb. If in doubt, use **avere** and don't worry! Again, developing the habit of listening to Italians is important. Gradually, with experience, you will develop a sense of what is right, based on what you have heard.

The overall pattern

The overall pattern then can be presented thus:

capire	arrivare	accorgersi
ho capito	sono arrivato/a	mi sono accorto/a
hai capito	sei arrivato/a	ti sei accorto/a
ha capito	è arrivato/a	si è accorto/a
abbiamo capito	siamo arrivati/e	ci siamo accorti/e
avete capito	siete arrivati/e	vi siete accorti/e
hanno capito	sono arrivati/e	si sono accorti/e

The perfect infinitive

The perfect has an infinitive: **avere finito** *to have finished*, **essere arrivato** *to have arrived*. It is formed with **avere** or **essere** and the past participle. It is used after a preposition or after a verb which can be followed by an infinitive:

Dopo avere mangiato, sono   *After eating (having eaten)*
   usciti in giardino.   *they went out into the garden.*

Non è ancora arrivato Paolo.   *Paolo hasn't arrived yet.*
Deve essere partito in ritardo.   *He must have set off late.*

We have devoted quite a lot of space to the **passato prossimo** because it is a tense we use frequently. We often want to tell people not only our life story but what we have just done. It occurs frequently in newspaper reports, especially the **cronaca** section. Here is a selection.

SESSION 4

Reading

Here are some short newpaper items. Read them carefully, more than once. Don't forget to exercise your skills at guessing meanings before looking words up. Then answer the questions at the end of the extracts.

1 Due esplosioni:

Lo Stromboli si risveglia. Allarme sull'isola.

Ieri pomeriggio, intorno alle 17.30, due forti boati hanno annunciato una piccola eruzione nella zona Sud del cratere dello Stromboli, che ha provocato un incendio alla vegetazione del costone. Le fiamme sono state prontamente domate con l'intervento di un 'Canadair', mentre gli uomini della Protezione Civile perlustravano la montagna con un elicottero per soccorrere eventuali gitanti feriti e si tenevano in contatto con gli abitanti della frazione di Ginostra, raggiungibile solo via mare, isolata da due giorni per le cattive condizioni del mare.

(*La Stampa*, 24 agosto 1998)

Stromboli	island, part of the Eolian Islands, off the north-east coast of Sicily. The volcano of the same name which dominates the island is in almost constant activity.
boato	*loud, deep rumble*
costone	*ridge*
'Canadair'	a type of amphibious aircraft used in fire fighting, which can scoop up water from the sea or a lake to drop on the flames.
Protezione Civile	the corps responsible for rescue in the case of natural disaster.
gitanti	*people taking part in a* **gita**, *an excursion*. A favourite excursion in the Stromboli area is at night by boat to see the volcano throwing up sparks, etc.
frazione	*a fraction, part of a whole*, in this case, part of the **comune**, away from the main village.

Comprehension – Passage 1

1 Whereabouts on the mountain did the small eruption take place?
2 What was the consequence of the eruption?
3 What did the Canadair do?
4 Why did the Civil Protection squad search the mountain?
5 Ginostra already had other problems. What were they?

2   Con un coltello ha rapinato la Cariplo

Attimi di tensione e di panico l'altra mattina per una rapina avvenuta presso l'agenzia di Settimo Torinese della banca Cariplo ...

L'assalto è avvenuto verso mezzogiorno e mezzo. Un bandito solitario, a viso scoperto, armato di un coltello a serramanico, ha fatto irruzione nell'istituto di credito.

... Il rapinatore ha subito varcato il bancone, e si è diretto deciso verso gli impiegati. Li ha minacciati con la tagliente lama e li ha quindi costretti a consegnargli quindici milioni.

Il colpo è stato messo a segno in pochi minuti, dall'esterno nessuno si è accorto di nulla. Il bandito è così riuscito poi a dileguarsi a piedi nel centro.

Scattato l'allarme, sul posto sono accorsi subito i carabinieri che hanno immediatamente istituito alcuni posti di blocco. Ma del rapinatore, però, nessuna traccia.

(La Stampa, 4 gennaio 1998)

Settimo Torinese	a small town on the eastern outskirts of Turin
Cariplo	the name of a bank (**Cassa di Risparmio della Lombardia**)
rapina	*robbery* (c.f. **rapinare** *to rob*) Note past participle in title of piece.
quindici milioni	*15 million lire = €7,700 approximately.* The article was written before the introduction of the Euro.
messo a segno	*successfully completed;* **mettere a segno un colpo**: *to hit the target.*
dileguarsi	*to vanish*

Comprehension – Passage 2

1 How many robbers took part in the attack?
2 How much was stolen?
3 Why do you think no one noticed the robber(s) during the getaway?
4 What did the carabinieri do?

3   Incubo in ascensore

Prigioniero per 10 giorni: allucinante avventura di un ex attore, custode del Club Med a Sestriere.

Ha perso quindici chili ma si è salvato, i medici: 'Un miracolo'

Sestriere. L'hanno trovato ieri alle 13 i carabinieri. Vivo. Vivo dopo 10 giorni trascorsi chiuso dentro un ascensore guasto, senza né acqua né cibo. Armando Piazza, 64 anni, custode al Club Med, era entrato nella torre bianca dove ha sede il club, deserto d'estate, per ritirare alcuni fax. L'ascensore s'è bloccato a un metro e 70 dal primo piano e lui è rimasto là dentro fino a quando una barista ha dato l'allarme: 'Manca da troppo tempo, temo gli sia successo qualcosa'.

(La Stampa, 21 agosto 1998)

The above is the front page summary of a news item treated in greater depth inside the paper. Hence the rather 'telegraphic' style.

| Sestriere | a ski resort in Piemonte |
| torre bianca | *white tower* The Club Med centre in Sestriere is a circular white tower, in a prominent position and well known in the area. |

Comprehension – Passage 3

1 Where had Armando Piazza spent 10 days?
2 Why had he gone into the building?
3 What made the barmaid call in the carabinieri?

4 **Clandestino ritrova il papà dopo 15 anni Da Tunisi a Torino**

ROMA. È arrivato in Italia come clandestino dalla Tunisia per cercare il padre, un tunisino con passaporto italiano che vive da oltre 15 anni a Torino. Ma le forze di polizia lo hanno sorpreso in Sicilia senza permesso di soggiorno e, adesso, si trova nel centro di Ponte Galeria, in attesa di sapere quale sarà il suo destino. Una storia degna del libro 'Cuore'. Tajeddine Abdel Karim, che ha appena compiuto 18 anni, ha lasciato la madre per venire a trovare il padre. I militari e i volontari della Cri, che gestiscono il centro di accoglienza di Ponte Galeria, dopo lunghe ricerche sono riusciti a rintracciare, grazie anche alla collaborazione con l'ufficio immigrazione della Questura, il padre, che si è precipitato a Roma, con tutti i documenti necessari ad accertare la paternità del ragazzo. Il consolato tunisino sta lavorando per far sì che il ragazzo possa restare con il padre in Italia. [Ansa]

(*La Stampa*, 25 agosto 1998 – internet edition: www.lastampa.it)

centro di Ponte Galeria	a reception centre for illegal immigrants, near Rome
Cuore	Title of a well-known sentimental novel by E. de Amicis, published in 1886
Cri	**Croce Rossa Italiana**, *the Italian Red Cross*

Comprehension – Passage 4

1 Who has been living in Turin for 15 years?
2 Why did the police take the young man into custody and where?
3 What did the father do when he heard his son was in Rome?
4 What did he bring with him?

i Two aspects of Italy today are touched on in these passages: the risk of natural disaster and immigration. Italy is a high-risk country for natural disasters. Sadly there have been many in recent years. Much of the peninsula is potentially subject to earthquakes and there are areas of frequent volcanic activity. In addition a very high proportion of Italy is mountainous or hilly (one third mountain and one third hill, leaving only one third flat), leading to risks of landslide and flooding. This has been aggravated by the flight of the peasants from land which is difficult to farm so that the land is untended; by unwise building development; and lack of investment in geologists and appropriate personnel to manage prevention. Recent governments have appeared to take this more seriously than their predecessors but there is a long way to go and the basic nature of the land will mean the risk can never be eliminated.

Passage 4 relates to a fairly recent development. After the massive emigrations to the Americas in the late 19th and early 20th centuries and then the post-war flow of emigrants to other parts of Europe, Australia, and simply from one part of Italy to another (largely from South to North and from country to city), Italy is now learning to live with an unfamiliar phenomenon: immigration. This comes mainly from the former Communist countries of Eastern Europe and from North Africa. And much of the immigration is illegal. The long Italian coastline is difficult to patrol and in spite of unemployment, Italy seems to be a magnet, although undoubtedly many who land in southern Italy plan to move straight through to other parts of Europe. And as always in rich countries, there is work that the Italians prefer not to do. Reactions to immigration are mixed and there is no doubt that it is imposing strains on life, particularly in certain cities where racial tensions have led to disturbances.

It goes without saying that bank robberies are neither new nor specifically Italian. And being trapped in a lift is a common nightmare!

SESSION 5

Looking at the perfect in action

Let's return to the language of the passages in Session 4. How did that go? We hope you found you could get the meaning, even if you did not understand all the words. If you did, you can certainly get a lot from reading a newspaper. We will come back to the business of meaning shortly, but first let's look at the **passato prossimo** in the news items.

Activity 5

Read the news items again and pick out all the examples you can find of the **passato prossimo**.

More irregular past participles

You will have found irregular past participles not previously presented:

a **costretti** from **costringere** *to oblige, to compel*. This is often used when in English we might say '*I had to ...*' meaning there was no other option for me. The base verb is of course **stringere**.

b **rimasto** from **rimanere** *to remain*. This is also common since it is used in expressions such as:

Ci sono rimasto male.	*I felt badly about it.*
E' rimasto sorpreso dalla tua reazione.	*He was surprised by your reaction.*

There is a reference list of common irregular past participles in the **Reference grammar**.

The passive form

You may have wondered about **Le fiamme sono state domate** in Passage 1. This is a passive. *The flames were overcome.* You have the **passato prossimo** of **essere** plus the past participle of **domare**. There was a similar passive in another passage. Can you find it? (See Key.)

Agreement of the past participle in verbs forming the 'passato prossimo' with *avere*.

You will also have noticed past participle agreements with **avere**. We have not yet dealt with:

Li ha minacciati	*He threatened them*
li ha costretti	*he forced them*

Can you see what is happening in the examples which are from Passage 2? The past participle agrees with the object of the verb, the pronoun **li**, which refers to **gli impiegati della banca**. The subject of the verb is *the robber*, who is singular. This is the usual way for the past participle to behave with **avere**. It agrees with a direct object pronoun placed before the verb. But it is not a point you should worry about greatly until you are at quite an advanced stage. The important point is the use of the **passato prossimo** to recount the events in a story.

Activity 6

Now here are some things that have happened to you recently.

1 Yesterday you witnessed a road accident. A car didn't stop at a red light and hit a car which was crossing on green. Tell

your Italian friend about it. Example: **Ieri ho visto un incidente stradale. Una macchina ...**

2 You left your wallet on a table in the hotel bar last night. Tell the receptionist and ask if by chance it was found.

3 You had a lovely walk yesterday with Paolo and Marco. You took the path near the petrol station. You went up the hill and then into the woods. You followed the path as far as Castiglione. Write a postcard to your mother telling her so.

4 You telephoned Anna last night. Her mother has broken her arm. She fell over in the street. Anna told you to give her greetings to Mario. Tell Mario.

SESSION 6

Dealing with vocabulary again

The newspaper items required some vocabulary guesswork from you. Here are some comments.

1 Words whose precise meaning is not crucial

There were words in the passages the meaning of which was not crucial to your overall understanding. You could read and understand the passage and knowing the precise meaning of those words would make very little difference. For instance, in Passage 2: **coltello a serra-manico** – does it matter what a **serra-manico** means? Isn't it enough to know the attacker had a knife? Similarly we are told **Il rapinatore ha subito varcato il bancone.** If you know all the other words, not knowing **varcato** really doesn't matter. As you develop your reading skills, you need not look up every word. So long as you are getting the gist, it is more enjoyable to carry on at a reasonable pace. Don't worry too much about the odd word here or there if you are following the story. Other words in these passages that this might apply to are: in Passage 1 **perlustravano**; in Passage 4 **Questura**.

2 Guessable words

There were some good guessing words in the passages, for example:

a words guessable from similar English words
Passage 5 contained several which were so easy, it may seem hardly worth mentioning them (the words in brackets are the English words which come to our mind, not necessarily the best translation or even a translation at all): **clandestino** (*clandestine*), **permesso di soggiorno** (*permit* or *permission to*

sojourn/stay); **rintracciare** (*traces*) (cf. **traccia** in Passage 2); **collaborazione; ufficio immigrazione; accertare la paternità**. Or in Passage 1: **incendio** (*incendiary*).

b words guessable from Italian or a combination of Italian and English

In Passage 1 **gitanti** (Italian **gita turistica**); and **soccorre** (Italian **Pronto soccorso** *hospital emergency department* and English *succour*); in Passage 2 **viso scoperto** (English *visor* perhaps and Italian **coperto** *covered*: **scoperto**, *discovered, uncovered* (**s** prefix is often the equivalent of the English *un-, dis-*); in Passage 5 **ricerche** (Italian **cercare** and English *research*)

Sophisticated guessers may have been able to work out **costone** in Passage 1 from **costa** *rib* and the suffix -**one**, meaning *big*. It is a word with a dictionary entry (meaning *ridge*) but that is the way it is built up. There is a word built in a similar way in Passage 2. What is it?

3 More false friends

Eventuale is a false friend (**eventuali gitanti** in Passage 1). We mentioned these in Unit 1. They are Italian words that look like English words but which do not have the same meaning. **Eventuale** means here *possible*, i.e. any tourists who might have happened to be on the volcano and have been injured. The adverb **eventualmente** is fairly common. It means *if this should be the case*. For instance you might be asked to give your name and (**eventualmente**) the name of your spouse. Meaning *if you have one*. Try to collect 'false friends' and get their use right. *Eventually* could be translated: **alla fine, finalmente**.

Activity 7

1 How would you tell Arturo's life story from the information below?

Example: Mi chiamo Arturo Marullo, sono nato nel 1958 a Terni ...

Nome: Arturo	Cognome: Marullo
Nato: il 6 febbraio 1958	Luogo di nascita: Terni (PG)✶
Scuola elementare: Terni	
Scuola media inferiore: Terni	
Scuola media superiore: Liceo scientifico, Perugia	

Studi: Laurea in economia e commercio, Perugia, 1984

Primo lavoro: Fratelli Alberti, commercianti in vino, Orvieto (3 anni)

Secondo lavoro: Supermercati Gatti, Milano (7 anni)

Lavoro attuale: Direttore di marketing, Pasta Bastoni, Milano

★ PG = the province of Perugia

2 And now yours. Don't forget to say where you were born, where you went to school, and to tell us about any further studies and the various jobs you have held. Perhaps you might like to include the personal side: when you married (**mi sono sposato/a**), and who you married (**mi sono sposato/a con**), when your children were born etc. It's up to you! But make sure you do think it through.

Activity 8

Talking to yourself

1 Immagini di essere uno dei protagonisti di una o due delle storie in Session 4 e racconti quello che è successo dal Suo punto di vista. Per esempio, il bandito nel brano 2 (ho fatto irruzione …) o uno degli impiegati della banca (Che paura oggi! A mezzogiorno e mezzo è entrato un bandito e ci ha minacciato con un coltello …); o nel brano 4, Armando Piazza: Mi hanno trovato …).

2 Racconti a Sé stesso la storia della vita di altre persone: amici, parenti, personaggi famosi. Il motivo per farlo è sforzarsi di parlare (e pensare) in italiano, cercare di usare la lingua. Non ha importanza di quali persone sceglie di parlare: l'importante è che siano interessanti per Lei.

3 Esiste nel Suo paese il fenomeno di una notevole immigrazione? Che cosa ne pensa Lei? Chi sono gli immigrati? Perché vengono? Ne conosce alcuni? Quali problemi incontrano? E quali sono i problemi creati dal loro arrivo? E' mai stato residente all'estero anche Lei?

4 Quali sono i Suoi incubi ricorrenti? E i Suoi sogni?

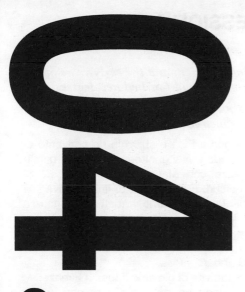

04

c'era una volta ...

In this unit we shall

- meet various Italians reminiscing about the past
- use the preposition **da** to say: *something to eat*, *nothing to do*, etc.
- say how things used to be, describe what people were like and what they were doing at a time in the past: a review of the imperfect – form and use
- look at the pronoun **si** used impersonally
- meet the pluperfect
- meet the gerund, the past continuous and the present continuous

SESSION 1

▶ Interview 1

Angioletta talks about being a student and the early years of her marriage. She married before she had finished her degree.

Listen several times, preferably without looking at the text and then answer the questions which follow.

Angioletta Ho studiato lingue a Pisa e stavo in un convento di suore che secondo i miei genitori era il posto giusto per una ragazza che stava fuori di casa ... Si sentivano più sicuri. E poi, prima di finire l'università mi sono sposata ... e siamo andati ad abitare a Firenze, dove lavorava mio marito.

Interviewer Ti sei trasferita all'università di Firenze?

Angioletta No, perché stavo finendo, non era conveniente e ho continuato ad andare a Pisa.

Interviewer Raccontami la tua vita di giovane sposa a Firenze.

Angioletta E' stato un periodo un po' difficile perché io ero abituata a stare con molta gente. Mi sono trasferita alla periferia di Firenze dove ho trovato grandi difficoltà a entrare, a fare amicizia con le persone vicine. Avevo un'amica molto cara che era una compagna dell'università anche, quindi passavo molto tempo con lei.

Interviewer Non lavoravi?

Angioletta Non lavoravo. Avevo ... facevo lezioni private. E studiavo. E soffrivo di solitudine, devo dire. Ho trovato molto difficile fare amicizia. Dicono che sia difficile per i toscani con i fiorentini e non avevo questa percezione, non l'avevo provata ... E facevo molto da mangiare. Cucinavo tantissimo, a me piaceva sperimentare ... e pulivo la casa, ero una padrona di casa molto attenta, lucidavo tutto, davo addirittura la cera alla cucina ... (*ride*) che è una cosa molto ...? Secondo me ora ...

Interviewer Quanto tempo siete rimasti a Firenze?

Angioletta Due anni.

Interviewer E Annalisa?

Angioletta Annalisa è nata a Firenze. Due anni e mezzo veramente. Annalisa è nata a Firenze e poi noi ci siamo trasferiti quando lei aveva sei o sette mesi. Siamo venuti ad Arezzo.

non l'avevo provata	Note the agreement of the past participle (see Unit 3). The pronoun **l'** stands for **la** and refers to **percezione** (f).

Comprehension 1

1 Where did Angioletta live in Pisa and why?
2 Why did she move to Florence when she married?
3 She could have transferred to the University of Florence but didn't. Why not?
4 What did Angioletta most miss living on the outskirts of Florence?
5 Why should she not have been surprised at how difficult it was to get to know people?
6 Who did she spend a lot of time with?
7 Did she have a job?
8 How did she console herself in her loneliness?
9 How long did she live in Florence?
10 Her daughter was born there. What did they do when Annalisa was six or seven months old?

SESSION 2

The use of prepositions *da* and *di* after certain adjectives and pronouns

The use of prepositions is possibly one of the most tricky areas when you are learning a foreign language. Of course, they often translate neatly on a one-to-one basis.

| Da dove vieni? | *Where do you come from?* |
| Il negozio è aperto dalle otto all'una. | *The shop is open from eight to one.* |

But there are also idiomatic usages, i.e. usages where there is not a straight translation. **Da** probably has more of these than other prepositions. You were reminded in Unit 2 of:

| Studio italiano da due anni. | *I've been studying Italian for two years.* |

Here is another idiomatic use of **da**. It is sensible to keep a section in your notes (just as you should have one for false friends) for these usages.

Certain indefinite adjectives and pronouns words are followed by **da** plus an infinitive. (Indefinites are a group of adjectives and pronouns which, as their name implies, are generally imprecise about number.)

qualcosa		**mangiare**	*something*	*eat*
niente/nulla		**bere**	*nothing*	*drink*
molto	__DA__	**fare**	*much/a lot*	__TO__	*do*
tanto		**dire**	*so much*	*say*
troppo		**vedere**	*too much*	*see*

But note also:

qualcosa		**bello**	*something*	*lovely*
niente/nulla		**nuovo**	*nothing*	*new*
molto	__DI__	**buono**	*much that is*	*good*
tanto		**importante**	*so much that is*	*important*
troppo		**sicuro**	*too much that is*	*certain*

Can you spot where the difference lies? **DA** + verb; **DI** + adjective.

Tricky translations

Even as we translated from Italian to English in the previous section, we came up against the point that word-for-word translation does not always work, or produces a stilted result.

At the level of individual words, another point to look out for when learning any foreign language is that words are often not precise equivalents because no two countries are the same. They have different histories, different rates of development, different terrain, climate etc. And words which may perhaps have the same origin, get used in different ways in different countries. This is an interesting point. Here are a couple of examples:

periferia: Italian cities do not really have suburbs. You are either in the centre (**in centro**), often **nel centro storico** meaning in the old, usually picturesque part; or **in periferia** on the outskirts but still within the city limits. Or else you go and live in another **comune** where you have a different local administration etc.

conveniente: *convenient* in English clearly has the same Latin origin as **conveniente** in Italian. However in Italian the word is often used colloquially to mean **vantaggioso dal punto di vista economico, adatto alle circostanze** – it seems to us that if you lived in the Florence area, it would be more convenient to be at university in Florence but Angioletta explained that she was so near the end of her course in Pisa it did not make sense to transfer. It was not convenient in the sense that she would have wasted time getting to know people and places and generally getting herself organized. Probably in English one would say: *advisable*.

SESSION 3

The imperfect tense

You will have noticed that, when talking about what they did, the stages in their career, our Italian speakers sometimes used another tense, not the perfect, **passato prossimo**. Much of what Angioletta says in Interview 1 is expressed in this other past tense which you may already know as the imperfect, l'**imperfetto**. Here are some examples from the part of the interview in which Angioletta is talking about the first year or two of her marriage:

Non **lavoravo**. **Avevo** ... **facevo** lezioni private. E **studiavo**.
E **soffrivo** di solitudine, devo dire ... E **facevo** molto da mangiare. **Cucinavo** tantissimo, a me **piaceva** sperimentare, ... e **pulivo** la casa, **ero** una padrona di casa molto attenta, **lucidavo** tutto, **davo** addirittura la cera alla cucina.

Activity 1

A different tense must imply a different meaning. Try translating some sentences and phrases from Interview 1 given again below. The imperfect has been underlined to draw your attention to it. Can you work out why it is being used? Can you convey that in your translation?

Example: Poi, prima di finire l'università, mi sono sposata ... e siamo andati ad abitare a Firenze, dove lavorava mio marito.
Then, before I had graduated from the university, I got married ... and we went to live in Florence where my husband was working/worked/used to work. (worked is a very acceptable translation, was working captures the meaning of the imperfect better in this case than used to work)

1 Mi sono trasferita alla periferia di Firenze dove ho trovato grandi difficoltà a entrare, a fare amicizia con le persone vicine. <u>Avevo</u> un'amica molto cara che <u>era</u> una compagna dell'università anche, quindi <u>passavo</u> molto tempo con lei.

2 <u>Facevo</u> molto da mangiare. <u>Cucinavo</u> tantissimo, a me <u>piaceva</u> sperimentare ... e <u>pulivo</u> la casa, <u>ero</u> una padrona di casa molto attenta, <u>lucidavo</u> tutto, <u>davo</u> addirittura la cera alla cucina.

3 Annalisa è nata a Firenze e poi noi ci siamo trasferiti quando lei <u>aveva</u> sei o sette mesi.

Do you think you understood intuitively why a different tense was being used in that activity? As we show in our suggestions in the Key, English offers more than one possibility when it comes to translating. And here lies the key to understanding. The way the past is conveyed in English and Italian does not correspond exactly. Each language has its own system and it is not helpful to think from one language to the other – even though, as a language learner, you inevitably will to some extent.

Two past tenses in Italian

In Italian there are the two basic past tenses: the **passato prossimo** or *perfect* and the **imperfetto** or *imperfect*. The difference between them lies in *point of view*. Is the important aspect that the action was done once and completed? Or is that not what you are trying to convey? A clue lies in the names. The *imperfect* is not a bargain basement, 'only one tiny flaw' tense. The word comes from Latin and means incomplete. *Perfect* means completed. When what happened, happened once and is viewed as finished and done with, we use the *perfect*. The *imperfect* is used when the speaker is focussing on another aspect of the past event.

It may help to look at certain verbs where the force of the meaning is thrown into relief when translating as you really need different words in English, so different is the meaning. Compare:

Sapevo che Elena stava male.	*I knew Elena was ill.* (i.e. it was something I knew)
Ho saputo che Elena stava male.	*I learned/heard Elena was ill.* (i.e. knowing it was an event which happened at a precise moment and then it became part of my knowledge)

Conoscevo poche persone *I knew few people in Florence/*
a Firenze. *I didn't know many people in Florence.*

Ho conosciuto mio marito *I met my husband in Florence*
a Firenze. (i.e. that was where I met him
for the first time. It was an
event which happened once –
and changed my life! Well, no,
perhaps it doesn't quite say
that much!)

Gabriella, whom you can see here with her husband Gianni,
told us:

Ho conosciuto mio marito *I met my husband at a*
a una gita della parrocchia. *parish outing.*

Some learners find it useful to think of time as a line. The
imperfect would fade in and out imperceptibly, while the perfect
would be for specific chunks of time, points in time, with a clear
beginning and end; the amounts of time can be longer or shorter,
but the start and finish are clear.

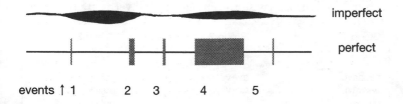

The uses of the imperfect

The imperfect is used in three main ways (all our examples here are taken from what Angioletta said above):

1 for repeated, habitual actions – finished, yes, but done many times:

> non lavoravo; studiavo; facevo lezioni private; cucinavo tantissimo; pulivo la casa; lucidavo tutto

2 for describing what a person or a thing was like at a point in the past:

> Ero una padrona di casa molto attenta.

3 when the verb is conveying things that happened but the start and finish of the action is not relevant, the action is seen as going on over an unspecified period, a background to other things:

> dove lavorava mio marito; avevo un'amica molto cara; soffrivo di solitudine

With practice and familiarity, you will develop a feeling for it. In this unit you will get a good amount of practice.

Activity 2

This Activity is mostly for learners who have not met the imperfect before or who feel unsure of it. Forming the imperfect is easy. You can probably work it out for yourself from the examples you have already met. Try. First pick out all the imperfects in Interview 1. Then sort them into verb groups according to the characteristic vowel. Then sort by subject pronoun so that you get all those verbs in -**are** of which the subject is '**io**' together etc. See how much you can work out for yourself about the form of the imperfect on this basis. It is a useful exercise, so try it, and consult the Key before reading on.

Forming the imperfect

Each of the three verb groups keeps the characteristic vowel from its infinitive but otherwise the endings for all verbs are the same:

Group 1	Group 2	Group 3
passare	**avere**	**pulire**
passavo	avevo	pulivo
passavi	avevi	pulivi
passava	aveva	puliva
passavamo	avevamo	pulivamo
passavate	avevate	pulivate
passavano	avevano	pulivano

The verb **essere** is totally irregular: **ero, eri, era, eravamo, cravatc, crano.**

Otherwise, very few verbs are irregular in the imperfect: they are the ones which have a contracted infinitive (see Unit 3, Session 3).

fare (facere)	facevo, facevi, faceva, facevamo, facevate, facevano
dire (dicere)	dicevo, dicevi, diceva, dicevamo, dicevate, dicevano
bere (bevere)	bevevo, bevevi, beveva, bevevamo, bevevate, bevevano
porre (ponere)	ponevo, ponevi, poneva, ponevamo, ponevate, ponevano
tradurre (traducere)	traducevo, traducevi, traduceva, traducevamo, traducevate, traducevano

Note: In the 3rd person plural of all verbs the stress falls on the third syllable from the end.

As we said you need to become familiar with the imperfect in use, so to give you that practice, several reminders follow in the remainder of this Unit.

SESSION 4

▶ Interview 2

Listen and answer the questions which follow. Try to listen without reading the text.

For many years Carlo worked for various Italian and foreign companies in Italy and abroad, in Brazil, Venezuela and Spain. Today he is Managing Director of Stock, a long established firm in Trieste. Here he is talking about his early days.

Carlo Sono nato in un tipico ambiente astigiano di provincia, da genitori che erano figli di contadini e cercavano di emergere e hanno cominciato con una piccola attività commerciale con tante difficoltà, con tanta ristrettezza all'inizio. Era gente molto laboriosa che grazie alle prime economie ha permesso ai loro figli di fare i primi studi ad Asti. Si andava ad Asti in corriera, a circa quindici, venti chilometri, e si tornava la sera. Ed è in questo ambiente che evidentemente poi mi sono formato. D'estate si andava per nidi, si andava a pescare nei fiumi, si andava a pescare anguille. Ho imparato a nuotare nei ruscelli. Quelli erano praticamente i nostri svaghi. Si andava per tartufi, c'era sempre un vecchio che conosceva ...

astigiano	*from the Asti area.* Asti (of **spumante** fame) is a town in Piemonte to the southeast of Turin; it is the main town of the province of Asti.
era gente molto laboriosa	**Gente** is a feminine singular noun and is accompanied by a singular verb (**era**).
si andava per tartufi	*we went truffle hunting.* The area where Carlo lived, is famous for its highly prized white truffles (**tuber magnatum**).

Comprehension 2

1 Carlo has had a successful career as a businessman. What did his grandparents do?
2 What seems to have been his parents' ambition?
3 What did they do to further their ambitions and what does their life seem to have been like?
4 Where did he go to school and what did that involve?
5 Carlo has fond memories of his childhood leisure activities. What were they?

Impersonal *si*

Carlo says: **si andava ad Asti ...** *Si*, the pronoun, has many functions. Here it is used impersonally (like English *one*). Carlo means: **noi andavamo ...** He is including siblings and friends. We shall meet this again in this Unit.

Another use of impersonal **si** where in English we might use a passive:

Qui si parla italiano.   *Italian is spoken here.*

In English we also use <u>you</u>, meaning people in general:

Una piccola trattoria dove si   *A little restaurant where*
mangia bene e si paga poco.   *you eat well and where*
the price is reasonable
(you pay little).

Something Italians are always trying to find. Aren't we all?

Activity 3

Pick out the verbs in what Carlo says (Interview 2). First make a list of the verbs in the perfect or **passato prossimo**. If you reflect on each, you will see that it refers to something which was done once and is finished. Then make a list of the imperfects which might be said to describe; those which convey habitual, repeated actions; and those which are describing the background.

We hope you found that useful. It takes time and practice to get the feel of the **imperfetto**. The **passato prossimo** is much more straighforward. Try to keep thinking about it as you listen and read. Here is some more practice.

SESSION 5

▶ Interview 3

In Unit 1, Gabriella told us that her Italian father and English mother lived in France, that when war broke out her father had taken his family home to Italy and how difficult this was for her mother since, for Italy, Great Britain was an enemy country. Gabriella looks back at the war.

Gabriella Infatti, mio fratello che allora era molto piccolino non voleva più parlare con mia mamma perché diceva che era il nemico lei. E allora mio papà l'ha dovuto mettere in collegio, dalle suore, piccolino, perché temeva che dicesse cose … e … comunque tra una vicissitudine e l'altra … sono venuti fuori da questa guerra brutta per loro. Hanno perso la casa, han perso tutto, scappavano sempre; eravamo sfollati da tutte le parti e nessuno voleva darci da mangiare proprio perché mamma era inglese. E una volta mamma di notte si è alzata, è andata a mungere una pecora per darci del latte e le hanno sparato. Infatti questo pezzettino – non so come si possa dire – di pallottola ha sempre girato per casa, l'abbiamo sempre visto … Eravamo sfollati a Villafranca Piemonte, eravamo sfollati lì. E io ricordo qualcosa vagamente. Non so se ricordo veramente o a furia di sentire raccontare … Però qualcosa ricordo di questa guerra.

in collegio	*in a boarding school*. The school was run by nuns, **suore**.
han perso	Gabriella abbreviates **hanno**: Speakers do sometimes abbreviate and/or slur words as they talk.
sfollati	*evacuated*. They moved out of the city, which was a target for Allied bombing. Many families left the big cities.
a furia di sentire	*by dint of hearing*

Comprehension 3

1 Gabriella's brother was still very young and didn't understand. He used to say something which made her father fear the consequences. What did he say and what decision did their father take?
2 When they were evacuated, the fact that Gabriella's mother was English meant what for the family?
3 This drove her to do something unusual one night. What was it and what happened?
4 Does Gabriella have clear memories of the war? Why not?

Activity 4

As with Activity 3, examine the verbs in Interview 3 in the same way and make sure you understand the use of both the perfect and the imperfect.

Activity 5

As we said above, many Italians left the cities during the war. While they were living in the countryside they adapted to the new way of life and helped the local peasants in exchange for their hospitality. Here is a true story which happened to the Rossi family – yes, their name really was Rossi. Read the introduction and write the story using the verbs in brackets. Make appropriate use of the perfect and the imperfect.

Le tre bambine e le oche *The three children and the geese*
La casa della famiglia Rossi (padre, madre e tre figlie: Finetta, Cheche e Titti), a Torino, è stata bombardata e la famiglia Rossi ha perso tutto. Si sono rifugiati nel Monferrato, vicino ad Asti, in un piccolo paese di campagna, Quarto. A Quarto, vivevano ospiti in una fattoria. Le tre bambine andavano alla scuola elementare del paese la mattina, e il pomeriggio portavano a pascolare le oche del contadino.

| **Rossi** | The name (like Smith and Jones) is often given to fictitious Italians because it is very common. |
| **una fattoria** | *a farm*. A 'false friend'. |

Your story starts:

Era una bella giornata di primavera ...

Il sole (1 splendere). Le tre bambine (2 tornare) da scuola e (3 decidere) di portare le oche a pascolare al di là del fiume.

La riva al di là del fiume (4 essere) pericolosa. Spesso i partigiani (5 combattere) contro l'esercito tedesco. Le tre bambine (6 sapere) che non (7 dovere) andarci, ma (8 essere) curiose.

Mentre le oche (9 pascolare), le tre bambine (10 giocare) nel prato.

All'improvviso, le tre bambine (11 sentire) degli spari e (12 buttarsi) in un fosso con le oche.

Poco dopo, (13 arrivare) i partigiani e i tedeschi. Finetta e Titti (14 avere) paura e (15 volere) scappare; Cheche, invece, (16 dire): 'Voglio restare: non ho mai visto una battaglia vera!'

I partigiani (17 sparare) contro i tedeschi; i tedeschi (18 sparare) contro i partigiani. Le oche (19 essere) terrorizzate. Le bambine (20 prendere) in braccio le oche per tranquillizzarle.

Dopo qualche minuto, la sparatoria (21 finire) e gli uomini (22 andare) via. Tutto (23 essere) calmo di nuovo; le tre bambine e le oche (24 uscire) dal fosso: (25 essere) tutte salve. Le tre bambine (26 tornare) a casa e (27 decidere) che probabilmente non sarebbero mai più andate a pascolare le oche al di là del fiume ...

i For the student who wants to pursue the topic of Italy during the Second World War, there is a considerable body of good writing on the subject. The incident which inspired the exercise brings to mind *La casa in collina* by Cesare Pavese.

SESSION 6

▶ Interview 4

Here, as well as noting the imperfect/perfect relationship, think further about describing people. And of course listen as often as you need. Gabriella remembers her mother.

Gabriella   Mia mamma era una persona eccezionale, silenziosa, tranquilla, comunque non usciva mai, raramente, però sapeva tutto, leggeva tanto, sapeva tutti i film, ci raccontava tante cose, era una donna molto istruita ma purtroppo me ne sono accorta troppo tardi, di questo. Era la prima ad alzarsi e l'ultima ad andare a letto. Mamma è mancata che io avevo quarant'anni e posso dire d'averla vista in camicia da notte solo quegli ultimi giorni in ospedale. In tutta la mia vita non l'ho mai vista in camicia da notte. Se io mi dovevo alzare presto, io o i miei fratelli, per qualche motivo, lei si alzava un'ora prima di noi. E quando ci veniva a svegliare, prima di sentire la sua voce che ci chiamava, sentivo il profumo della saponetta. E l'ultima ad andare a letto. Sempre. Era molto rigida nelle sue idee che poi portava avanti senza ... cioè non è che lei pensasse: io devo fare così. No, no, no, era il suo modo di ... E si alzava presto al mattino per fare le cose che le piacevano: fumarsi una sigaretta, bere una tazza di caffè e fare le parole incrociate.

Interviewer　In italiano?

Gabriella　In italiano, e mio papà diceva sempre che era un'inglese sbagliata, che ... (ride) le piaceva anche molto bere il vino, l'apprezzava a tavola, ci preparava delle bellissime colazioni, tutti sempre a tavola, presenti, dovevamo essere a colazione, anche se non avevamo impegni, sempre, e vestiti. Mai in camicia da notte, mai in vestaglia. Cos'altro posso dire di mia mammina? Un'altra cosa curiosa di mia mamma è che verso le quattro e mezza del pomeriggio, lei si cambiava, si cambiava, e mi sono accorta quando mamma è mancata che in fondo lei non aveva niente, aveva poche cose: tre o quattro camicette, due magliette, però erano sempre in ordine, pulite, stirate, collettini ben lavati e stirati. Lei verso le quattro e mezza si ritirava, si lavava, si cambiava come se dovesse uscire e finiva lì la sua giornata perché aveva già organizzato la cena e allora parlava con noi, cantavamo, si suonava il piano, era una vita un po' particolare, infatti le mie compagne di scuola venivano volentieri a casa per vedere questa vita un po' strana che noi conducevamo, che io pensavo essere tipicamente inglese. Però quando poi sono andata in Inghilterra mi sono accorta che era una vita di mia mamma, non era una vita proprio inglese, era lei, così.

Mamma è mancata	**Mancare** is the usual way of saying *'pass away, die'* in Italian. Few people use **morire** referring to a recent death or the death of a loved one. Newspapers often report deaths using the verb **scomparire**: *È scomparso X ...*

che io avevo quarant'anni	**che** *when*. An idiomatic way of expressing the idea but one which is easily understood by the foreign learner.
per qualche motivo	*for some reason*. Note that **qualche** must always be followed by a singular, whereas in English it is more usually followed by a plural. A useful way of remembering this is via a frequently used phrase such as **qualche volta** *sometimes*. **Volta** is patently singular.
fumarsi una sigaretta	Making **fumare** reflexive underlines the enjoyment Gabriella's mother found in this quiet cigarette before the start of the day.
mammina	The diminutive accentuates how very much Gabriella loved her mother. Notice Gabriella consistently uses the simple possessive with no article with **mamma, papà, mammina** (see Unit 2)
come se dovesse uscire	**dovesse** is an imperfect subjunctive (see Unit 8).
si suonava il piano	Here is the impersonal **si** again, meaning *we*.

Comprehension 4

1 Gabriella regrets that she didn't realize something about her mother until it was too late. What was it?
2 What point do you think Gabriella is making by drawing attention to the fact that she had not seen her mother in a nightdress until her final illness in hospital?
3 What were her mother's little pleasures which she enjoyed before the family got up?
4 What sort of behaviour does she seem to have demanded from her children?
5 What habit of her mother's does Gabriella remember as being curious – and, she thought, typically English?
6 What picture do you get of her mother?

Activity 6

Examine the text of Interview 4 for imperfects and perfects.

SESSION 7

Saying something had happened: the pluperfect

Activity 7

finiva lì la sua giornata perché **aveva** già **organizzato** la cena

Aveva … organizzato *she had … organized*. This is moving one stage back in time. It is called the pluperfect, **il trapassato**, and is formed … Well how do you think it is formed, judging from this example? Check in the Key – there is a further question for you there.

Forming the pluperfect

Verbs which make the perfect with **avere**	Verbs which make the perfect with **essere**
avevo finito	ero uscito/a
avevi finito	eri uscito/a
aveva finito	era uscito/a
avevamo finito	eravamo usciti/e
avevate finito	eravata usciti/e
avevano finito	erano usciti/e

If you look back to Gabriella's account of her family during the war, you will notice she says:

Eravamo sfollati a
   Villafranca …

*We had moved away
   to Villafranca …*

She uses the pluperfect. The verb **sfollare**, involving as it does movement, is conjugated with **essere**.

Activity 8

The story of the three little girls and the geese (Activity 5) can also be told using the pluperfect. It is a question of style. Try telling it again, leaving all the imperfects as they are and using the pluperfect for each perfect.

Further practice of the imperfect

Activity 9

Practise forming the imperfect, using Gabriella's description of her father. We have put nearly all the verbs which Gabriella used into the infinitive and we want you to find the correct form. ONE only was in the perfect. Which one was it and what would the form be? We have left other verbs, e.g. a subjunctive, unchanged. Think hard about the subject of numbers 7, 8 and 11; 9 has a different subject again and it is not **papà**.

Mio papà (1 essere) un gran buffone, gli (2 piacere) gli scherzi, (3 scherzare) sempre, (4 organizzare) riunioni in casa, parenti, feste, pranzi, gli (5 piacere) far da mangiare, era un gran cuoco ... e ci (6 portare) sempre in giro ... (7 avere) un giorno della settimana che era il nostro giorno, (8 uscire) con papà. Non (9 capire) mai se era il nostro giorno di libertà con papà o era il giorno di libertà di mia mamma .... Non (9 capire) mai. Papà (10 dedicarsi) alla spesa, (11 fare) sempre la spesa con papà perché mamma un po' per via della lingua o ... oppure perché a papà (12 piacere). E questo (13 essere) molto strano perché parlo di quarant'anni fa quasi, anche di più per cui ... allora gli uomini in Italia non (14 aiutare) in casa. Invece papà (15 fare) tutto in casa, tutto ... perché gli (16 piacere), non perché volesse aiutare mamma, perché gli (17 piacere).

Activity 10

A little more practice. In the following sentences, choose for each verb which tense, perfect or imperfect, makes sense. Then put the verb given into that form.

1 Mentre io (tornare) a casa l'altra sera tardi, (vedere) un riccio (*a hedgehog*) che attraversava la strada.
2 Quando Gianni (abitare) qui vicino, noi lo (vedere) spesso. Ora lo vediamo raramente, ma l' (incontrare) giovedì. (Uscire) dalla banca.
3 Questa (essere) la casa dei nonni ma noi la (ristrutturare). Loro (avere) qui la sala da pranzo ma noi la (trasformare) in una grande cucina, come vedete.
4 I nonni (cucinare) su un forno a legna. Alla nonna (riuscire) a perfezione certi piatti cotti a fuoco lento.

Saying what was going on in the past: the past continuous

Look back to what Angioletta said at the beginning of Unit 4 about her move to Florence while she was still a student in Pisa. She was asked whether she transferred to the University of Florence and said:

No, perché stavo finendo ...   *No, because I was finishing ...*

She uses the imperfect of **stare** plus **finendo** to underline that she really was in the process of finishing at that time, there wasn't much left to do. You may or may not have met this type of imperfect. Just as in English you can say (indeed, have to say) *I was finishing* using a form which underlines that the action was going on at that time, so you can in Italian. You use the imperfect of **stare** plus what is called the **gerund**. The name may be unfamiliar but it is very easy to form. The root (the first part) is the same as for the imperfect and you add **-ando** for Group 1 verbs and **-endo** for all the rest.

Group 1	Group 2	Group 3
parlare → **parlando**	decidere → **decidendo**	partire → **partendo**

The verbs which are irregular in the imperfect (and you remember that is very few indeed) are also irregular in the gerund:

fare → facendo
dire → dicendo
bere → bevendo
porre → ponendo
tradurre → traducendo

And **essere** is NOT irregular!

essere → essendo

Activity 11

Try emphasizing that the actions in the following sentences were in progress at a time in the past.

Anna was preparing the supper.
Anna stava preparando la cena.

1 John was finishing a letter.
2 The train was coming into the station.
3 Father was reading the newspaper.
4 Mother was having a shower. (fare la doccia)

The tense lends itself to a murder mystery situation. The suspects are being interrogated by the police to discover what they were doing at the moment the murder was being committed and each has an alibi. X was doing this and Y was doing that ... Why not have some fun in your imagination and work out such a situation! Of course, the simple imperfect conveys the same idea, but **stare** + gerund emphasizes the action as ongoing at that point in time.

The present continuous

You can also use a form to say actions are ongoing in the present. If you haven't already met it, you might guess what it is. You use the present tense of **stare** and the gerund.

Sto studiando.	*I am studying.*
Stiamo cercando di risolvere un problema.	*We are trying to resolve a problem.*

SESSION 8

Reading

This is an extract from another essay by Natalia Ginzburg written in Rome in the autumn of 1944. During the war her first husband, Leone Ginzburg, a former university teacher of Russian and a Jew, was sentenced to internal exile, **confino,** *a punishment much used by the Fascist authorities for political dissidents. He was required to leave Turin and live in a small village in the mountainous Abruzzo region, at that time very much undeveloped and remote even though it is not far from Rome. His wife and three small children went too. For Natalia, used to big-city life, it was a different world.*

Quando la prima neve cominciava a cadere, una lenta tristezza s'impadroniva di noi. Era un esilio il nostro: la nostra città era lontana e lontani erano i libri, gli amici, le vicende varie e mutevoli di una vera esistenza. Accendevamo la nostra stufa verde, col lungo tubo che attraversava il soffitto: ci si riuniva tutti nella stanza dove c'era la stufa, e lì si cucinava e si mangiava, mio marito scriveva al grande tavolo ovale, i bambini cospargevano di giocattoli il pavimento. Sul soffitto della stanza era dipinta un'aquila: e io guardavo l'aquila e pensavo che quello era l'esilio. L'esilio era l'aquila, la stufa verde che ronzava, era la vasta e silenziosa campagna e l'immobile neve. Alle cinque suonavano le campane della chiesa di Santa Maria, e le donne andavano a benedizione, coi loro scialli neri e il viso rosso. Tutte le sere mio marito ed io facevamo una passeggiata: tutte le sere camminavamo a braccetto, immergendo i piedi nella neve. Le case che costeggiavano la strada erano abitate da gente cognita e amica: e tutti uscivano sulla porta e ci dicevano: 'Con una buona salute'.

Qualcuno a volte domandava: 'Ma quando ci ritornate alle case vostre?' Mio marito diceva: 'Quando sarà finita la guerra'. 'E quando finirà questa guerra? Te che sai tutto e sei un professore, quando finirà?' Mio marito lo chiamavano 'il professore' non sapendo pronunciare il suo nome, e venivano da lontano a consultarlo sulle cose più varie, sulla stagione migliore per togliersi i denti, sui sussidi che dava il municipio e sulle tasse e le imposte.

This short extract evokes the monotony and melancholy of Natalia's time of exile in a haunting, poetic style. The whole essay is not long and you may enjoy reading it. In the last paragraph you learn that Leone died in prison in Rome, a prisoner of the occupying Germans by then, not long after they left the village. The essay ends:

Allora io avevo fede in un avvenire facile e lieto, ricco di desideri appagati, di esperienze e di comuni imprese. Ma era quello il tempo migliore della mia vita e solo adesso che m'è sfuggito per sempre, solo adesso lo so.

'Inverno in Abruzzo' (written in 1944) in Natalia Ginzburg,
Le piccole virtù, Einaudi 1962

s'impadroniva di noi	Note the word **padrone** seems to be in this word. So 'the sadness became our ...'?
ci si riuniva ... **si cucinava ...** **si mangiava**	This is the impersonal **si** we met earlier in the unit (Session 4). Note, however, that **riunirsi** is reflexive, which means if you use the impersonal **si** you have two identical pronouns together. Italian avoids this by changing the first **si** to **ci**.
gente cognita	You may not know the meaning of **cognita** but you do know **conoscere** and the expression **incognito**. Can you guess? **cognita** is however very literary. More usual: **conosciuta**.
venivano a consultarlo	It is difficult today to imagine the simple faith country people like these placed in someone who obviously knew a lot and probably didn't make

	any charge for the benefit of his advice. Since he knew a lot, he was expected to know everything. Similar experiences are described by Carlo Levi, Torinese sent into internal exile, further south in the Basilicata, in his book *Cristo si è fermato a Eboli* (Christ Stopped at Eboli).
tasse ... imposte	The latter are general taxes payable to the state such as income tax whereas the former are taxes on specific services or provisions and payable to specific agencies, for instance on cars, on school attendance (effectively *fees*), etc.
desideri appagati	*wishes granted, fulfilled*

Comprehension 5

1 Natalia felt herself exiled from real life (**una vera esistenza**). What did she miss from the existence she had left behind?

2 How large a house do they seem to have had at their disposal?

3 Where did Natalia see an eagle and what did it come to symbolize for her?

4 What do you learn about the appearance of the women of the village?

5 What sort of advice did people come to seek from Leone Ginzburg?

Activity 12

Talking to yourself

Ora tocca a Lei! Now it's your turn. Think out how to talk (to yourself or someone else) about:

1 La Sua prima scuola. Com'era? Chi erano i Suoi amici? Che cosa Le piaceva fare? Che cosa detestava fare?

2 La vita della Sua famiglia quando era bambino/a. I Suoi genitori, fratelli, sorelle ... La casa dove vivevate. Le vacanze. Ricordi felici (o tristi, se vuole).

3 E' abbastanza anziano/a da ricordare la Seconda Guerra Mondiale? Che cosa si ricorda? Forse Lei ha avuto la sfortuna di vivere anche un'altra guerra. Ripensi alla Sua esperienza, e immagini di raccontarla a qualcuno, in italiano.

4 Cambiamenti nel corso della Sua vita. Com'era la Sua città (o il Suo paese) quando era bambino/a?

The more practice in reminiscing you can give yourself the better – remember the advice on language learning in Unit 1. But of course we don't know your life story. So you choose what to focus on and tell yourself what you used to do, what things and people were like ...

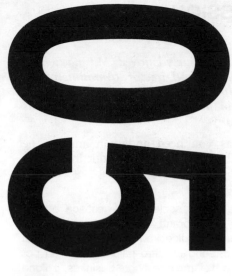

05

al lavoro

In this unit we shall learn
- how to talk about businesses and jobs
- how to express frequency and approximate amounts
- more prepositions: **fra/tra; in/a** + place
- relative pronouns: **che, quello che, cui,** etc.
- how to say *both ... and, either ... or, neither ... nor*
- the present subjunctive
- how to talk about repeated actions: **andare** + gerund
- how to say *'having done this, I ...'*: past participles
- the conditional perfect
- the use of **tu** and **Lei**

SESSION 1

▶ Interview 1

*Italian food is well known and widely enjoyed. Marina, whom we met in Unit 3, is Managing Director (**Amministratore Delegato**) of a chain of self-service restaurants, which aim to serve classic Italian food in pleasant surroundings. She was asked to describe the company.*

As usual, listen as often as you need and then answer the comprehension questions. If you can do so without looking at the text, you are giving yourself valuable practice at real-life situations.

Marina Beh, la società è una società che gestisce questa piccola catena di ristoranti. Sono in tutto quindici ristoranti, apriremo il sedicesimo a Roma fra un paio di settimane. Poi ci sono un altro paio di locali un po' diversi, insomma diciamo che il core business, il filone principale è questi ristoranti self-service. Sono dei self-service un po' più di lusso del self-service classico, dove cioè cerchiamo di dare di più sia nella qualità del prodotto, di quello che prepariamo da mangiare, sia nell'allestimento, nell'arredo dei ristoranti. E' una formula che funziona abbastanza bene anche se sono ristoranti molto grandi che hanno bisogno di investimenti piuttosto alti e hanno dei costi anche di gestione alti dunque funzionano solo se riescono a garantire un certo livello di attività. Che è abbastanza difficile da originare quindi si possono aprire solo in posti abbastanza particolari. Non è una formula che si presti a uno sviluppo a tappeto sul tipo McDonalds, ma a uno sviluppo un po' più lento.

Interviewer Quanti ne avete aperti nei nove – dieci anni che ci lavori?

Marina Una decina, circa uno all'anno, uno e mezzo all'anno che non è moltissimo. Nello stesso periodo McDonalds ne apre mille probabilmente, anche forse di più. Ma è una cosa diversa. E' un po' il problema, diciamo, di questa formula che non riesce ad espandersi a dei ritmi molto veloci. Comunque, insomma, in complesso è una cosa che funziona quindi. Il primo ristorante è stato aperto a Trieste ma la sede del gruppo è in Veneto e diciamo che da lì, ci stiamo lentamente espandendo sul resto del territorio. Adesso abbiamo più o meno coperto il Nord Italia –

beh, insomma siamo nelle principali città – e quindi ci stiamo un po' espandendo verso sud adesso.

Interviewer La sede del gruppo è in Veneto?

Marina Sì, vicino a Venezia. Io ho questo piccolo ufficio qui perché la mia famiglia, quella di mio marito, è qui a Milano, quindi è una base. Io sto qui anche se faccio poi abbastanza la pendolare, perché ogni settimana passo almeno un paio di giorni in sede.

Interviewer Il tuo lavoro in che cosa consiste?

Marina Sono amministratore delegato, quindi diciamo che mi occupo un po' di tutti gli aspetti di gestione della società da un punto di vista strategico se vogliamo, cioè non entro negli aspetti operativi, non li gestisco direttamente. Mi occupo abbastanza intensamente di tutto quello che è lo sviluppo, cioè la ricerca di nuove posizioni, contatti con controparti che ci offrono queste posizioni, la verifica se sono adatte o meno all'insediamento di nuovi ristoranti, lo studio … purtoppo per trovare una posizione che vada bene per un Brek, ne dobbiamo vedere cinquanta per cui è un'attività che porta via molto tempo, anche perché sono posti cosparsi per tutt'Italia qualche volta anche all'estero ci propongono delle cose, quindi devo viaggiare, girare.

sviluppo a tappeto	Marina is coining a phrase here. The expression **bombardamento a tappeto** meaning *blanket bombing*, has this dictionary definition: **lancio di grandissime quantità di bombe su una delimitata zona in modo da distribuirle egualmente dappertutto** (*lo Zingarelli 2004*). What Marina means is development leading to dense coverage.
Io ho questo piccolo ufficio qui	Marina was interviewed in Milan.
la pendolare	*commuter.* Don't forget your guessing skills. What does *a pendulum* (**pendolo**) do? It moves back and forth on the same path …
Sono amministratore delegato	It is not usual to form a feminine for *managing director*.
adatte o meno	*suitable or not* (lit: *suitable* or *less suitable*.) **Meno** means less.

Marina Bastianello
Amministratore Delegato

20122 Milano
Via dell' Unione, 3
Tel. e Fax (02) 867466

Brek Ristoranti s.p.a.
30038 Spinea (Ve)
Via delle Industrie, 8
Tel. (041) 5496111
Fax (041) 5496176

Comprehension 1

1 How many restaurants are there in the chain?
2 Is this all the company runs?
3 In what ways does the company consider it offers something special?
4 What is the problem which Marina seems to consider very important in ensuring that the company is profitable?
5 What kind of rate of expansion does Marina reckon the company is able to maintain?
6 Does she seem worried about the company?
7 There are two main reasons why Marina has to travel a lot. What are they?
8 One aspect of the company's business above all takes a lot of her time. What is it?

SESSION 2

Vocabulary for business

Often the words for talking about business are guessable, the English words having Latin origins and therefore being similar to the Italian, since Italian is close to its Latin parentage. Sometimes, however, you will find Italians use English words for standard concepts in the business world, which were usually first mooted in USA. There was an example in what Marina said.

Activity 1

Pick out words relating to business and commerce in the text of Interview 1. Using your knowledge and guessing skills, make a list with translations. Then consult the Key at the back of the book. It will help you with any you couldn't manage.

Activity 2

Here is a list of expressions related to the world of work (**Il mondo del lavoro**). They are divided into two groups, nouns (**nomi**) and verbs (**verbi**). For each noun, find the corresponding verb and for each verb the noun. You could use a dictionary if you get stuck.

> Example: **nome:** una società → verbo corrispondente: associarsi
>
> **verbo:** gestire → nome corrispondente: la gestione

Nomi: il prodotto – l'allestimento – il costo – il livello – lo sviluppo – l'amministratore – la ricerca – l'insediamento
Verbi: garantire – fondare – istituire – prestare – espandersi – investire – verificare – valutare

Activity 3

In Interview 1 Marina uses some of the points we have looked at in previous units.

1 Find an example of **stare** + gerund, the present continuous. In fact Marina uses the same expression twice.
2 Find examples of the preposition **da**: (a) used after an indefinite, as described in Unit 4 (**qualcosa da mangiare**); (b) used after an adjective and followed by an infinitive.

3 Pick out at least three words or expressions which you think are characteristic of spoken language, words used by Marina as she hesitates, thinks, etc. For instance, when you first met Marina in Unit 3 we pointed out her use of **diciamo**.

Expressing frequency

Notice this idiomatic use of **a**:

uno all'anno (ristorante)	*one (restaurant) a year*
cinque riunioni alla settimana	*five meetings a week*
una volta al giorno	*once a day*

Activity 4

How then would you say in Italian:

1 once a week
2 three times a day
3 twice a month?

Activity 5

Here is part of a feature from a magazine:

Conducete una vita sana? Siete in forma? Scopritelo rispondendo a queste domande! *Do you lead a healthy life? Are you fit? Find out by answering these questions!*

Quante volte alla settimana (o al mese) ...

1 ... vai a lavorare a piedi?
2 ... fai sport?
3 ... vai a dormire prima di mezzanotte?
4 ... mangi verdura fresca?
5 ... mangi frutta fresca?
6 ... vai a passeggiare?

More prepositions: a special use of *fra/tra*

You probably know **fra/tra** meaning *between*:

fra amici	*between friends*
fra Pisa e Firenze	*between Pisa and Florence*
tra la vita e la morte	*between life and death,* i.e. *dying*
tra mezzogiorno e l'una	*between 12 o'clock and one*

Notice this use of **fra/tra**:

apriremo il sedicesimo a Roma *fra* un paio di settimane	*we shall open the sixteenth in Rome **in** a couple of week's time*

With an expression referring to an amount of time, **fra/tra** means *in ...* (amount of time) *'s time*. **Fra** is interchangeable with **tra**. The choice of one rather than the other depends on which sounds best, i.e. to avoid repeating **f** or **t**.

fra tre giorni	*in three days' time*
fra un mese	*in a month's time*
fra poco	*in a short time, shortly*

Activity 6

It's the beginning of the new working year. Marina has a meeting with her colleagues to inform them about the new commitments and dates. Look at the notes she has written in her diary before the meeting and complete what she says at the meeting.

---

10 gennaio 2004

Ore 10.00 – riunione

Date da ricordare:

- apertura sedicesimo ristorante Brek a Roma, 25 gennaio '04

- apertura primo ristorante Brek all'estero (Germania, Monaco), gennaio 2005

- sopralluogo locali Brek di Monaco e conferma definitiva dell'accordo, prima settimana febbraio '04

- inizio lavori di ampliamento Brek Vicenza, settembre '04

- inizio lavori di ristrutturazione Brek Torino, Carlo Felice, giugno '04

Example: **Tra un paio di settimane,** il 25 gennaio, apriremo a Roma il nostro sedicesimo ristorante.

1 .... apriremo il nostro primo ristorante all'estero, a Monaco, in Germania.

2 .... faremo un sopralluogo per i locali del Brek di Monaco. Se va tutto come stabilito confermeremo definitivamente l'accordo.

3 Per quanto riguarda lavori su ristoranti già esistenti, quelli di ampliamento del Brek di Vicenza saranno iniziati

.... Invece i lavori di ristrutturazione del Brek Torino, quello in Piazza Carlo Felice, inizieranno ....

More prepositions: *a/in* used with places

Don't forget that the way **a** and **in** work with places is different from the English *in/to*. In English whether you mean going to the place or being there affects your choice of preposition:

a Londra	*to London / in London*
in Italia	*to Italy / in Italy*

In Italian what is relevant is whether the place is a *village/town/city* or a larger area such as an Italian *region* or a *country*. Use **a** with the name of a village, town or city, **in** with a larger area:

Vado a Venezia.	*I'm going/I go to Venice.*
Sono a Venezia.	*I'm in Venice.*

Vado in Toscana e poi in Francia.	*I'm going to Tuscany and then to France.*
Abito in Toscana. Mio fratello abita in Francia.	*I live in Tuscany. My brother lives in France.*

Activity 7

You have just had a lovely holiday, a cruise up the Po in northern Italy. You visited various interesting towns in the three regions you went through: Milano, Cremona, Mantova in Lombardia; Parma and Ferrara in Emilia Romagna; and Verona, Padova and Venezia in Veneto. Write a postcard to some Italian friends telling them where you went, using the information from the tour brochure opposite and using **a** and **in** correctly.

GIORNO 1	Arrivo all'aeroporto di Venezia. Notte a bordo della motonave Venezia.
GIORNO 2	Visita guidata di Venezia: Basilica di S. Marco, Piazza S. Marco e il Palazzo Ducale, il Canal Grande, il Ponte di Rialto. In serata possibilità di andare in gondola.
GIORNO 3	Partenza per Murano e Burano e poi Chioggia; gita facoltativa a Padova: Basilica di S. Antonio (bronzi di Donatello) e Cappella degli Scrovegni (affreschi di Giotto).
GIORNO 4	Comincia il viaggio sul Po. Escursione: Ferrara: Palazzo dei Diamanti e Castello Estense.
GIORNO 5	Continua il viaggio sul Po. Escursioni: Mantova: Palazzo Ducale e Palazzo Te; Verona: Arena – con teatro lirico in serata.
GIORNO 6	Continua il viaggio. Escursione: Parma: Duomo e Battistero.
GIORNO 7	Arrivo: Cremona. Piazza del Comune, Duomo.
GIORNO 8	Viaggio in treno: Milano. Visita della città, shopping. Notte in albergo.
GIORNO 9	Partenza.

Expressions of approximate amounts

un paio	*a pair*
una decina	*about ten*
una dozzina	*a dozen, about 12*
una quindicina	*about fifteen*
una ventina	*about twenty*

The suffix **-ina** can be added to any of these round numbers: 20, 30, 40, 50, 60, 70, 80, 90. It means '*about* that number' and it is more common with those up to and including 50.

Siamo a una quarantina di chilometri da Firenze.	*We are about forty kilometres from Florence.*

Compare **quarantina** (*about forty*) with **quarantena** (*quarantine*), which was originally 40 days. At 'a hundred', the suffix for expressing approximation changes:

un centinaio	*about a hundred*
un migliaio	*about a thousand*

The plural is irregular and feminine:

Centinaia di vespe hanno invaso il giardino.	*Hundreds of wasps invaded the garden.*

Migliaia di tifosi stanno arrivando per la partita.	*Thousands of fans are arriving for the match.*

The noun **un paio** works the same way. How would you say: *two pairs of shoes?* **due paia di scarpe.**

Activity 8

In your office there are a couple of terrible gossips. All day they ask each other about other colleagues. And if they don't know the information requested, they have a guess. Below are some of the questions. Answer them as they do, using one of the approximate quantity words just studied and the information given in brackets.

Example: Quanti anni pensi che abbia Carla? (40)
  Non lo so ... credo **una quarantina** ...

1 Quanti anni pensi che abbia Marco? (30)
2 Quanti anni pensi che abbia Paola? (50)

Example: Quanti soldi pensi che guadagni Carla al mese? (2 milioni)
  Non ne sono sicuro/a ... forse un paio di milioni ...

3 Quanti soldi pensi che guadagni Marco all'anno? (30 milioni)
4 Quanti soldi pensi che guadagni il nostro capo al mese (10 milioni)

Example: Quanti giorni di ferie ha preso Paola quest'anno? (10)
  Mah ... mi sembra **una decina.**

5 Quanti giorni di ferie ha preso Marco quest'anno? (2)
6 Quanti giorni di ferie ha preso Carla quest'anno? (15)

Example: Quante volte hai chiesto a Carla di non fumare in ufficio? (100)
  Almeno **un centinaio!**

7 Quante volte hai chiesto al tuo capo di darti un permesso per uscire prima il mercoledì? (1000)
8 Quante volte hai chiesto a Marco di non lasciare la porta del suo ufficio aperta quando è al telefono con le sue amanti? (100)

SESSION 3

Relative pronouns ('who', 'which', etc.)

There are a number of examples in what Marina said. Relative pronouns are used to join two clauses or phrases so as to tell you more about the first. They are straightforward in Italian once you understand them.

Che

It can refer to people or things and be the subject or object of the clause which follows it, so that it can mean *who, whom, which* or *that*. In other words, it's much easier in Italian!

Marina è una persona che ama mangiare bene. (refers to a person, Marina, and is subject of **ama**)
Marina is someone who loves to eat well.

La società, che possiede ora quindici ristoranti self-service, cresce a un ritmo costante. (refers to a thing and is subject of **possiede**)
The company, which owns fifteen self-service restaurants now, is growing at a steady rate.

Marina, che conosco molto bene, abita a Milano. (refers to a person, object of **conosco**)
Marina, who(m) I know very well, lives in Milan.

La società che lei gestisce è ben conosciuta in Veneto. (refers to a thing, object of **gestisce**)
The company (which/that) she manages is well known in the Veneto.

Note: the relative pronoun can sometimes be omitted in English. Che must be present in Italian.

Activity 9

Match each person in the list on the left with the description of his or her profession (list on the right). Make a sentence, using the relative pronoun **che** to connect the two halves.

Example: Il direttore d'orchestra / dirigere l'orchestra
Il direttore d'orchestra è la persona che dirige l'orchestra.

Il cantante d'opera
Lo scrittore
L'amministratore delegato
Il cuoco
Il controllore
Il calciatore
Il dentista

amministrare l'azienda
giocare in una squadra di calcio
controllare i biglietti sul treno
curare i denti dei suoi pazienti
cantare l'opera nei teatri
cucinare i pasti in un ristorante
scrivere libri

Cui

Cui is used instead of **che** after a preposition. Marina says (of the difficulty of selecting sites for the company's restaurants):

per trovare una posizione ... ne dobbiamo vedere cinquanta, per cui è un'attività che porta via molto tempo	to find a place ... we have to see fifty, so it is a task which takes a lot of time.

In this case, **cui** does not refer to a specific word, more to the whole problem. **Per cui**, is in fact often used to mean *therefore, on account of which*. Cui can however refer to specific words, denoting people or things:

E' una persona <u>con cui</u> non mi sento a mio agio.	He/she is a person with whom I don't feel at ease.
La casa <u>in cui</u> abita quell'amico è nuova.	The house that friend lives in is new. (the house in which that friend lives ...)
dei self-service <u>in cui</u> cerchiamo di dare di più ...	self-service restaurants in which we try to give more ...

You can use **dove**, as Marina does, instead of **in cui**. If the preposition is **a** it can be omitted, although this is perhaps more usual in written than spoken Italian:

La signora cui ho parlato del Suo progetto era molto entusiasta.	The lady I spoke to (to whom I spoke) about your plan was very enthusiastic.

Activity 10

Marina, a busy woman, often gives her secretary detailed instructions to do what she will not have time to do herself. Read the instructions and transform them into a single sentence, using the relative pronoun **cui**, preceded by a preposition; in one case you can omit the preposition. Note: she uses **tu** to her secretary.

> Example: Telefona all'Ingegner Rossi. Devo prendere un appuntamento con **lui** entro la fine della settimana.
> Telefona all'Ingegner Rossi **con cui** devo prendere un appuntamento entro la fine della settimana.

1 Manda un fax alla Dottoressa Paolini. Devo sapere **da lei** se i lavori procedono regolarmente a Torino.
2 Telefona all'Avvocato Franceschi. Devo discutere **con lui** riguardo al nuovo contratto per il Brek di Monaco.

3 Scrivi una lettera di sollecito al Ragionier Barbato. Devo ricevere **da lui** i preventivi per i lavori al Brek di Vicenza entro la fine del mese.

4 Telefona all'Architetto Cappelli. Devo restituir**gli** i disegni e i progetti per il Brek di Roma con le correzioni al più presto.

Il cui, la cui, i cui, le cui

All these mean *whose* and the article should be that of the person or thing possessed:

Il mio amico Paolo, <u>il cui</u> padre è un noto scultore, mi ha invitato ad una mostra.

My friend Paul, whose father is a well-known sculptor, invited me to an exhibition.

Il viaggiatore, <u>la cui</u> valigia è stata smarrita dalla compagnia aerea, era furibondo.

The traveller whose suitcase was mislaid by the airline was furious.

Il quale, la quale, i quali, le quali

These can replace **che** or **cui** and are useful in particular to avoid ambiguity, since they show gender. Sometimes a speaker or writer will use them simply to avoid repetition of **che**.

La sorella del mio amico, <u>la quale</u> studia a New York, ci ha ospitati nel suo appartamento. (**la** shows it is the sister, not the friend, who is studying in New York.)

My friend's sister, who is studying in New York, put us up in her apartment.

Chi

What you need to remember, especially if you have studied French, is that **chi** is not commonly used as a relative pronoun. It is an interrogative pronoun, meaning *who?* As a relative pronoun it has very specific uses:

a Chi ... chi ... = *some ... others ...*

Chi ballava, chi cantava, chi stava a guardare ...

Some were dancing, some singing, others watching ...

Chi dice una cosa, chi un'altra.

Some say one thing, others another.

b To convey the idea *he who, she who, people who* as in sayings like:

Chi mai semina, mai raccoglie.

He who doesn't sow, doesn't reap.

(You've got to put
something in to get
something out!)

Chi dorme non piglia pesci.   *He who sleeps doesn't catch*
any fish. (Keep alert if you
want results)

Also in ordinary speech:

Può venire chi vuole.   *Anyone who wants to can come.*

Activity 11

Here is a series of Italian proverbs and sayings. They have been
split into two and the right-hand list is not in the correct order.
Try matching them. Can you guess at the English equivalent?

Example: Chi dorme non piglia pesci.
He who sleeps doesn't catch any fish.

Chi dorme ...	... la vince.
Chi tardi arriva ...	... raccoglie tempesta.
Chi va all'osto ...	... male alloggia.
Chi va piano ...	... l'aspetti.
Chi la fa ...	**... non piglia pesci.**
Chi va al mulino ...	... di spada perisce.
Chi semina vento ...	... s'infarina.
Chi la dura ...	... va sano e va lontano.
Chi di spada ferisce ...	... perde il posto.

Quello che, ciò che, quelli/quelle che

Quello che, ciò che both mean *what*, in the sense of *that which*.
Tutto quello che means *everything that* (*all that which*). The
first two examples are from Marina's description of her work.

... nella qualità del prodotto,   *... in the quality of the*
quello che prepariamo   *product, what we prepare*
da mangiare.   *to eat (the food we prepare).*

Mi occupo di tutto quello che   *I deal with everything*
è lo sviluppo.   *related to development*
    (all that is related to ...)

Non capisco quello che dice.   *I don't understand what*
    he says.

Quello che mi preoccupa è la   *What worries me is his/her*
sua impetuosità.   *impetuousness.*

Quello che can also refer to a person (*the one who*). The plural
is **quelli che, quelle che, tutti quelli che**.

Gianni è quello che indossa una maglia rossa.

Gianni is the one wearing a red sweater.

Tra i nostri clienti, quelli che non pagano puntualmente sono in genere i più benestanti.

Among our customers, those who (the people who …) don't pay punctually are generally the most comfortably off.

Activity 12

Look at this photo. Say who's who, following the example:

Fausto — Antonio

Papà   Claudio   Anna   Mamma

Example: **Quello che indossa la giacca a quadri è mio fratello, Claudio.**

1 (Anna – sorella)
2 (la mamma)
3 (papà)
4 (Fausto – cugino)
5 (Antonio – il ragazzo di Anna)

Activity 13

Choose the correct relative pronoun from those explained above to complete the following sentences, which are taken from earlier chapters in the book.

Example: Amo le donne interessanti, **quelle che** non trovi nelle sale da ballo.

1 Mah, io potrei dire .... dico di solito ai miei studenti.

2 Se sentivo qualcuno .... parlava inglese tentavo di attaccare discorso.

3 Mamma non ha mai imparato bene l'italiano per .... la prendevamo in giro.

4 Ho un nipotino .... vedo pochissimo.

5 Ho avuto i problemi nella vita .... tutti hanno avuto.

6 Silvia è molto seria, molto ligia al dovere, ... deve fare, lo fa.

7 Barbara capisce tante più cose che non Silvia a .... abbiamo sempre attribuito doti (di intuito).

8 Gli stipendi vanno pagati a .... lavora.

9 Non c'entra assolutamente niente con .... avevo fatto prima.

10 Contrariamente a .... si può pensare una gran parte (degli esami) erano teorici.

11 Armando Piazza, custode del Club Med, era entrato nella torre bianca .... ha sede il Club.

12 Tajeddine Abdel Karim, ... ha appena compiuto 18 anni, ha lasciato la madre per venire a trovare il padre.

sia ... sia both ... and ...

Marina says:

> cerchiamo di dare di più **sia** nella qualità del prodotto, di quello che prepariamo da mangiare, **sia** nell'allestimento, nell'arredo dei ristoranti.

sia ... sia ...	*both ... and ...*

You can also say: **e ... e ...**

> *Either ... or ...* is **o ... o ...**
> *Neither ... nor ...* is **né ... né ...**

This is another case of English and Italian working differently. In Italian you have the same word for both parts, in English, two different words. You can however use **che** as the second word if the first is **sia**.

Activity 14

Marina is constantly on the lookout for suitable places to open a new Brek. Imagine a meeting with the local council officers in a place which Marina considers suitable. Marina describes and promotes the hallmark characteristics of the restaurants in the Brek chain. Using the information given, construct sentences using **sia ... sia ...** correctly.

Example: self-service / locali di altro tipo (gestire)
> Il nostro gruppo **gestisce sia self-service sia locali di altro tipo.**

1 cibo di ottima qualità / ambiente elegante (garantire)
2 servizio veloce / salette da pranzo tranquille e silenziose (offrire)
3 costi di gestione alti / investimenti alti (avere)
4 nel Nord Italia / nel Centro-Sud (volere espandersi)

Activity 15

Re-read or listen again to what Marina said. Then close your book and try to summarize it in Italian using your own words. Here are some questions to guide you:

1 Qual è l'attività principale della società Brek?
2 Quanti ristoranti ci sono?
3 Che tipo di ristoranti sono?
4 Che cosa cercano di offrire?
5 Perché è importante garantire un certo livello di attività in un ristorante Brek?
6 In quale città è stato aperto il primo ristorante?
7 Perché Marina fa la pendolare tra Milano e la zona di Venezia?
8 Di che cosa si occupa soprattutto lei?
9 Perché porta via molto tempo la ricerca di posizioni adatte ad un ristorante Brek?

SESSION 4

▶ Interview 2

The Italians were the first bankers. Emanuela, whom you met in Unit 1, is a branch manager in a small private bank (i.e. neither publicly owned nor quoted on the Milan Stock Exchange). We expected to find her rather pleased to have been made a manager.

Emanuela	Io lavoro in una banca, una banca privata, e attualmente dirigo una piccola agenzia. Molto piccola, siamo solo cinque elementi. Sono molto stanca, pagata poco e …
Interviewer	Dunque non sei molto contenta in questo momento?
Emanuela	No, non sono molto contenta perché non ho uno stipendio adeguato alla mia qualifica e quindi sto

	aspettando che loro decidano di cambiare il livello della mia posizione quindi di darmi lo stipendio giusto che è previsto per la legge. Sto aspettando da un anno.
Interviewer	Questo è perché sei una donna?
Emanuela	No, non è questo. Ci sono anche altri tre ragazzi che hanno lo stesso problema … Sono maschi, sono l'unica, diciamo, l'unica … be' ragazza, ormai non posso più dire … visto che ho trentacinque anni mercoledì prossimo … ma l'unica donna che nella nostra banca, a parte una signora molto più vecchia che ha una qualifica di alto livello …. gli altri che hanno la mia funzione sono tutti maschi. Anche loro purtroppo – sono tre ragazzi che hanno il mio stesso problema, fanno lo stesso tipo di lavoro, stesso tipo di impegno, lo stesso tipo di responsabilità, però lo stipendio non è quello previsto correttamente per la legge.
Interviewer	Ma sono molte le donne direttori di banca in Italia?
Emanuela	Qualcuna c'è. Io ne conosco diverse. Cassa di Risparmio, San Paolo, ne vedo diverse, ce ne sono abbastanza. Non credo che sia una, ci sia una discriminazione … Ammesso che si abbia il tempo e la voglia di dedicare di più dell'orario normale, previsto, per il lavoro. Però non credo ci siano problemi di … forse più per i clienti … magari vengono, trovano una donna giovane, è una cosa che non tutti apprezzano. Magari pensano sia necessario avere più il fisico del ruolo, no? Vecchiotto, capelli grigi, uomo. Questa è una cosa che disorienta un po' il cliente, trovo. Vengono, mi chiedono: 'Dov'è il direttore?' 'Mi dica!' 'No, volevo parlare con il direttore.' (ride) E' un po' … però …

lo stipendio giusto previsto per la legge	The correct salary as laid down by law. This may in fact be a trades union agreement (**un accordo sindacale**) rather than a law.
Cassa di Risparmio, San Paolo	These are the names of banks.
Mi dica	Lit. *Tell me!* The standard expression to indicate to a customer that a shop assistant, bank clerk etc. is ready to attend to his/her needs. Perhaps: *How can I help you?* The familiar (**tu**) form of this is: **dimmi!**

Comprehension 2

1 How many staff are there in the branch of the bank which Emanuela manages?
2 Emanuela is not happy. Why?
3 Is she the only woman manager in the small private bank she works for?
4 Does she feel there is sex discrimination (a) in the matter of her salary? (b) in the appointment of women bank managers generally?
5 What problem does she think a woman manager poses to the bank customers?

SESSION 5

False friends again

Add these to your collection:

attualmente	*at the present time, at this moment, nowadays*
attualità	*current events*
attuale	*present, contemporary, current. (actual:* **reale, vero, effettivo;** *actually:* **di fatto, in verità, effettivamente, in effetti;** *actuality:* **realtà, verità, condizioni reali)**
stipendio	*salary.* The Italian word doesn't have the limited use of *stipend* in English. But, once again, the link makes it guessable. Note: **salario** *wages*, i.e. the pay of manual workers.

Activity 16

Below is a summary of Emanuela's interview. Read it and think hard about its meaning. We want you to translate it into English and to think particularly about the translation of the words in bold type.

Tra il dire e il fare c'è di mezzo il mare

(Lit: *between saying and doing lies the ocean*)

1 Emanuela lavora in banca. Ha una posizione di una certa responsabilità, e si aspetterebbe di ricevere uno stipendio piuttosto alto. **In realtà** il suo stipendio è abbastanza basso.
2 Il motivo di questo stato di cose è che è stata solo recentemente promossa di livello, per cui **attualmente** non viene ancora pagata secondo quanto prescrive la legge. In futuro, però, verrà pagata di più.

3 Per quanto riguarda la sua credibilità, come donna, di fronte ai clienti uomini, Emanuela pensa che la condizione **attuale** delle donne lavoratrici in Italia sia migliore che nel passato, e non si ritiene discriminata.

4 Tuttavia, nonostante Emanuela sia ottimista a questo riguardo, la discriminazione sessuale sui posti di lavoro **in effetti** è un problema vivo. Del resto, lei stessa dice che molti uomini che arrivano nella sua banca si stupiscono di trovare un direttore donna.

The present subjunctive

Earlier in this unit we met: **sia ... sia**, meaning *both ... and*. So what is meant when Emanuela says:

Non credo **sia** una ... ci **sia** una discriminazione ...

Sia here is clearly a verb: Emanuela in fact corrects herself to add **ci**. You might have expected, if you think about it, that she would use **c'è**. But she says: **non credo ci sia una discriminazione**. She uses the subjunctive. You can probably guess that the verb is **essere** and this is the present subjunctive. Why does she use it? What is this subjunctive which strikes fear into the heart of many a language learner? First let us say it should not do that! Like any part of the language, it needs to be studied, Italians need to be listened to and imitated, and gradually the learner will find it becomes a part of his/her Italian.

General remarks about the subjunctive

When analysing Italian verbs grammarians divide them into *moods*, **modi** in Italian. The subjunctive is a mood, as is the indicative (see **Grammar – the technical jargon explained**). As a general rule, the subjunctive is associated with subjectivity, point of view, not being categorical. The indicative is factual, the subjunctive deals with areas of doubt, possibility, uncertainty. The third mood, the conditional, deals with the hypothetical. The term *mood* as applied to the subjunctive may help you to remember it is related to feelings, uncertainties. The term *mode* might be more suitable, as it is perhaps more a question of *point of view*, the way the action is viewed. We should add that it is often said that the use of the subjunctive is diminishing. Maybe, but it is still widely used and not just by highly educated people. It still needs to be learned by the foreign student who aspires to a good command of Italian.

The subjunctive mood has four tenses: present, imperfect, perfect and pluperfect. It is not in itself a tense. For the moment we will stay with the present subjunctive, which is what Emanuela uses in the sentence we picked out. Emanuela says she doesn't think there is discrimination against women on the banks' part. She does not want to be categorical, it is her opinion. And the subjunctive brings that home.

The uses of the subjunctive

The most satisfactory way to approach the uses of the subjunctive is to consider them as you meet them, although we have put a reference list in the **Reference grammar** at the back of the book for you to consult when you need. For the moment we will draw your attention to the uses in the texts in *Improve Your Italian* as we meet them.

We must first be clear: the subjunctive is not normally used in main clauses. It is almost always used in a subordinate clause, that is a clause which doesn't stand by itself, but is introduced by something in the main part of the sentence. For instance in the sentence we have already looked at, the main clause is **Non credo**, and **credo** leads us into a subordinate clause. In almost all cases the subordinate clause starts with **che**. Emanuela happens to use two verbs (**credere, pensare**) which can be used without **che**, although other speakers use **che**; it's a matter of personal style. Let's look at more examples of the subjunctive in what Emanuela says, and a couple in what Marina says.

Emanuela:

sto aspettando che loro **decidano** di cambiare il livello della mia posizione.
I am waiting for them to make up their minds to change the level of my post.
Ammesso che si **abbia** il tempo e la voglia ...
Given that one has the time and the desire to ...
Però non **credo** ci **siano** problemi di ...
However, I don't believe there are problems of ...
Magari **pensano sia** necessario avere il fisico del ruolo.
Perhaps they think it is necessary to have the physical appearance for the role.

Marina:

Non è **una formula che si presti** a uno sviluppo a tappeto.
It's not a formula which lends itself to blanket development.
per trovare **una posizione che vada** bene per un Brek ...
to find a location suitable for a Brek ...

The subjunctive for opinions and beliefs

Of the examples we have, three involve verbs meaning thinking, believing. When you say you think something is – or isn't – the case or that you believe something is true or otherwise, you are expressing an opinion, not offering the thought as fact. Doubt, uncertainty, avoiding being categorical – all cases for the subjunctive. So it will be associated with verbs such as **pensare, credere, dubitare** (*to doubt*), **sperare** (*to hope*), **temere** (*to fear*), **avere paura** (*to fear, be afraid*) etc. and expressions with similar meanings.

The subjunctive in clauses describing a type or category

per trovare **una posizione che vada** bene per un Brek.
to find a position suitable for a Brek.
Non è **una formula che si presti** a uno sviluppo a tappeto
It isn't a formula which lends itself to blanket development.

To go back to Marina's words, what sort of **posizione** is so difficult to find? Not a healthy one, not a quiet one, but one which is a good one for a Brek. The phrase **che vada bene per un Brek** describes the location just in the same way as the adjectives 'healthy' or 'quiet' might. This is why grammarians call this an 'adjectival phrase or clause'. It is describing a type of, rather than a specific, location; 'una posizione' rather than 'la posizione'.

Grammarians call the word (**una posizione**) that the relative pronoun (**che**) refers to 'the antecedent'.

When the antecedent does not refer to a specific person or thing, they call it an 'indefinite antecedent'. Such expressions tend to occur after verbs related to looking for, wanting, needing, etc. And they are followed by a subjunctive. The second example from Marina is similar.

Look at two sentences and try to sense the difference:

| Leggo un romanzo che stimola la curiosità. | *I'm reading a novel which stimulates curiosity.* |
| Cerco un romanzo che stimoli la curiosità. | *I'm looking for a novel which stimulates curiosity.* |

(NB The translation here and below is word for word rather than the best possible.)

In the first sentence the words following **che** describe a specific novel and the quality it is known to have. In the second sentence the words after **che** describe the type of novel I am looking for. But I don't know whether or not there is one such available. Try two more:

Vado da uno psicologo che mi dà fiducia.	*I go to a psychologist whom I can trust.* (A fact. I am happy with my psychologist.)
Cerco uno psicologo che mi dia fiducia.	*I'm looking for a psychologist whom I can trust.* (This is the sort of psychologist I am hoping to find.)

And these. The first comes from the speech made by a new Prime Minister to Parliament when seeking its acceptance of the government he had just formed:

In una fase successiva è maturato l'accordo che consente oggi al Governo di presentarsi davanti alle Camere.	*In a subsequent phase the agreement which allows the Government to present itself to the (two) Chambers came into being.*

And here is what he might have said earlier, in the period in which he was canvassing support from various parties as he tried to form the government:

Ci vuole un accordo che consenta al Governo di presentarsi davanti alle Camere.	*We need an agreement which will allow the Government to present itself to the Chambers.*

In our experience the subjunctive in adjectival clauses is fairly common, but grammar books often leave it to last and skate over it when presenting the subjunctive, possibly because, as you will agree, it is not easy to explain!

Other cases

In our collection of examples we had two other types. For the moment we will just say that certain other categories of verb are followed by the subjunctive (e.g. **aspettare che**) and also that certain conjunctions are followed by the subjunctive (e.g. **ammesso che**).

LANGUAGE LEARNING TIP   It is helpful to collect examples of the subjunctive. This is also true for other points you particularly want to remember. But it seems to us particularly useful with the subjunctive, which ultimately you will develop a feel for. Noting examples, thinking about them, going over them when you are revising, can help develop that feel. We recommend it.

SESSION 6

The form of the present subjunctive

All this is very well, you are probably saying, but how about the form of the subjunctive? Analyzing the use of the subjunctive may be tricky. Happily, forming it is not. Verbs divide into two types: (a) Group 1 verbs (-**are** type) (b) All other verbs.

	Group 1	Group 2	Group 3	Group 3
	parl**are**	decid**ere**	cap**ire**	part**ire**
io	parl**i**	decid**a**	cap**isca**	part**a**
tu	parl**i**	decid**a**	cap**isca**	part**a**
lui/lei	parl**i**	decid**a**	cap**isca**	part**a**
noi	parl**iamo**	decid**iamo**	cap**iamo**	part**iamo**
voi	parl**iate**	decid**iate**	cap**iate**	part**iate**
loro	pa̱rl**ino**	deci̱d**ano**	capi̱s**cano**	pa̱rt**ano**

As in the present indicative, the stress in the third person plural is on the antepenultimate syllable: **pa̱rlino, deci̱dano, capi̱scano, pa̱rtano**. Note also that verbs like **capire** have -isc- inserted where they would have it in the present indicative.

Activity 17

Study the tables and answer the following:

1 Why did we say verbs divide into two types in the present subjunctive? What is the characteristic of each type?
2 Which form is identical to the present indicative (the usual present you already know)?
3 Why do you think it is fairly common to use a subject pronoun with the singular forms of the present subjunctive?
4 Which forms have the same ending in both groups?

Irregular verbs

A number of verbs are irregular. Among the common ones are:

essere	avere	andare	dare	dire	fare	venire
sia	abbia	vada	dia	dica	faccia	venga
sia	abbia	vada	dia	dica	faccia	venga
sia	abbia	vada	dia	dica	faccia	venga
siamo	abbiamo	andiamo	diamo	diciamo	facciamo	veniamo
siate	abbiate	andiate	diate	diciate	facciate	veniate
siano	abbiano	vadano	diano	dicano	facciano	vengano

(Underlining indicates irregular stress.)

Notice the endings are the same for all irregular verbs and as we said are like Groups 2 and 3 verbs. This means if you are given the first person singular present subjunctive of an irregular verb, you should be able to work out the other persons. Try it.

It is also the case that for many irregular verbs the first person singular of the indicative has the same root as the subjunctive. Unfortunately it doesn't always work but it may be helpful to try this. For instance in the group above it is true for **andare**, **dire**, **fare** and **venire**.

Activity 18

Here are the infinitives of some irregular verbs and the first person singular, present subjunctive. Write out the complete form of the present subjunctive for each:

> potere **possa**; sapere **sappia**; tenere **tenga**; volere **voglia**;
> uscire **esca**; dovere **debba**; produrre **produca**;
> piacere **piaccia**.

Note: verbs such as **uscire** and **dovere**, which have a vowel change in the present indicative, have a similar vowel change in the present subjunctive. Similarly verbs with soft **c**, **g**, **sc**, before any **i** in the endings of the present indicative (**tu**, **noi** endings) have the same sound change in the present subjunctive where the ending starts in **i**. **Piacere** is of course mostly used in the 3rd persons, singular and plural, but the other forms exist and can be used: **Non credo che tu piaccia ai miei genitori.**

Activity 19

Study the following sentences and decide whether the verb should be indicative or subjunctive; then choose that form for the verb indicated.

1 Pensi che (essere) vero?
2 Sono certo che (essere) falso.
3 Marta è una persona che (dimostrare) sempre molta pazienza.
4 Ci vuole una persona che (avere) molta pazienza.
5 Non credo che il pranzo (essere) pronto.
6 So che il pranzo non (essere) pronto.
7 Credo che il direttore (avere) torto.
8 Il direttore è una persona che (dire) sempre quello che pensa.
9 La società ha bisogno di personale che (fare) il lavoro con entusiasmo e professionalità.
10 Mauro pensa che il direttore (volere) cambiare il sistema.

Activity 20

Che cosa ne pensano i clienti? *What do the customers think?*
On the one hand, Emanuela says there is no discrimination in her workplace. On the other hand, she tell us how some male customers are sometimes not entirely pleased to find the bank manager is a woman. Write down the thoughts of one male customer after he has met Emanuela, using the information given below and deciding whether to use the present subjunctive or the present indicative. You are practising using the subjunctive after certain verbs.

Example: Penso / una donna (essere) in gamba come un uomo.
Penso che una donna **sia** in gamba come un uomo.

1 Mi hanno detto / questa direttrice (avere) sufficiente preparazione ed esperienza.
2 Credo / le donne (essere) intelligenti e affidabili come gli uomini.
3 Però so anche / ad alti livelli le donne (non ricevere) rispetto e attenzione.
4 Ho paura / una donna (non avere) abbastanza autorità quando deve difendere gli interessi dei suoi clienti.
5 Spero / (non essere) vero, ma temo / un direttore donna (non garantire) i miei investimenti come un direttore uomo.

Activity 21

Complete the following sentences choosing whether to use the present subjunctive or the present indicative. You are practising using subjunctives to describe a type or category.

> Examples: Lavoro in una banca che (essere) è molto piccola.
> (Not a type – it's the one I work in)
> Sto cercando un posto di lavoro in una banca che non (essere) **sia** troppo piccola. (That is the type of bank I want to work in).

1 Attualmente, ho uno stipendio che non (essere) .... adeguato alle mie responsabilità.

2 Voglio uno stipendio che (essere) .... adeguato alle mie responsabilità.

3 Molti clienti uomini vogliono un direttore che (sapere) .... difendere i loro interessi ad alti livelli, e pensano che una donna non sia adatta a questo compito.

4 Molte banche, tuttavia, hanno un direttore donna che (sapere) .... svolgere il proprio lavoro professionalmente proprio come un direttore uomo.

5 E' necessario un nuovo contratto di lavoro che (garantire) .... agli impiegati di banca lo stipendio adeguato al loro livello.

6 Al momento, abbiamo un contratto che (non garantire) .... agli impiegati uno stipendio adeguato.

Activity 22

You're chatting to a colleague and you discover that your ideas on your working conditions differ. Answer each of his/her remarks as shown in the example, using the correct form of the present subjunctive.

Example: **Il Suo collega**   La pausa pranzo è troppo corta!
Lei   (essere abbastanza lunga) Non sono d'accordo! **Penso che** la pausa pranzo **sia** abbastanza lunga.

1 **Il Suo collega**   Nel nostro ufficio l'aria condizionata non funziona: fa freddo in inverno e caldo in estate!
Lei   (funzionare benissimo; fare caldo in inverno; essere fresco in estate)

2 **Il Suo collega**   Il nostro direttore non dà mai ascolto alle nostre richieste!

Lei	(dare sempre ascolto; fare attenzione ai problemi di tutti)
3 **Il Suo collega**	I colleghi più giovani non sanno fare il loro lavoro e vengono sempre a chiederci aiuto perché non hanno voglia di fare niente!
Lei	(saper fare il loro lavoro; venire a chiedere aiuto per imparare)
4 **Il Suo collega**	Il personale che fa le pulizie deve lavorare di più: escono troppo presto la sera e arrivano troppo tardi la mattina!
Lei	(non dovere lavorare di più; tenere gli uffici molto puliti; uscire all'ora prevista dal loro contratto di lavoro)

SESSION 7

▶ Interview 3

*Felicità Torrielli is an example of an entrepreneur, **un imprenditore**, running a small business. Italy tends to produce energetic entrepreneurs and small businesses. Signora Torrielli created her own business 25 years ago and makes ready-to-wear garments for some well known designer labels, including Valentino and Ungaro. Here she answers a question about the aims of her firm.*

Signora Torrielli	Lo scopo, quando uno fa un'azienda, è quello di creare della produttività e quindi dei posti di lavoro. Io ho cominciato con un'unica dipendente, nel secondo mese siamo diventati due, nell'arco di dieci anni siamo diventati 20 e attualmente siamo al venticinquesimo anno e siamo 30.
Interviewer	Mi racconti: come ha cominciato?
Signora Torrielli	Io volevo separarmi da mio marito, e non avevo nessun tipo di mestiere in mano, la cosa che mi piaceva di più fare era cucire i vestiti. Allora sono andata in una scuola di taglio e cucito e ho detto alla direttrice che avrei seguito i suoi corsi ma non come le altre ragazze, perché io, che ero giovane, ma non ero più una ragazza, non volevo nessun tipo di diploma, avrei seguito i suoi corsi, ma a modo mio; cioè io entravo in una lezione, se lì insegnavano a tagliare una gonna, io

appena avevo capito come si taglia una gonna, non avrei proseguito per settimane a fare gonne, sarei passata all'altra aula dove insegnavano a fare giacche o pantaloni, così, perché io volevo una infarinatura. Fatto questo tipo di scuola, ho assunto un maestro di taglio, ho comprato dei tessuti e ho cominciato a fare dei modelli. Poi ho fatto delle telefonate, ho detto alle mie amiche che io avevo aperto, allora si chiamava una sartoria, avevo aperto una sartoria e io ho cominciato.

Subito dopo però ho capito che questa cosa non mi piaceva come tipo di lavoro perché era troppo personale, non era una cosa che mi dava soddisfazione, a fare un vestito, ho capito che mi piaceva la produzione. Allora mi sono affittata un piccolissimo laboratorio, ho messo dentro due persone di cui una era una tagliatrice, c'è ancora, la prima persona c'è ancora, e ho cominciato a fare dei piccoli modelli che sono andata a vendere nei negozi e di lì ho cominciato.

Abbiamo avuto una crescita abbastanza limitata, se vogliamo, perché il campo della moda è così tanto cambiato in questi anni che la nicchia che noi c'eravamo riservata, che era quella di fare del pronto ad alto livello, è andata esaurendosi.

Interviewer Come mai?

Signora Perché le grandi firme, trovando difficoltà a vendere ai
Torrielli loro prezzi alti, tutti quanti hanno fatto delle seconde linee, che si avvicinavano molto al nostro prodotto. Noi facevamo la nostra linea, che aveva praticamente i loro costi ma non poteva uscire ai loro costi perché non aveva il nome né il marchio. Quindi la nostra nicchia nel mercato è andata esaurendosi, perché fra comprare una giacca mia che costa 300.000 lire e comprarne una di Valentino che ne costa 420, beh, la gente, a questo punto, preferisce prendere quella firmata anziché quell'altra che ha forse il tessuto più bello, forse … Allora la nostra azienda si è cambiata e, anziché produrre una linea propria, è diventata un, come si chiama, un terzista e noi lavoriamo solo per le grandi firme che sono Valentino, Ungaro, Mila Schön, adesso.

lo scopo	Another 'false friend' for your collection. It means *aim*.
posti di lavoro	*jobs*
un/una dipendente	*an employee*
nell'arco di dieci anni	*over a period of ten years*
a modo mio	*in my own way*
una infarinatura	literally *a light dusting of flour* (**farina**). Signora Torrielli really wanted to be sure she had sufficient understanding of each process to be able to manage others doing it.
assunto	irregular past participle of **assumere** (Unit 3 – Mario uses **assumere**)
nicchia	*niche*
il pronto	*ready-to-wear*; more usually Italians use the French expression **prêt-à-porter**.
marchio	*brand-name*, or simply *name* in this context
le grande firme	literally *signature* (**firmare** *to sign*, **una firma** *a signature*) but in this context, *designer label*. Yet another 'false friend'.
tutti quanti	*all of them, the lot of them*
300.000 lire ... 420	This interview was done before the introduction of the Euro in 2002.

Comprehension 3

1 How many years has Signora Torrielli been in business and how many people does she employ?

2 Why did she choose to set up this particular kind of business rather than one in another field?

3 What was untypical of her as a student in the dressmaking school she attended?

4 How did she launch her dressmaking business?

5 What did she very quickly realize?

6 Signora Torrielli started production of clothes (as opposed to dress-making) with two employees. What is she rather proud of?

7 Business hasn't been plain sailing for Signora Torrielli. In what way has her firm had to adapt to market conditions?

SESSION 8

Activity 23

Look at the interview with Signora Torrielli in Session 7.

1 Can you pick out any examples of the gerund, the form ending in **-ando** or **-endo**?
2 Can you find a past participle which seems not to have **avere/essere** with it?
3 Look also for any examples of the pluperfect (imperfect of **avere/essere** + past participle).
4 You should be able to find what looks like the conditional (see Unit 1) but with a past participle. Can you?

Gerund with *andare*

Firstly, when an object or reflexive pronoun is used with the gerund, it tacks on to the end, hence the **si** attached to **esaurendo**. The use of **la nostra nicchia ... è andata esaurendosi** underlines that it was a gradual process: *our niche gradually disappeared.*

You remember **stare** + gerund to form the present continuous and the past continuous (Unit 4). You can also use **andare** with a gerund, to convey the idea of repeated action:

andare facendo, dicendo,   *to be continually doing,*
   scrivendo ...   *saying, writing ...*

Activity 24

Every day Signora Torrielli has to face a series of problems. Here are some of the problems. Express each in a single sentence using **stare/andare** + gerund.

Example: le tasse / aumentare
        Le tasse **stanno aumentando** / Le tasse **vanno aumentando**.
        Taxes are going up.

1 Le stoffe / rincarare.
2 La concorrenza / crescere.
3 Il mercato / saturarsi.
4 Il campo della moda / cambiare.
5 La produzione / rallentare.
6 Le grandi firme / invadere il mercato del prêt-à-porter.
7 I guadagni / diminuire.
8 La situazione / peggiorare.

Past participles without an auxiliary verb

Fatto questo tipo di scuola ...   *Having attended this type of school ...*

Finita la cena, la famiglia si è riunita attorno alla TV per la partita.   *Having finished supper/ supper being finished/ when supper was finished, the family gathered round the TV for the match.*

The past participle is used as a neat way to join up the account of two past actions rather than say: I did this and then I did that. It is a stylistic device. Notice the participle behaves like an adjective, agreeing with the noun. (Those who know Latin will realize this derives from the ablative absolute.)

Notice also how Emanuela said:

Visto che ho trentacinque anni mercoledì prossimo ...   *Seeing that I am thirty-five next Wednesday ...*

Ammesso che si abbia il tempo e la voglia ...   *Given that one has the time and the desire to ....*

Here the past participle links with **che** and becomes a conjunction.

Activity 25

Read the following instructions for making a skirt. Change them using the past participle as in the example and then link with the next instruction.

Example:

Scegli una stoffa che ti piaccia e che sia adatta al tipo di gonna che vuoi tagliare.
Una volta scelta la stoffa, prendi le tue misure.

1 **Disegna il modello della gonna su carta,** facendo attenzione a seguire le misure che hai preso. Una volta ...
2 **Riporta il modello su stoffa,** seguendo con più precisione possibile il disegno su carta. Una volta ...
3 **Taglia la stoffa,** lasciando almeno due centimetri di margine per le cuciture. Una volta ...
4 **Cuci la gonna a mano,** usando il filo per imbastire: comincia dalla gonna vera e propria, per poi passare alla cintura e alla cerniera. Una volta ...
5 **Indossa la gonna** per controllare che vada bene. Una volta ...

6 Cuci la gonna a macchina. Una volta ...
7 Stira la gonna.

Revision of the pluperfect

ho detto alle mie amiche che   ...I *told my friends that I*
<u>avevo aperto</u> una sartoria.   *had opened a*
   dressmaker's business.

A straightforward use of the pluperfect, as you have seen in Unit 4 Session 7.

The conditional perfect in reported speech

This is another case where English and Italian differ. The use of the conditional with a past participle forms another tense, called the **conditional perfect**. Its name matters little. It is the use which matters: Signora Torrielli reported to us what she said to the principal of the dressmaking school she attended. When speaking she would have used the **future tense**, saying:

Seguirò i Suoi corsi ... non proseguirò per settimane ...
passerò all'altra aula ...
I shall follow your courses ... I shan't continue for weeks ...
I shall move on to the next classroom ...

We will meet **the future** in full in Unit 6, but note that when putting into reported speech words which were originally said in the future, Italians use the conditional perfect, whereas in English we use the conditional.

ho detto alla direttrice che <u>avrei seguito</u> i suoi corsi ... non <u>avrei proseguito</u> per settimane a fare gonne ... <u>sarei passata</u> all'altra aula ...
I told the principal I <u>would follow</u> her courses ... I <u>wouldn't continue</u> for weeks making skirts ... I <u>would move</u> on to the next classroom ...

Activity 26

Signora Torrielli often has meetings with a representative of Valentino, the fashion house, to agree about arrangements for production of the garments she makes for them. Read the following conversation and then imagine how Signora Torrielli reports it to her workforce so that they know what the firm's commitments and deadlines are. You will need to use the conditional perfect for the numbered verb phrases, as in the example.

Example: Line 5: Per quando **vorrete** il prodotto finito?
Ho chiesto alla rappresentante di Valentino per quando **avrebbero voluto** il prodotto finito.

Rappresentante	Questa è la collezione donna per il prossimo autunno-inverno: un modello per tailleur, una gonna sportiva, un vestito da sera, jeans, cappotto, camicette, ...
Torrielli	Sì ... per quando vorrete il prodotto finito?
Rappresentante	Entro metà agosto? Poi bisognerà farlo arrivare ai distributori e poi i distributori ai negozianti ...
Torrielli	Beh, se è entro metà agosto ... allora ... avremo bisogno (1) della stoffa in maggio ... almeno per i capi eleganti, il tailleur e il vestito da sera, le camicette.
Rappresentante	Ai primi di maggio ... va bene ... e per gli altri capi forse un po' più tardi?
Torrielli	Sì, ma non troppo ... dovremo cominciare (2) a lavorarla entro fine maggio, sicuramente. Se rispettiamo queste date, potremo garantire (3) un primo lotto di capi finiti ... diciamo per fine luglio ...
Rappresentante	Andrebbe benissimo.
Torrielli	... e poi saremo in grado (4) di consegnare il resto entro metà agosto, come dicevamo ... Ma, senta, per le consegne ai distributori?
Rappresentante	Nessun problema ... ci rivolgeremo (5) sempre allo stesso corriere. Dovrete risolvere (6) solo i problemi logistici, a quel punto.
Torrielli	Non c'è problema. Solo una cosa: sarà più pratico (7) dare direttamente il numero di telefono del magazzino, invece che quello del mio ufficio. Il responsabile per il magazzino si occuperà (8) di tutto.

Tu or *Lei*?

You may perhaps have noticed that our interviewees so far have mostly used **tu** to the interviewer, and vice versa. An exception was Signora Torrielli. She is also the only interviewee who has been referred to by her surname. This is simply because of the relationship of the interviewer with the various people. Mostly they are friends, in some cases old friends. They always use **tu** to each other. In the case of Mario Rotondale, it is more a case of usual practice. Mario runs a gym and tennis club and he very quickly finds himself saying to the members: **diamoci del tu**. In

English, you would probably say: *my name is Mario, call me Mario* ... and you would use first names to each other. He finds, with the many members he has and, particularly in the gym, the friendly relationship which develops, that it is best to use **tu** with everyone, regardless of age or status. The interviewer's relationship with Signora Torrielli, however, has always been formal. They originally met at a dinner party and the interviewer has subsequently been a customer of Signora Torrielli's factory. Neither is young and they would have to meet socially much more for there to be a move to **tu**. Emanuela is an interesting case. Her husband and the interviewer were once colleagues. Colleagues almost always use **tu** to each other. But Emanuela has been brought up not to use **tu** a great deal, especially to people older than herself. There is therefore a situation where the interviewer uses **tu**, considering her a friend, but she does not reciprocate, aware of the age difference. This will also happen between adults and children: children have to be taught to use **Lei** because they don't always do so.

We were uncertain how to address you, dear learner, in the *Talking to yourself* suggestions. Had you been a class sitting before us, we would have used the collective **voi**. To each of you individually we would probably use **tu** (and first names). But in a book, we felt **tu** was too familiar; on the other hand **Lei** seems very formal. However since it is important for you to learn **Lei** so as not to give offence in casual encounters in Italy, we decided to use **Lei**.

This gives the impression that the whole situation is fraught. This is not really the case. When you do not know a person, you must use **Lei**. But in many relationships, when you are working or enjoying yourselves together, Italians are quick to say: **Diamoci del tu**. It is the Italian equivalent of using first names. They usually add: **è più facile**. For you as a student of Italian, that may not be the case, but try! And allowances will of course be made for you.

Remember that when you write **Lei**, formal *you*, and its related **La, Le, Suo/a** etc, there is a convention of using a capital letter. This is important in letters in particular since it is considered a mark of courtesy.

There has certainly been a shift in the way **tu** and **Lei** are used in the last twenty, thirty, forty years. The use of **Lei** is deferential, polite, distancing yourself out of courtesy, respect. **Tu** marks solidarity, closeness, friendship, affection. In the Fascist period **voi** was the compulsory mark of respect and the use of **Lei** was at one point forbidden as foreign – a mistaken view. **Voi** continued to be used for the formal *you* in rural areas for some time although it is unlikely you will hear it now, except perhaps in the south.

It may be of interest to know that Cesare Romiti (see Unit 2), who worked closely with Gianni Agnelli for some 25 years, for most of which Agnelli was President of Fiat and Romiti Managing Director, apparently always used **Lei** when addressing Agnelli. This is worthy of comment in the press, in other words Italians find it unusual.

LANGUAGE LEARNING TIP In one of the activities in this Unit we chose sentences from interviews or texts in previous units. Have you looked back at the earlier units recently? We strongly recommend you have a pattern of revision of earlier units, at least re-reading texts or listening again to the recording. We have purposely not simplified the Italian of the interviews and therefore, as the exercises made clear, points crop up before they are explained. Looking again helps to reinforce your understanding. Going over familiar texts also reinforces your memory of words and structures. If you haven't already tried it, why not give it a go? See if you can find any subjunctives!

Activity 27

Talking to yourself

Possible topics for your conversations in Italian with yourself – or if you are lucky, with the person or people studying with you – might be:

1 Descriva il Suo lavoro attuale e l'organizzazione (la ditta, la compagnia, l'ente ...) per cui lavora.

2 Le piace l'abitudine di dare del tu? Trovi degli esempi di situazioni in cui si usa il 'tu' invece che il 'Lei' in un modo che è inappropriato. Per esempio, in ospedale un dottore potrebbe dare del tu a un paziente anziano che non aveva mai incontrato prima. Secondo Lei, ci sono situazioni in cui dare del tu rende la vita più facile o più difficile?

3 Il cibo italiano: le piace? Quali piatti preferisce? Perché? Mangia spesso nei ristoranti italiani? Come sono? Ne consiglierebbe alcuni?

4 Le piacciono i self-service? Quali sono i vantaggi e gli svantaggi dei self-service? Mangia mai da McDonald? Che cosa pensa della loro rapida diffusione? In Italia, sono spesso situati in posizioni di spicco, per esempio nelle piazze centrali di città famose. Certe persone pensano che rovinino la bellezza e lo stile della piazza: Lei, che cosa ne pensa?

5 Donne direttori di banca: ne conosce qualcuna? Che cosa pensa, in generale, delle donne con responsabilità manageriali? E delle donne in politica? Al momento, quasi nessuna donna, in Italia, ha ancora raggiunto posizioni di vero potere in politica. La sorprende? Pensa che sia più facile per le donne nel Suo paese raggiungere posizioni di potere in politica?

6 La moda italiana: le piace? Che cosa pensa della moda italiana per uomo? Lei si veste secondo la moda o si lascia guidare da altre considerazioni nella scelta dei vestiti?

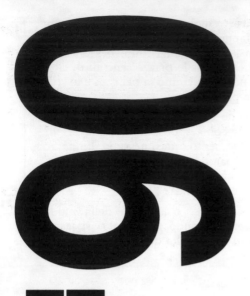

06 problemi di lavoro

In this unit we shall learn
- about some of the problems Italians face in the workplace
- how to talk about what we intend to do in the future: the future tense
- how to say something is likely: a special use of the future
- how to say something must be done: the passive with **andare**
- another way of saying things are being done: the passive with **essere** and **venire**

SESSION 1

▶ Interview 1

You remember Emanuela was feeling tired and undervalued. We asked her about problems specific to work in an Italian bank.

Emanuela   Sì, diciamo che ... mah, ci sono problemi che adesso la concorrenza è diventata più agguerrita, arriveranno le banche europee, quindi sarà introdotto l'euro, quindi saranno anni un po' particolari per il sistema bancario italiano, anni in cui dovranno cambiare tantissime cose, e allora è richiesto uno sforzo grande, uno sforzo grande, una grossa attenzione, molto lavoro, questo credo in tutte le banche italiane. Tutte ... dobbiamo veramente uscire dal medioevo. (*Ride*) Sì, è vero, abbiamo un sistema proprio arretrato e quindi dovremo lavorare molto.

We then asked Emanuela whether she derived any satisfaction from her work and she said (perhaps you can guess):

Emanuela   (*Ride*) In questo momento vorrei una soddisfazione economica. Vorrei una soddisfazione economica perché è lo stupido parametro con cui misuriamo il nostro valore. Io sono apprezzata, lavoro tanto, quindi loro mi paghino ... e questo perché vorrei comprare una bella casa, vorrei avere un futuro ... più facile, no? per mia figlia, quindi vorrei più ... più soldi.

sarà introdotto l'euro	Emanuela was interviewed in the summer of 1998.
una soddisfazione economica	We would add, though Emanuela might not agree, the employees of Italian banks have, in recent years, enjoyed favourable conditions in terms of hours and remuneration compared with bank staff in other EU countries.
uscire dal Medioevo	*come out of the Middle Ages*. We would agree, from personal experience and as customers used to other banking systems, that Italian banks have rather out-of-date ways, although, as in many aspect of Italian life, things are gradually changing.

loro mi paghino	*let them pay me*. An example of a subjunctive used in a main clause. It is in effect a third person imperative: the third person imperative is made using the present subjunctive.

Comprehension 1

1 Why does Emanuela think that in Italian banks there are difficult years ahead which will require much work and effort?
2 Why does she want what she calls 'economic satisfaction'?

SESSION 2

The form of the future

Emanuela looks ahead to the next few years and uses the future tense.

arriveranno le banche europee	*the European banks will come in*
sarà introdotto l'euro	*the euro will be introduced*
saranno anni un po' particolari per il sistema bancario italiano	*they will be rather unusual years for the Italian banking system*
anni in cui dovranno cambiare tantissime cose	*years in which so many things will have to change*

The future is formed on the same root as the conditional (Unit 1). Do you remember? For Groups 2 and 3 verbs, the base is the infinitive without the final -e and for Group 1 verbs the infinitive without the final -e and with the **a** of the ending changed to **e**.

arrivare	decidere	partire
arriverò	deciderò	partirò
arriverai	deciderai	partirai
arriverà	deciderà	partirà
arriveremo	decideremo	partiremo
arriverete	deciderete	partirete
arriveranno	decideranno	partiranno

The endings are the same for each group and for all verbs. Some verbs are irregular in that the first part, the root, is not formed as described above. These irregulars are exactly the same verbs as for the conditional, with the same irregularities.

1 **essere: sarò, sarai, sarà, saremo, sarete, saranno**

2 verbs whose infinitives contract:

andare: andrò
avere: avrò
cadere: cadrò
dovere: dovrò
potere: potrò
sapere: saprò
vedere: vedrò
vivere: vivrò

3 verbs in which there is a contraction and a consonant change:

bere: berrò
tenere: terrò
venire: verrò
volere: vorrò
rimanere: rimarrò

4 As in the conditional, the following are **NOT** irregular:

dire: dirò
fare: farò
stare: starò

It may be helpful at this stage for you to compare the future and the conditional endings. We have not yet taken you through all the persons of the conditional, only first and third person singular, which you looked at in Unit 1. Here is the full picture.

Future		Conditional	
capirò	*I shall understand*	**capirei**	*I should understand*
capirai	*you will understand*	**capiresti**	*you would understand*
capirà	*he will understand*	**capirebbe**	*he would understand*
capiremo	*we shall understand*	**capiremmo**	*we should understand*
capirete	*you will understand*	**capireste**	*you would understand*
capiranno	*they will understand*	**capirebbero**	*they would understand*

Note: the third person plural of the conditional has the irregular stress usual in that person in most tenses: **arriverebbero**. The third person plural of the future is stressed on the **a** of -**anno**, i.e. is regular.

Activity 1

Study the above table comparing the endings of the two tenses. Where in particular are you going to have to be very careful how you pronounce the two tenses to avoid saying the wrong one?

The uses of the future

1 It is used to express intended future actions, as Emanuela does. However, it is also common, as in English, to use the present to express what are in effect future plans:

La settimana prossima, vado in Francia per lavoro.	*Next week I am going to France for work reasons.*
Andiamo al cinema stasera. Vuoi venire anche tu?	*We are going to the cinema this evening. Do you want to come too?*

Note also, Italians use the present tense with **subito** to express something that they are about to do.

Vengo subito.	*I'll come immediately.*

2 A special case is the use of the future to express probability. This is different from English and like other such cases needs special attention.

A	Dov'è papà?	*Where's dad?*
B	Sarà in officina.	*He's probably in the workshop.*
A	Portiamo delle mele dai nonni?	*Shall we take some apples to the grandparents?*
B	Ne avranno già tante; i loro vicini gliene danno sempre.	*They're sure to have lots; their neighbours always give them some.*
A	Che ore sono?	*What's the time?*
B	Saranno le otto.	*It must be eight o'clock.*

The implication is that it is probable, likely, but can't be stated as fact.

Activity 2

Complete the following by putting the verbs in brackets into the correct person of the future tense. Then say what it all means.

Speaker A Senz'altro, con un nuovo amministratore delegato, ci (1 essere) dei cambiamenti.

Speaker B   Sì. Sappiamo già che (2 modernizzare) il sistema di gestione. (3 Introdurre) per i vari direttori un sistema di traguardi da raggiungere. (4 Stabilire) con ogni direttore i suoi obiettivi e poi gli (5 lasciare) una grande libertà di decisione. Se il direttore (6 riuscire), (7 ricevere) un compenso a fine anno. Sennò …

Speaker A   Certo che questo (8 piacere) ad alcuni ma ad altri (9 mancare) la struttura attuale.

Activity 3

How would you put the following conversations in Italian?

1   A Strange, there's a light on in Gianni's house. He went to the United States.
   B He must have come back.
   A I don't think so. It must be burglars.

2   A Look, isn't that Pietro in that Mercedes at the traffic lights?
   B Yes. Perhaps he has won the lottery.
   A Or else it's his American uncle's car. He is in Italy at the moment.

Activity 4

Can you find any relative pronouns in what Emanuela says in Interview 1?

SESSION 3

▶ Interview 2

Marina too was asked about problems at work.

Marina   Beh diciamo che ci sono soprattutto due ordini di problemi. Uno riguarda un po' l'Italia in generale, nel senso che lavorare in Italia è molto difficile perché ci sono moltissimi vincoli legislativi, burocrazie, permessi, leggi poco chiare che vanno sempre interpretate, quindi non si è mai sicuri di fare la cosa nel modo migliore e infatti, nel nostro settore in particolare, c'è la difficoltà anche di competere con degli operatori che sono in media molto piccoli, perché tipicamente il bar e la trattoria sono gestiti a livello familiare, che tendono a ignorare (*ride*) la buona gestione, quindi hanno dipendenti in nero, non pagano i contributi, non battono gli scontrini, non pagano le tasse, cioè è evidente che lì c'è una struttura di costi completamente diversa. E' molto difficile per esempio assumere il personale perché il personale che lavora nel settore della ristorazione è abituato ad essere pagato in nero e essere pagato con delle cifre molto alte proprio perché sono in nero. Quindi è difficile attirare le persone e farle venire a lavorare da noi con dei salari decisamente più bassi però con i costi per l'azienda che sono molto alti perché bisogna aggiungere le tasse, i contributi, ecc. Questo sicuramente è un problema non tanto specifico nostro ma insomma un po' dell'Italia in generale.

E per me poi c'è forse un po' il problema di avere questa commistione tra il lavoro e la famiglia, cioè avere un intreccio di rapporti personali e professionali del lavoro che può essere un po' difficile da gestire, insomma, è un po' diverso avere a che fare con persone estranee, anonime o avere a che fare con i familiari. Delle volte questo facilita le cose, delle volte invece …

Interviewer Perché questi ristoranti fanno parte …

Marina Del gruppo di famiglia. Quindi ci sono sempre rapporti con mio padre, con i miei fratelli, con persone familiari o comunque persone diciamo con cui c'è un rapporto personale prima che professionale e questo appunto può essere qualche volta un po' difficile da gestire …

Interviewer Mi puoi dare un esempio?

Marina Mah, per esempio, mio padre quando tratta con me, è evidente che non tratta con me come la manager di un'azienda ma tratta con me come sua figlia, per cui mi tratta come figlia e quindi … (*ride*) quindi insomma è un rapporto diverso che … delle volte magari non c'è il rispetto che avrei se fossi un'estranea con cui c'è un rapporto di un altro livello.

nel senso che	Another little phrase much used in spoken Italian (lit: *in the sense that*)
vincoli legislativi	*legal constraints.* **Vincoli** are *chains*, of a restricting type, *bonds, fetters.*

non si è mai sicuri	*one is never sure.* With impersonal **si** any adjective is made masculine plural. If this seems odd, all we can say is that the reason lies in the history of Italian.
dipendenti in nero	Employees who do not appear on the firm's books, who are paid in cash. No **contributi** *contributions for social security* are paid for them.
non battono gli scontrini	Bars, restaurants and shops are required to give customers a **scontrino**, *fiscal receipt.*
avere a che fare con **fratelli**	*to deal with, to have dealings with* *brothers* but includes *sisters* if there are any.

Comprehension 2

1 Marina sees problems at work as being of two sorts. The first are, she says, specifically Italian. What, in broad outline, are they?

2 What does Marina say, in detail, about employment practices in the restaurant business in Italy? Why does Brek find it difficult to compete for staff?

3 The second category of problem which she experiences is peculiar to her situation. What is it?

i Marina's remarks touch on several aspects of Italian life. First the questions of laws and permits. It seems Italy has a very large number of laws on its statute book compared to other Western European states. And the procedures for doing things are often complicated and full of pitfalls. The Prodi government made a start on simplifying many procedures with the two Bassanini laws (**leggi Bassanini**), so called after the Minister who saw them through Parliament.

Lavoro nero, *black work*, has long been a feature of the Italian economy although a moment's reflection will confirm that it is not unknown in other countries. It seems that the costs to an employer of the social charges he has to pay on each employee are higher in Italy than in most countries of Western Europe and there is therefore a temptation to avoid them. This is particularly true in the case of small firms. An organization the size of the one Marina works for would not, of course, employ people this way. **Lavoro nero** would also include the plumber who charges you less if you pay cash and the employee who moonlights. The high costs of employing workers – and indeed the difficulty of getting rid of them should you need to – has also led to giving work to consultants, sometimes in cooperatives of young people, rather than employing them direct.

Italy has a general problem with tax evasion. One aspect of it is the service industries. When you buy something in a shop or eat a meal in a restaurant you should be given a **scontrino** or **ricevuta fiscale**. Technically you can be fined if you leave the premises without one. The trader who fails to give you a receipt possibly does not put the transaction through his books, cheating on VAT (**IVA – imposta sul valore aggiunto**) and other taxes. In the early 90s, in a drive to stamp out such tax evasion, there were some well publicized cases of customers being stopped and fined: children who had bought lollipops and not demanded **scontrini**, for instance. The fines on the traders are far heavier than on the customers. You can imagine the scandalized tone adopted by reporting journalists, which of course brought the clamp-down to public attention – presumably as was intended – and probably reduced avoidance. You may, therefore, as someone unused to picking up a till receipt when buying very inexpensive items, be surprised to find the shop assistant calling you back to take your receipt. We would not wish to give the impression that most Italians are dishonest. Our experience is rather the opposite. And dishonesty knows no frontiers.

The firm Marina works for is part of a family group. Family businesses are a well-documented feature of the Italian economic scene, as readers may be aware. Famous family firms include Benetton, Ferragamo, and, possibly infamous and certainly no longer owned by the family, Gucci.

SESSION 4

Unfinished sentences – more about the spoken language

You may notice that Marina doesn't finish the sentence:

Delle volte questo facilita le cose, delle volte invece …

Sometimes this makes things easier, at other times, on the other hand …

Nor does the interviewer finish the sentence which follows:

Perché questi ristoranti fanno parte …?

Because these restaurants are part of …?

In both cases the two speakers understand each other without having to spell everything out. This happens in the spoken language, any language. And the better two people know each other, the more this will occur. You may be able to turn this to good effect, saving yourself the trouble of finishing every sentence in Italian. This will tend to be in informal situations.

The passive with *essere*

The story of the passive in Italian is broader than in English and incorporates some useful shades of meaning. First, what do we mean by the passive? Verbs can be either active or passive. Here are some examples:

Active:

Subject   Verb   Object (direct)

Il Papa ha ricevuto oggi il Presidente degli Stati Uniti.
The Pope today received the President of the United States.

Subject   Object (direct)   Verb

La moglie del Presidente lo accompagnava.
The President's wife accompanied him/was with him.

Passive:

Subject   Verb   Agent

Il Presidente degli Stati Uniti è stato ricevuto oggi dal Papa.
The President of the United States was received by the Pope today.

Subject   Verb   Agent

Il Presidente era accompagnato dalla moglie.
The President was accompanied by his wife.

In the active, the subject of the verb does something to a direct object. In the passive the sentence is turned round and the object is made the grammatical subject, with the former subject becoming what is called the agent, in other words, something introduced by the word *by* (in Italian **da**). It sounds very convoluted but we all use the passive frequently:

Subject   Verb   Agent

Il libro è stato comprato da oltre un milione di lettori entusiasti.
The book has been bought by over a million enthusiastic readers.

Subject   Verb

|Il prodotto| |sarà richiamato| dopo la scoperta dell'errore.
The product will be recalled after the discovery of the mistake.

The point of putting the idea this way round is to highlight the subject of the passive verb, in the examples above, **il libro** and **il prodotto**, rather than **oltre un milione di lettori entusiasti**. Indeed in the second sentence who was going to recall the product (the agent) is left unstated.

In English the passive is formed with *to be* and a past participle. In Italian, you can use **essere** and the past participle but another possibility with a special shade of meaning is illustrated below.

The passive with *andare*

Marina, talking about unclear laws, says:

leggi poco chiare che vanno   *laws which are not clear*
    interpretate   *and which have to be*
                                                    interpreted

She uses **andare** not **essere**. The force of this is: **le leggi devono essere interpretate.** *The laws must/have to be interpreted.* Forming the passive with **andare** rather than **essere** conveys what *should be done*, obligation.

Lo spumante va servito fresco.   *Fizzy wine must be/should*
                                                     be served cool/chilled.
Va ricordato che ...   *It must be/should be*
                                                     remembered that ...

This latter type of phrase is very common in discussion or where you are arguing a point.

va sottolineato che ...   *it should be emphasized*
                                                    (underlined) that ...
va detto che ...   *it has to be said that ...*

Activity 5

Can you find any passives in what Marina said in Interview 2? Reread her words and then check the Key.

Activity 6

Here are some statements in the active voice. Rephrase them in the passive, according to the example.

Example: **Active:** La polizia ha arrestato un giovane tunisino che è arrivato in Italia come clandestino.

Passive: Un giovane tunisino che è arrivato in Italia come clandestino è stato arrestato (dalla polizia).

1 Dei volontari hanno rintracciato il padre del giovane.
2 La banca ha risolto il problema di Emanuela.
3 Ha cambiato il livello del suo lavoro e aumentato il suo stipendio di conseguenza.
4 Un'eruzione dello Stromboli ha provocato un incendio nei boschi.
5 Le cattive condizioni del mare hanno isolato per due giorni la frazione Ginostra.

Activity 7

And now a little practice of the passive with **andare**. Continue the following exchanges on the lines of the example and say what the last sentence in each case means:

Example: **A** E' stato rintracciato il padre?
      B No, signore.
      A Allora va rintracciato al più presto.
      Then he must be found as soon as possible.

1 **A** E' stato isolato il malato?
  B No, dottore.
  A Allora …

2 **A** E' stato liberato il prigioniero?
  B No, signore.
  A Allora …

3 **A** E' stato firmato l'assegno?
  B No, signora.
  C Allora …

4 **A** E' stato dato l'allarme?
  B No, professore.
  A Allora …

The passive with *chiedere, dare, dire,* etc.

The last question in this activity however requires a cautionary note. There are a number of common verbs which we frequently use in the passive in English and which cannot be used in the passive in the same way in Italian. **Dare** is one of them. We are thinking of sentences like:

He was given a present.
They were asked to arrive early.
I was told he had arrived.

This is because the equivalent verbs in Italian work thus:

	Direct	Indirect
Verb	Object	Object

| dare | un regalo | a qualcuno |

		Indirect
	Verb	Object

| chiedere/domandare | a qualcuno | di fare qualcosa |

	Indirect	
Verb	Object

| dire | a qualcuno | di fare qualcosa. |

In each case, **qualcuno** is an indirect object (the **a** is the clue). Italian doesn't allow an indirect object to become the subject of a passive. So what do you do? You have to find another way of expressing the idea, for instance, making the subject **loro** *they*, i.e. some vague, unspecified people.

I.O.	Verb	Direct Object

| Gli | hanno dato | un regalo. |

I.O.	Verb

| Gli | hanno chiesto | di arrivare in anticipo. |

I.O.	Verb

| Mi | hanno detto | che era arrivato. |

Activity 8

Can you find any relative pronouns in what Marina says in Interview 2?

SESSION 5

▶ Interview 3

Our interviewer found Signora Torrielli weighed down by her problems and very much in need of the holiday which she would be taking in a few weeks. The problems are so numerous, we have divided the interview into two parts (see Session 7).

Signora Torrielli	Le problematiche di quest'azienda sono il fatto che non viene più pagata l'idea, non viene pagato più niente ma viene solo pagato il minuto/lavoro. Quindi a noi arriva la giacca, il rotolo di tessuto, Il rotolo dei modelli, i fili e i bottoni e noi abbiamo 100 minuti per rendere questa cosa appesa ad un attaccapanni imbustata e pronta per la spedizione. Non ci vengono più riconosciute le nostre – volevo chiamarle bravure artigianali – perché si pretende da noi l'industria con incluso il risultato dell'artigiano, quindi siamo proprio in una profonda crisi ... Non si può ottenere il massimo del prodotto con il minimo dei minuti. Da me vogliono il massimo della ... non della produttività ma della qualità e non mi danno il tempo per farlo. E quindi l'azienda è in crisi per questa ragione. Per fare quel lavoro in 100 minuti non ci stiamo, noi andiamo non fuori mercato ma andiamo in perdita.
Interviewer	Dunque la trovo in un momento difficile.
Signora Torrielli	Certo. Anche perché non vedo quale possa essere la soluzione. Siccome tutti avranno sempre meno soldi, potranno sempre spendere meno, però saranno sempre più sollecitati dalla pubblicità, dai giornali, da tutti a volere quelle firme lì e quelle firme lì per poter vendere continueranno a discapito della qualità del tessuto, della qualità della confezione, così, a scendere nei prezzi e quindi la gente, sì, metterà un capo firmato ma non avrà più il valore di quella firma perché il capo non viene più fatto come dovrebbe essere fatto. Se si parla di prêt-à-porter. Se si parla di alta moda è un altro discorso, ma quello non facciamo, insomma, quindi ...

le problematiche	**il complesso dei problemi.** Sig.ra Torrielli has more than one problem!
imbustata	*bagged,* i.e. in its plastic wrapping for transport
si pretende da noi l'industria con incluso il risultato dell'artigiano	Another 'false friend' **pretendere** is more to do with having pretensions, laying claims, than with make-believe. Here: *they expect us to produce in an industrial way but wanting the finished product of a craftsman.*
non fuori mercato	*not out of business*
ma andiamo in perdita	*but we are going to make a loss*
non ci stiamo	*we can't do it*
a discapito di	*to the detriment of*
un capo firmato	*a designer label garment*
è un altro discorso	*it's another matter*
alta moda	*haute couture*

Comprehension 3

1 Describe the process which is undergone when Signora Torrielli produces a jacket for Valentino or another well-known firm. e.g. who supplies what, who does what.
2 Signora Torrielli complains that the firms are expecting something they do not any longer really pay for, or in Emanuela's terms, recognize economically. What is it?
3 Why do the firms need to cut costs so fiercely?
4 What consequence does this have on the finished article, in the case of ready-to-wear?
5 What area of fashion does Signora Torrielli say is not affected by this constant lowering of quality, value?

SESSION 6

Activity 9

Can you find anything that looks like the passive in what Signora Torrielli said in Interview 3? Check the Key to see if you were right.

The passive with *venire*

Il capo non viene più fatto come *The garment is no longer*
dovrebbe essere fatto.   *made as it should be (made).*

Several times in this interview, Signora Torrielli uses a very
common form of the passive, made with **venire** (not **essere**) + the
past participle. You will find that this is much used by Italians,
but it can only be used in simple (one word) tenses. It is not used
with compound tenses such as the perfect, where you need
essere. Otherwise **essere** and **venire** are interchangeable,
although possibly **venire** is used to suggest process, action, while
essere is to do with state. For example, Signora Torrielli could
have equally said:

Il capo non è più fatto come dovrebbe essere fatto.

Here is another example:

Il panettone viene mangiato a Natale. *Panettone is eaten at Christmas.*

(**Panettone** is a cross between a very light bread and cake, made
of a yeast dough and containing candied peel.)

So there are three ways of forming the passive:

essere
venire   } + past participle
andare

but the meaning when **andare** is used, is distinctly different, as
we saw in Activity 7.

Activity 10

Suggest how you might say:

1 Here's the coffee. It's hot. It should be drunk immediately.
2 The situation is difficult. It should be said that John is a
  stubborn person.
3 Usually in Italy meals are accompanied by wine.
4 The long working day is recognized in our remuneration.
5 Our work is valued.
6 The price must be increased.

Activity 11

In Interview 3 Signora Torrielli uses some of the forms we have
just been working on.

1 Can you find examples of the future in what she says?
2 How about the present subjunctive?
3 She also uses the impersonal si. Can you find any examples?

SESSION 7

▶ Interview 4

More aspects of Signora Torrielli's crisis. We should explain the interviewer had met Signora Torrielli for the first time the previous year.

Interviewer E' molto cambiato dall'anno scorso?

Signora No, no, no. Assolutamente. E' proprio una cosa che è
Torrielli in escalation da anni, questa, perché tutti trovano meno mercato, allora diminuiscono i prezzi, diminuiscono la qualità dei tessuti, diminuiscono la qualità della produzione, sempre però a discapito dell'ultimo che è quello che produce. Non a discapito della fotomodella, non a discapito del servizio fotografico, non a discapito di … a discapito però dell'ultimo che mette insieme il capo, che è quello che non può difendersi. Che per lo meno si difende molto poco anche perché ci sono tutti i mercati emergenti che producono – non ancora bene – ma che produrranno nel giro di poco tempo bene. Dunque l'Italia, se non fa qualche cosa, perderà completamente tutta questa fascia di … e le persone perderanno i posti perché non ci sarà più il mercato per fare questo tipo di lavoro. Tutti quelli che hanno potuto, proprio per tutte le grane sindacali, per tutti gli obblighi sindacali, per tutti gli obblighi di legge, per l'USSL e tutte quelle altre cose … tutti quelli che avevano la potenza, quindi quelli più grossi, sono andati, hanno trasferito le loro produzioni, all'estero, e il governo non ha fatto niente per tenerli in casa. Dalle scarpe alle borse, le confezioni, le maglierie, tutti. Noi facciamo ancora quest'élite di firme ma sicuramente quest'élite di firme, le loro linee più basse sono già state portate sicuramente fuori Italia a fare. Invece noi siamo a Torino, abbiamo la fortuna di essere a Torino … abbiamo certamente un mercato più favorevole perché siamo su Torino ma credo che a Torino nel giro di quest'anno abbiano chiuso cinque o sei laboratori.

Interviewer Mi è sembrato l'anno scorso, quando L'ho incontrata per la prima volta, che Lei era molto orgogliosa della Sua azienda ...

Signora Torrielli Sono orgogliosa ma non sono più gratificata, allora quando uno non viene più gratificato ... quando si deve combattere contro ... i minuti, proprio il minuto, che non può permettere a una ragazza di andare due volte a prendere l'acqua perché Lei, vedendo fare quello, sa che quella giacca non esce più in 100 minuti, esce in 102, e siccome tutte vanno due volte, non è più 102, ma 130 minuti. 130 minuti e noi ci abbiamo rimesso 30 minuti, 30 minuti vuol dire moltiplicato per 35 moltiplicati per 22 giorni di lavoro e noi alla fine andiamo a meno anziché a più.

Difficilissimo già trovare ragazze che hanno voglia di fare questo lavoro. Forse hanno ragione loro perché è un lavoro di grande impegno, bisogna avere la testa tutto il giorno, non è una fabbrica dove uno schiaccia il bottone o ... Con i contratti che i dipendenti ormai hanno, loro si attengono strettamente al contratto e non c'è più il rapporto interpersonale se non raramente, no, no, perché se loro decidono che non vogliono fermarsi un'ora di più perché quell'ora di più – giustamente hanno fatto otto ore di lavoro – non si fermano e non gliene importa niente se andiamo in mora perché siamo in ritardo.

Quando ho iniziato non era così ... Devono diminuire i prezzi e dove loro possono sicuramente stringere più facilmente è solo sull'ultimo gradino che è la produzione.

Domanda Ma non è la cosa più importante?

Signora Torrielli Certo ma non è che la gente capisca la differenza ... Basta che ci sia il nome, per loro il marchio è la garanzia, quindi chi vede quello crede che sia già stato fatto tutto dentro quel marchio, invece dentro quel marchio è stato fatto tutto per risparmiare, per permettere gli utili a quel marchio.

in escalation	Another English phrase in an Italian business context
nel giro di poco tempo	*very soon* (**nel giro di 3 mesi** *within three months*)
grane sindacali	*troubles caused by the unions* (**sindacati**)

USSL	**Unità Socio – Sanitaria Locale** *the local Health Authority*
30 minuti ... moltiplicato per 35 ...	The working week is 35 hours and there are 22 working days in a month ... That would seem to be the calculation Signora Torrielli is doing. We confess to not quite understanding the 130 minutes – perhaps it is 2 minutes for each of 15 workers – but understand the overall problem.
non gliene importa niente	*they couldn't care a jot.* (lit: *nothing of it matters to them*)
andare in mora	Signora Torrielli's contracts will specify a delivery date and she probably *incurs a penalty for lateness*. **Mora** is a legal term for unjustified lateness in fulfilling an obligation, contract etc. but is often used to mean the penalty which that incurs.
chi vede quello	*the person who sees that* (the name label) (this is the relative **chi**, see Unit 5)
gli utili	*profits*

Comprehension 4

1 Which elements in the chain which is involved in producing designer label garments does Signora Torrielli say are exempt from the economy measures? Which areas suffer from savings being made?

2 She fears competition from which quarter?

3 What does she say the most powerful firms are doing?

4 What has happened to five or six workshops similar to hers in Turin this year?

5 What other problems does she consider Italian employers have to contend with, which lead to their moving production away from Italy?

6 The interviewer found her to be very proud of her business last year but thinks this might be no longer the case. What is Signora Torrielli's comment?

7 Apart from the time problem, what staff problems does Signora Torrielli mention?

SESSION 8

Activity 12

Look through Interview 4 for examples of some of the points we have dealt with recently:

1 Relative pronouns   2 The subjunctive
3 The passive   4 The future

Reading

And finally, here's a happy worker. It's someone you've already met.

Il mio mestiere è quello di scrivere e io lo so bene e da molto tempo. Spero di non essere fraintesa: sul valore di quel che posso scrivere non so nulla. So che scrivere è il mio mestiere. Quando mi metto a scrivere, mi sento straordinariamente a mio agio e mi muovo in un elemento che mi par di conoscere straordinariamente bene; adopero degli strumenti che mi sono noti e familiari e li sento ben fermi nelle mie mani. Se faccio qualunque altra cosa, se studio una lingua straniera, se mi provo a imparare la storia o la geografia o la stenografia o se mi provo a parlare in pubblico o a lavorare a maglia o a viaggiare, soffro e mi chiedo di continuo come gli altri facciano queste stesse cose, mi pare sempre che ci debba essere un modo giusto di fare queste cose che è noto agli altri e sconosciuto a me. E mi pare d'essere sorda e cieca e ho come una nausea in fondo a me. Quando scrivo invece non penso mai che c'è forse un modo più giusto di cui si servono gli altri scrittori. Non me ne importa niente di come fanno gli altri scrittori. Intendiamoci, io posso scrivere soltanto delle storie. Se mi provo a scrivere un saggio di critica o un articolo per un giornale a comando, va abbastanza male. Quello che allora scrivo lo devo cercare faticosamente come fuori di me. Posso farlo un po' meglio che studiare una lingua straniera o parlare in pubblico, ma solo un po' meglio. E ho sempre l'impressione di truffare il prossimo con delle parole prese a prestito o rubacchiate qua e là. E soffro e mi sento in esilio. Invece quando scrivo delle storie sono come uno che è in patria, sulle strade che conosce dall'infanzia e fra le mura e gli alberi che sono suoi. Il mio mestiere è scrivere delle storie, cose inventate o cose che ricordo della mia vita ma comunque storie, cose dove non c'entra la cultura ma soltanto la memoria e la fantasia. Questo è il mio mestiere, e io lo farò fino alla morte. Sono molto contenta di questo mestiere e non lo cambierei per niente al mondo.

'Il mio mestiere' (written in 1949) in Natalia Ginzburg,
Le piccole virtù, Einaudi 1962

mestiere	*trade* (rather than *job*). Italian definition from *Lo Zingarelli 2004*: **esercizio di una attività lavorativa, spec. manuale, frutto di esperienza e pratica, a scopo di guadagno.** N. Ginzburg indeed refers to holding her tools nice and firmly in her hands.
frainteso	*misunderstood*
qualunque altra cosa	*any other thing whatsoever*

Comprehension 5

The questions are in Italian. Mostly a small change to the original sentence will produce the answer. Your reply need not be a complete sentence, just a natural answer.

1 Che cosa sa da molto tempo Natalia Ginzburg?
2 Su che cosa dice di non sapere nulla?
3 Come si sente quando scrive?
4 Che cosa adopera per fare il suo mestiere?
5 Che cosa succede se prova a studiare una lingua straniera o a parlare in pubblico, ecc?
6 Scrive di tutto, Natalia Ginzburg?
7 E' più brava a scrivere articoli per un giornale o a parlare in pubblico?
8 Con quali immagini spiega le sensazioni che prova (a) quando scrive un articolo (b) quando scrive una storia.
9 Come sappiamo che le piace il suo mestiere?

Written style

Natalia Ginzburg's hallmark is a simple, direct style of writing. Nevertheless you will probably realize that when Natalia Ginzburg writes, the style is more literary than when one of our interviewees speaks. A simple example in the first few lines is the abbreviation of the present tense of **parere: par** instead of **pare**.

This may also be done in speech. And of course the sentences are carefully structured, balanced, finished.

You may notice too that in this passage there are subjunctives underlining her uncertainty about how various activities are best carried out.

... mi chiedo come gli altri **facciano** queste stesse cose, mi pare sempre che ci **debba** essere un modo giusto di fare queste stesse cose ...

Activity 14

Talking to yourself

1 In banca: tutti noi abbiamo qualche storia da raccontare: il Bancomat che non funziona proprio quando non ne possiamo fare a meno, il Bancomat ci ha 'mangiato' la carta, la banca non ha pagato le nostre bollette da un anno o altri errori della banca ... Racconti le Sue disavventure!

2 Imprese/attività a conduzione familiare: ne conosce qualcuna? Quali sono i vantaggi? Quali gli svantaggi?

3 Lavorare con il marito, la moglie o con un altro familiare o parente. Quali sono i pro? E quali i contro?

4 Il distacco generazionale e i rapporti tra genitori e figli. I Suoi rapporti con gli anziani della famiglia o con la famiglia del Suo coniuge/partner. Racconti le Sue esperienze.

5 Lavora troppo, Lei? Fa troppi straordinari? Il Suo datore di lavoro riconosce il lavoro che fa? Come sono cambiate le Sue condizioni di lavoro nel corso della Sua vita lavorativa? Ne parli!

6 Forse Lei è datore di lavoro: quali problemi ha con i Suoi dipendenti? E' facile o difficile trovare gli impiegati giusti, quelli con le caratteristiche di cui ha bisogno per la Sua attività? I Suoi dipendenti sono disposti ad essere flessibili quando ce n'è bisogno?

7 La Sua attività è minacciata dai concorrenti all'estero? Che cosa può fare per difendersi? Che futuro vede per la Sua azienda?

8 Compra vestiti firmati Lei? Perché? Quali stilisti Le piacciono? Secondo Lei, perché per molte persone la firma è così importante?

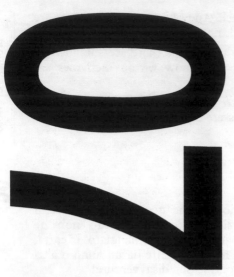

07

la persona e il lavoro

In this unit we shall
- look at the effect of work on the personal lives of some Italians
- look at the reality behind some Italian stereotypes: the Italian husband, 'la mamma italiana'
- look at the prepositions required after certain verbs, adjectives and nouns
- look further at the gerund and meet the present participle
- revise question words
- consider other uses of the subjunctive and ways to avoid it
- revise object pronouns and emphatic pronouns

▶ Interview 1

For the women we interviewed, managing family, home and career is a big preoccupation. First Marina who is married and has two daughters, 8 and 6. She was asked how she managed to combine career and family.

Marina	Eh, ci si arrangia, insomma. Come tutte le donne, trovo in qualche modo delle soluzioni. Io ho la fortuna di avere un marito che è molto bravo con le bambine, quindi quando sono via, il che succede abbastanza spesso, si occupa lui della gestione domestica in un certo senso. Non è molto contento di questo ma insomma lo fa. E poi ho una serie di aiuti quindi, ho una ragazza alla pari per le bambine, una signora che viene a fare le pulizie ...
Interviewer	Dunque tuo marito forse non è tipico?
Marina	Mah, insomma anche gli uomini italiani si stanno evolvendo. Sì, credo che ormai, non tutti ma insomma ... sicuramente rispetto a qualche anno fa sono molto cambiati, partecipano alla vita domestica. Mio marito comunque ha avuto un'educazione molto spartana, è sempre stato abituato ad arrangiarsi anche in casa, aveva i genitori separati, quindi è sempre stato allevato in modo molto ... molto poco italiano, non c'è dubbio. Non c'era questa figura della mamma che pensa a tutto, che si occupa di tutto ... Però ripeto, sì, penso che mio marito forse sia meglio da questo punto di vista, però io vedo che gli uomini, gli uomini giovani insomma ... D'altra parte non c'è scelta, se la donna lavora credo non ci sia alternativa ...

---

ci si arrangia	**arrangiarsi** to manage, to find a solution somehow, to get by somehow. Note: **arrangiarsi** is a reflexive verb. Marina uses it with the impersonal **si** (one). Italian avoids **si si**: the first **si** is made into **ci**. Hence: <u>**ci si**</u> **arrangia**. We mentioned this in the note to the N. Ginzburg passage at the end of Unit 4.

il che	*which,* referring to **quando sono via**
una ragazza alla pari	*an au pair girl*
una signora che viene a fare le pulizie	*a lady who comes to clean.* Often referred to as **una donna di servizio**, often simply **una donna**. For instance you offer to help your hostess and she will say: **No, no, lo farà la donna.** See also **colf**, *home help* (formed from <u>col</u>laboratrice <u>f</u>amiliare).
rispetto a	*compared with*
sono molto cambiati	*they have changed a lot.* Note: **cambiare** when intransitive forms the **passato prossimo** with **essere**.

Comprehension 1

1 Marina seems to have things very much under control. What makes one think it isn't as easy as all that?
2 Does Marina think Italian men help on the home front?
3 Why is her husband better prepared than many for having a wife with a successful career?
4 What notion of the typical Italian mother do you get from what Marina says?

SESSION 2

Verbs requiring prepositions before following infinitives
Notice how Marina says:

una signora che <u>viene a</u> fare le pulizie

Already in Unit 1 we met **dovere, potere, volere** and of course **piacere (mi piace, mi piacerebbe)** followed by the infinitive. We mentioned in passing that other verbs needed a preposition before a following infinitive. We drew attention to **mi rifiuto di comprare** and **non credo di essere molto brava. Rifiutarsi** and **credere** both need **di** before an infinitive which follows them. Many verbs require **a**, for instance, **venire** (see above). We have provided a list in the **Reference grammar**. Sometimes expressions like this form up into a chain of prepositions:

| Devo <u>cercare di</u> <u>ricordarmi di</u> fare la spesa prima della riunione. | *I must try to remember to do the shopping before the meeting.* |

Hai voglia di <u>andare a</u> vedere un film?	*Do you want to go and see a film?*

Adjectives and nouns requiring prepositions before following infinitives

Similarly, certain adjectives and nouns require an **a** or a **di** when an infinitive is to follow. Marina says of her husband:

è sempre stato <u>abituato ad</u> arrangiarsi	*he's always been used to managing by himself*

She could have said:

non è <u>contento di</u> farlo ma insomma lo fa	*he's not pleased to do it but he does it*
è <u>capace di</u> cucinare	*he can cook/he is capable of cooking*

Verbs requiring a preposition before a following noun

The learner needs also to be aware that some verbs require a preposition before their object (usually a noun). Examples in what Marina says are:

... la mamma che <u>pensa a</u> tutto, che <u>si occupa di</u> tutto.	*... the mother who takes care of everything, who looks after everything*

You will notice that the two phrases are similar in meaning but different in structure, one using **a**, the other **di**. If there is to be a pronoun instead, the preposition will affect the choice of a pronoun. For example, if you are making plans for something and you offer to look after a certain aspect, you may say:

<u>Ci</u> penso io.	*I'll take care of it* (lit: *I'll think of it*). (**ci** because it is **pensare a** ...)
Me <u>ne</u> occupo io.	*I'll look after it.* (**ne** because it is **occuparsi di** ...)

You need to note particularly those verbs which work differently from their English equivalent. There is a list of some common ones in the **Reference grammar**. You need to be especially careful when trying to express the passive with verbs which take an indirect object in Italian (**a** + noun; or indirect object pronoun). It can't be done as you have seen in Unit 6, Session 4.

Direct Object	Indirect Object
The manager answered my letter.	**Il direttore ha risposto alla mia lettera**.
My letter was answered by the manager.	This cannot be translated directly. The letter is the direct object in English, but the indirect object in Italian.
Emanuela often asks John to do the shopping.	**Emanuela chiede spesso a John di fare la spesa**.
John is often asked by Emanuela to do the shopping.	No direct translation is possible.

There are also cases when a preposition is needed in English and not in Italian.

| ascoltare qualcosa, qualcuno | *to listen to something, someone* |
| cercare qualcosa, qualcuno | *to look for something, someone* |

LANGUAGE LEARNING TIP We would not advise attempting to learn lists of points, unless you are quite sure that that suits your style of learning. However, what we suggest strongly is that you try to be observant when listening to Italian, reading etc. and try to absorb the whole package rather than just the single word, e.g. **ascoltare qualcuno** ... rather than just **ascoltare**. It may also be helpful to make your own lists as you go along. Dictionaries usually tell you how a particular word functions.

Activity 1

Hai provato a ... ? *Have you tried ...?*

One of your friends has a husband who doesn't help in the home at all. She telephones you often to talk about the situation. This is one of your conversations. Complete it by filling in the gaps. Use the following expressions for her: **cominciare a; accorgersi di; continuare a; essere abituato a; rifiutarsi di; essere contenta di** and these for you: **provare a; fare finta di; essere stufa di.**

Example:	**Amica**	Non ne posso più! **Sono** veramente **stufa di** dovere fare sempre tutto io!
	Lei	Secondo me dovresti **smettere di** lamentarti con me e **cominciare a** lamentarti con tuo marito ... !

Amica	Ci ho provato, sai?! Il risultato è che dice che gli dispiace, ma poi (1) .... comportarsi esattamente come prima!
Lei	E allora, senti, fai così: (2) .... fare finta di dimenticarti che ci sono dei lavori da fare ...
Amica	Non conosci mio marito! Lui proprio non (3) .... quello che c'è da fare in casa! Non li vede neanche, i lavori da fare!
Lei	Ma scusa, perché tu non glieli fai notare?
Amica	Quando glieli faccio notare, lui (4) .... farli, perché dice che lavora già abbastanza fuori casa, e che non (5) .... fare i lavori domestici, dice che sono cose da donne!
Lei	Secondo me tu non sei abbastanza furba ... io ogni tanto (6) .... non stare bene ... che so ... di avere un gran mal di testa ...
Amica	E tu dici che lui ci crederebbe?! No, guarda ... io le bugie non le so dire ... e poi, scusa, non (7) .... ottenere il suo aiuto in questo modo ... vorrei che cambiasse per davvero ... forse un giorno (8) .... capire il mio punto di vista ...
Lei	Aspetta e spera! Da quello che mi dici di tuo marito, è il tipo che non cambierà mai! E per di più, io (9) .... dover ascoltare ogni giorno le tue lamentele!

Activity 2

Mr Rossi is very disorganized. He always has good intentions at the beginning of the week but he rarely manages to do what he has decided to do. Imagine what he says to himself on Friday evening when he looks back over what he intended to do but didn't.

Example: lunedì pomeriggio – avere intenzione di andare a trovare la zia Franca – non riuscire a trovare il tempo – mettermi ad aggiustare un rubinetto che perdeva

Lunedì pomeriggio <u>avevo intenzione di andare a trovare</u> la zia Franca, ma non <u>sono riuscito a trovare</u> il tempo perché all'ora di pranzo <u>mi sono messo ad aggiustare</u> un rubinetto che perdeva e quando ho finito il lavoro era troppo tardi per uscire!
On Monday afternoon I meant to go and see Aunt Franca

but I didn't manage to find the time because at lunch-time I started to see to a leaking tap and when I had finished the job it was already too late to go out.

1 martedì mattina – avere intenzione di comperare un regalo per il compleanno di mia figlia – non riuscire a trovarlo – dimenticarmi di chiedere a mia moglie in che negozio lo vendevano

2 mercoledì sera – avere intenzione di andare allo stadio con gli amici per vedere insieme la partita di calcio – non riuscire a organizzare la serata – dimenticarsi di comperare i biglietti

3 giovedì mattina – avere intenzione di andare alla Posta per pagare la bolletta del telefono – non riuscire a pagarla – accorgersi troppo tardi di non avere abbastanza contanti nel portafoglio

4 venerdì pomeriggio – avere intenzione di prenotare le vacanze per l'estate – non riuscire ad andare all'agenzia di viaggi – cominciare a leggere un libro molto interessante e dimenticarsi di uscire

SESSION 3

▶ Interview 2

Emanuela has a daughter, Anna, aged 5, and as we have said, her husband, John, is American. Not being so high on the career ladder, she doesn't have the paid help Marina has, but her parents, now retired, live close by and help to some extent. She was asked whether in fact she saw herself as a career woman.

Emanuela	In un senso mi piacerebbe, certe volte mi sembra una cosa che posso apprezzare. Altre volte quando magari al mattino mia figlia non vuole lasciarmi uscire, vuole andare a spasso, un periodo in cui ha molto bisogno di suo papà, di sua mamma, vorrei non lavorare. Sto pensando che perdo, lavorando, gli anni più belli della mia famiglia, quello è brutto. Spero che lo sforzo valga la pena, ecco non sia inutile ...
Interviewer	Dunque veramente il problema di abbinare famiglia e lavoro per te ...
Emanuela	E' difficile, è difficile, sì, devo dire che dopo cinque anni sono proprio stanca, è difficile e, purtroppo, anche chiacchierando con altre amiche che hanno più o meno la mia età, hanno bambini piccoli, loro hanno lo stesso problema. Nel lavoro è richiesta molta competizione, molte ore, un grosso sforzo e comunque la famiglia ha delle esigenze che non possono essere disattese. E quindi è una cosa che pesa a tutte, ecco.
Interviewer	Hai un marito americano, lo conosco, so che in casa lui condivide ...
Emanuela	Sì, lui è bravissimo, no, non voglio dire bravissimo, lui fa esattamente quello che io penso sia il dovere di ogni coniuge. Mio marito è molto apprezzato dalle mie amiche, mi dicono che sono molto fortunata, che è bravissimo, che è un tesoro, che è un papà magnifico. E' vero, credo sia un bravissimo papà, è un marito che condivide assolutamente l'impegno della casa. Però anche gli altri mariti che hanno una moglie che lavora devono per forza aiutare, non c'è scelta, è un obbligo perché la giornata è veramente troppo pesante, quindi ... C'è qualche scemo ... Si può dire scemo?
Interviewer	Perché no?
Emanuela	C'è qualche scemo che non aiuta e questo è causa di problemi familiari seri. Perché sono situazioni che poi danneggiano l'armonia familiare.
Interviewer	Allora l'uomo italiano giovane veramente ...
Emanuela	Sì, sì, io trovo che i nostri coetanei, se non altro, magari non si occupano specificatamente della casa però comunque fanno la spesa, lasciano il bagno in ordine, guardano i bambini, li portano al parco, vanno a prenderli in piscina, non è proprio più concepibile,

lavorando tutti e due, avere una sola persona che si occupa della casa e dei figli. Non è assolutamente possibile. Mio cognato non fa nulla in casa perché mia sorella non lavora, quindi l'impegno della famiglia è esclusivamente quasi di mia sorella. Però lei ha la grossa fortuna di non dover lavorare fuori casa quindi ... Suo marito ha una giornata molto intensa, molto stressante, tutto il carico familiare è suo, di lei, ecco. Però quella è una cosa anche equa, potendo permettersi di mantenere la moglie a casa ...

Interviewer E anche a te, piacerebbe stare a casa?

Emanuela Sì, sicuramente sì. E' una scelta che scontenterebbe mia mamma che non ha lavorato fuori casa dopo il matrimonio e lei trova l'indipendenza economica assolutamente necessaria. Evidentemente, pur essendo lei l'amministratrice delle finanze familiari, il fatto di non poter essere lei una fonte di guadagno autonoma forse pensa abbia limitato le sue scelte. Io in questo momento baratterei l'indipendenza economica che ho con più tranquillità, con una vita più semplice.

Interviewer Sì?

Emanuela Sì. Invece di avere una vita costantemente impegnata, organizzare la giornata, cosa farò questa sera per cena, chi va a prendere mia figlia? chi la porta in piscina? cosa facciamo adesso che lei è in vacanza? Quindi una continua rincorsa all'organizzazione familiare, ecco. Sacrificando tante volte anche la bambina che invece avrebbe bisogno di avere più tempo con noi. Potrei rinunciare al lavoro tranquillamente oggi, oggi in particolare ... (*ride*) Oggi in particolare. Io starei qui volentieri una settimana senza vedere nessuno, senza lavarmi neanche la faccia proprio, niente make-up, niente tailleur, niente scarpe con tacco alto. Starei qui una settimana ad andare in bicicletta, fare dei pranzi semplici, qua è molto tranquillo, svegliarsi al mattino, andare a prendere i lamponi e non fare niente tutto il giorno. Mi piace tanto questo posto.

coniuge	*spouse* i.e. *husband or wife*; *Lo Zingarelli 2004*: **ciascuna delle due persone unite in matrimonio (sia il marito che la moglie).** Latinists will have found guessing easy. **Coniugato** means *married* and in official documents **già coniugato** is sometimes used rather than **divorziato**; also **libero/a di stato.**
si può dire ...?	*can you say* (lit: *can one say?*). **Si può** is neater than **è possibile** which learners sometimes use. Try to adopt it!
scemo	*fool, silly person* (*Lo Zingarelli 2004*: **che manca di giudizio, di senno, di intelligenza**). Emanuela's hesitation in using the word would seem to be related to her personal judgment of what might be described as lazy, thoughtless or selfish husbands. Here she is saying that they haven't the sense to understand the consequences of their behaviour.
coetani	A good one for guessing: **co** + **età**. *People of the same age as us.*
scontenterebbe	Can you guess? **contento**, preceded by the **s** which makes it negative: *it would make (my mother) unhappy.*
Oggi in particolare ... lo starei qui ... questo posto	The interview took place on a lovely Sunday late in June, in the attractive hills of the Alte Langhe (southern Piemonte) where Emanuela's ancestors used to farm and where her parents still have a rather dilapidated, very old house. The idea of being back in the noise of the city and going to work the next morning was obviously not appealing!
lamponi	*raspberries.* Emanuela and her family have a kitchen garden at the farm, with some particularly prolific raspberry canes.

Comprehension 2

1 From what is said here, summarize Emanuela's attitude to being a career woman.

2 What is her big worry?

3 What does she find she has in common with friends of her own age?

4 Her friends think Emanuela is very lucky in her husband, but she takes back the word **bravissimo** which she initially uses to talk about his sharing of the household tasks. Why?

5 In talking about the husbands of working wives generally, she uses the same phrase as Marina. What is it?

6 What sort of tasks does she say young Italian husbands undertake?

7 Her life and her sister's are very different. What do you learn about her sister and her brother-in-law?

8 What seems to be the position of Emanuela's mother as regards working wives?

9 Emanuela is feeling particularly tired. What seems to plague her life?

10 What would Emanuela like to do for a week, rather than go back to the city and her job?

i The general opinion, when you ask various people, not just our interviewees who each had rather special situations, seems to be that sharing of domestic duties between husband and wife is still unequal in many cases even though the wife is, like her husband, trying to make a career. Italian women attribute this in part to **la mamma italiana** who – and this is a generalization of course – tends to be indulgent towards her sons and do everything for them while requiring her daughters to help in the house.

SESSION 4

The gerund again

You may have noticed both Marina and Emanuela use **stare +** *gerund* for on-going actions:

Marina

anche gli uomini italiani si stanno evolvendo.

Italian men too are evolving, making progress.

Emanuela

Sto pensando che ...

I keep thinking that ...

In the second case, in English we probably wouldn't say *I am thinking*. What Emanuela means seems to be that the thought recurs to her quite often, it is on-going in that sense.

But Emanuela uses the *gerund*, the form ending in -**ando**/-**endo**, several times without the verb **stare**:

Sto pensando che perdo, <u>lavorando</u>, gli anni più belli ...
I keep thinking that by working I am losing the best years ...

anche <u>chiacchierando</u> con altre amiche ...
also when chatting with other friends ...

non è proprio concepibile, <u>lavorando</u> tutti e due, avere una sola persona che si occupa della casa e dei figli.
it's not really conceivable, with both working/since both are working, to have one single person who looks after the house and the children.

tutto il carico familiare è suo, di lei, ecco. Però quello è una cosa anche equa, <u>potendo</u> permettersi di mantenere la moglie a casa ...
the whole burden of home and family falls on her. However that is also fair, since he can (afford to) maintain his wife at home ...

pur <u>essendo</u> lei l'amministratrice delle finanze familiari ...
even though she is the administrator of the family finances ...

From the above examples you can see that there is a variety of ways in which the gerund can be translated. It is used when in English you might say:

---

on
by } + verb + *ing*
when
since + clause with verb

Note that the subject of the gerund should be the same as that of the main verb. Emanuela says: **Sto pensando che perdo, lavorando, gli anni più belli**. She is thinking and she is working. Note: clarity is lost when this is not done, as in the last example but one.

Activity 3

In the sentences which follow, change the part in bold print to the gerund.

Example: **Dal momento che ha** un lavoro molto impegnativo, Emanuela non può passare molto tempo con sua figlia.

Avendo un lavoro molto impegnativo, Emanuela non può passare molto tempo con sua figlia.

1 Certe mattine Emanuela non vorrebbe andare a lavorare, **poiché sa** che sua figlia sentirà la sua mancanza.
2 La vita di Emanuela è al momento molto faticosa, **perché deve** abbinare famiglia e lavoro.
3 **Dal momento che condivide** tutti i lavori domestici con lei, il marito di Emanuela le è di grande aiuto.
4 Certi mariti non si rendono conto che, **se non aiutano** in casa, danneggiano l'armonia familiare e rendono la vita difficile a sé stessi prima ancora che alla moglie.
5 La maggior parte dei giovani mariti italiani è di sostegno alla moglie **perché lascia** il bagno in ordine, **fa** la spesa, **guarda** i bambini, **li porta** al parco, **li va** a prendere in piscina.
6 **Visto che non deve** lavorare fuori casa, mia sorella ha molto più tempo di me per badare alla casa e alla famiglia.

The adjectival form: the present participle

The gerund is a verbal form. The *-ing* ending in English can be adjectival and there is also an adjectival form in Italian ending in **-ante** (Group 1, **-are** verbs) and **-ente** (all other verbs). Its technical name is the present participle. This is a tricky area and we suggest you limit yourself to using present participles you have met, in similar contexts to those in which you met them.

un'esperienza sconvolgente   *a shattering experience*
(*Lo Zingarelli 2004*: sconvolgere: metere in disordine, in agitazione, in scompiglio)

un fatto raccapricciante   *a horrifying fact*
(*Lo Zingarelli 2004*: raccapricciare: provare orrore, turbare profondamente)

Here the *-ing* word (-**ante**/-**ente** word in Italian) tells us more about the noun. The Italian has a plural form in **-i**: **scene commoventi** *moving scenes*.

As with other adjectives, this form can be used as a noun. Indeed some are also nouns: **un credente** *a believer*; **un principiante** *a beginner*.

Activity 4

Change the expression in bold print to the correct form of the present participle.

Example: Un risultato **che incoraggia**. Un risultato **incoraggiante**.

1 Una persona **che resiste** a grandi fatiche. = Una persona ...
2 Un rumore così forte da **assordare**. = Un rumore ...
3 Un oggetto **che pesa** molto. = Un oggetto ...
4 Un calciatore **che ha la funzione di attaccare**. = Un ...
5 Un vestito **che aderisce** al corpo. = Un vestito ...
6 Un film che non era bello come ti aspettavi e **che ti delude**. = Un film ...
7 Un criminale **che traffica** in armi. = Un ... d'armi.
8 Una persona **che presiede** un'associazione. = Un ...

The student may be perplexed occasionally to find a present participle which does not seem to obey the rules for its formation given above. This is because the Italian participle derives directly from the Latin participle, whereas the verb over the centuries has changed its form. One of the little fascinations of language study! Here are some examples:

Una persona **che prevede** i problemi e si organizza per tempo.
Una persona **previdente**. (**i** in participle, **e** in verb)

Un coltello affilato **che taglia** molto bene.
Un coltello **tagliente**. (**-are** verb but participle in **-ente**)

Una persona **che diffida** di tutto e di tutti.
Una persona **diffidente**. (**-are** verb but participle in **-ente**)

Question words – interrogative pronouns

Emanuela finds herself daily plagued by finding solutions to certain problems:

Cosa farò questa sera per cena?	*What shall I do for supper tonight?*
Chi va a prendere mia figlia?	*Who is going to fetch my daughter?*

This highlights the words used for asking questions, interrogative pronouns, the Italian equivalents of *who* and *what*. **Chi?** is *who?* and *whom?* i.e. subject or object.

Chi è?	*Who is it?* (subject)
Chi arriva?	*Who is arriving?* (subject)
Chi vedi?	*Who can you see?* (object)

| Con chi parli? | *Who are you talking to?* (object) |

Cosa? che cosa? or **che?** can all be *what?* Probably **cosa** is the most common in spoken, everyday Italian, while **che** belongs more to formal, even literary usage. All three can be subject or object:

Che cosa è?	*What is it?* (subject)
Cosa fai?	*What are you doing?* (object)
Con che cosa lo apri?	*What do you open it with?* (object)

There is a list of question words in the **Reference grammar**.

Questions which expect the answer *yes* or *no*, need no question word and are made by using the question intonation in speech, or in writing, adding a question mark.

Ti piace il formaggio?	*Do you like cheese?*
Conosci Anna Pavese?	*Do you know Anna Pavese?*
Hai visto il nuovo film di Benigni?	*Have you seen Benigni's new film?*

Activity 5

A very curious small child, who asks questions all the time, is plaguing you. Here are the replies you give him. Work out what his questions were. Use the interrogative pronouns **chi** and **che cosa**. A clue: all the questions are about types of work or workers.

Examples: E' la persona che ci consegna la posta ogni mattina.
Question: **Chi è il postino?**

Ci consegna la posta ogni mattina.
Question: **Che cosa fa il postino?**

1 Scrive gli articoli sui giornali che leggiamo ogni giorno.
Question:
2 E' la persona che vende la frutta e la verdura.
Question:
3 E' la persona che aggiusta i rubinetti quando sono rotti.
Question:
4 Suona il pianoforte.
Question:
5 Dipinge quadri.
Question:

SESSION 5

Personal pronouns: object, direct and indirect, and reflexive

These are usually covered in beginners' courses since you can't go far without them. There is a table in the **Reference grammar**, should you need it. Emanuela's interview however provides a useful springboard for reminding you about their place in relation to the verb. Study the following;

quando magari mia figlia non vuole lasciar<u>mi</u> uscire
when perhaps my daughter doesn't want to let me leave

Hai un marito americano, <u>lo</u> conosco
You have an American husband, I know him

(i nostri coetanei) guardano i bambini, <u>li</u> portano al parco, vanno a prender<u>li</u> in piscina …
(men of our age) look after the children, take them to the park, go and fetch them from the swimming pool

senza lavar<u>mi</u> neanche la faccia proprio
without even washing my face

Object pronouns, whether direct or indirect or indeed reflexive, usually precede the verb. However there are certain parts of the verb where they are attached to the end. Can you see some cases in the examples above? Yes, with the infinitive. This is also the case with the gerund:

Mio marito si occupa dei bambini, portando<u>li</u> al parco, prendendo<u>li</u> da scuola, accompagnando<u>li</u> dal medico.
My husband looks after the children, taking them to the park, picking them up from school, going with them to the doctor's.

Note that the stress does not change. Pronouns are also attached to the imperative:

dimmi	(**tu** form)	*tell me*
scusami	(**tu** form)	*forgive me, excuse me*
diamoci del tu	(**noi** form)	*let's use **tu** to each other*
ditelo con i fiori	(**voi** form)	*say it with flowers*

Note also that the formal, third person form of the command is really a subjunctive so this rule does not apply, hence:

mi scusi	*forgive me, excuse me*
mi dica	*tell me* (see Unit 5, Session 4)
s'accomodi	*please sit down*

Personal pronouns: subject, emphatic pronouns

Did you notice that both Marina and Emanuela used pronouns to stress and/or make clear who they are referring to?

quando sono via ... si occupa <u>lui</u> della gestione domestica
when I am away ... he takes care of the household management

Sì, <u>lui</u> è bravissimo, ... <u>lui</u> fa esattamente quello che <u>io</u> penso sia il dovere di ogni coniuge ...
Yes, he is very good, ... he does exactly what I think is every husband's duty

pur essendo <u>lei</u> l'amministratrice delle finanze familiari, il fatto di non poter essere <u>lei</u> una fonte di guadagno autonoma forse pensa abbia limitato le sue scelte.
even though she runs the family finances, perhaps she thinks that the fact of not being able, herself, to be an autonomous source of earning has limited her choices.

And in another place Emanuela puts in **di lei** to help clarify what would otherwise be ambiguous, although she still leaves the following sentence possibly unclear because the subject of the main verb, è, is not the same as that of the gerund, **potendo**. In the English translation the differentiation between the possessives, *his* and *her*, helps as does the avoidance of the gerund. When you feel the possessives are leading to a lack of clarity in Italian, you can put in: **di lui, di lei ...**, as Emanuela does.

Suo marito ha una giornata molto intensa, molto stressante, tutto il carico familiare è <u>suo, di lei</u>, ecco. Però quella è una cosa anche equa, potendo permettersi di mantenere la moglie a casa.
Her husband has very intensive, stressful days, and all the burden of the family falls on her. However that is only fair, since he is able to afford to keep his wife at home.

Activity 6

Emanuela is very lucky: her husband shares equally with her the responsibility for their home and for the upbringing of their daughter. Here is an imaginary conversation between the two of them. Emanuela suddenly remembers something urgent to do and her husband immediately offers the solution. Write the husband's answers, using personal pronouns correctly as in the example.

Example: **Emanuela**   Domani bisogna pagare la bolletta del telefono!
The telephone bill has to be paid tomorrow.

Suo marito   Non preoccupar<u>ti</u>! <u>La</u> pago <u>io</u>!
Don't worry. I'll pay it.

1 Emanuela: Domani bisogna portare la bambina in piscina!
  Suo marito:
2 Emanuela: Domani viene a cena mia mamma! Chi prepara la cena?
  Suo marito:
3 Emanuela: Domani bisogna spedire quelle lettere!
  Suo marito:
4 Emanuela: Domani dobbiamo andare a fare la spesa!
  Suo marito:

Activity 7

In this exercise you practise using personal pronouns both before and after verbs. The text is based on what Marina says and the pronouns (subject, direct and indirect object and reflexive) have been omitted. Your job is to provide them! You may find it useful first to glance at the table of pronouns in the **Reference grammar**.

La famiglia di Marina *Marina's family*

A Marina è una donna in carriera, che deve trovare ogni giorno una soluzione per conciliare la sua vita di mamma e moglie con la sua vita lavorativa. Si ritiene fortunata, perché suo marito **le** è di grande aiuto quando ___ (1) è via per lavoro, si occupa delle bambine, ___ (2) va a prendere a scuola, ___ (3) aiuta a fare i compiti, organizza la giornata per ___ (4). Spesso viene aiutato in questo da una ragazza alla pari, ma è ___ (5) che deve telefonar___ (6), discutere con ___ (7) la giornata e gli orari delle bambine, pagar___ (8).

B Marina e suo marito possono anche contare sull'aiuto di una donna delle pulizie, però non ___ (1) conoscono molto bene, quindi non si fidano di lasciare la pulizia della casa completamente nelle sue mani. Quando Marina non è via per lavoro, si occupa ___ (2) di dar___ (3) istruzioni e di mostrar___(4) quali sono i lavori più urgenti. Invece, quando Marina è fuori città, è il marito che deve preoccuparsene: è ___ (5) che deve aspettar___ (6) la mattina prima di uscire per andare al lavoro, è ___ (7) che deve scrivere per ___ (8) la lista dei lavori più urgenti, è ___ (9) che deve controllare che tutto sia stato fatto alla fine della giornata e che deve pagar___ (10) alla fine della settimana.

C A quanto pare, il marito di Marina non è entusiasta di tutto questo! ___ (1) adatta, perché sa di non avere scelta. Quando Marina è via, ___ (2) sveglia più presto del solito la mattina, sveglia le bambine, controlla che ___ (3) lavino, ___ (4) vestano, facciano colazione e arrivino in orario a scuola. La sera, quando torna dal lavoro, cucina per ___ (5) e per sé stesso e ___ (6) preoccupa di controllare che la loro giornata sia andata bene. Ha imparato a fare tutte queste cose perché non è mai stato viziato da sua mamma, ma in fondo in fondo pensa che la sua vita sarebbe molto più facile se avesse sposato una donna più tradizionale!

The subjunctive after *sperare* and other verbs

Emanuela refers to the difficulties of being a working mother and then says:

> Spero che lo sforzo valga la pena, ecco, non sia inutile.
>
> *I hope the effort is worth while, that it is not pointless.*

The subjunctive underlines her doubts, which come through the whole interview. She works in order to provide a better life for her daughter, but finds it all very stressful and wonders whether the game is worth the candle.

After **sperare**, the subjunctive is not always used. This may be partly a personal choice, part of the speaker's style. To use a subjunctive after **sperare** may however be subconsciously underlining one's uncertainty. Apart from the present indicative, the future is sometimes used after s**perare**:

> Spero che farà bel tempo domani.
>
> *I hope the weather will be good tomorrow.*

The subjunctive is used after other verbs which introduce an element of subjectivity. You have already met it after **credere**, **pensare**, in other words when opinions are involved. It is also required in clauses which follow verbs expressing other emotions such as wanting, regret, fear, doubt.

Voglio che dica la verità.	*I want him to tell the truth.*
Teme che il risultato sia negativo.	*He's afraid the result will be negative.*
Dubito che riesca a convincere sua moglie.	*I doubt he will succeed in convincing his wife.*

Do you appreciate that the first verb is introducing the subject's point of view on the second? I want him to tell the truth – that is my wish, but may not be his, or his boss's, etc. You will also realize there is some cross-over in the emotions. For instance, **non credo che** may well be expressing doubt as well as opinion.

Avoiding the subjunctive

If the subject of both verbs is the same, there is no need for a subjunctive:

Voglio dire la verità.	*I want to tell the truth.*
Teme di essere noioso.	*He's afraid of being boring.*
Dubito di convincere mia moglie.	*I doubt I'll convince my wife.*

And when giving your opinion you can always say:

| Secondo me, è un'impresa impossibile. | *In my opinion it's an impossible undertaking.* |

Activity 8

Imagine you are an Italian woman and you are very sceptical about the possibility of a change in the position of women in Italy. You have read an article in the newspaper which says that Italian men in the younger generation are changing. You decide to write a letter to the editor to put your point of view which is that Italian men are not changing at all and you see the future for Italian women as very black! Explain your ideas using the following expressions, followed by the subjunctive: **penso / non penso che ...; credo / non credo che ...; temo che ...; dubito che ...; ho l'impressione che ...; spero che ...**

Example: **Non credo che** gli uomini italiani della nuova generazione **siano** diversi da quelli delle generazioni precedenti.
I don't believe the new generation of Italian men is different from preceding generations.

The choice of arguments and words is yours, so we cannot give a right answer but there is a letter written by an Italian for you in the Key.

SESSION 6

▶ Interview 3

Signora Torrielli's two daughters now have children of their own and she is a grandmother. When she was younger, however, in addition to the difficulties of being a working mother, she had a sense of guilt, since she was a single mother. This was by choice, but didn't mean she was without regrets.

Interviewer	Lei tiene molto alla famiglia, vero?
Signora Torrielli	Sì. Io mi sono sposata, che ero molto giovane, ho avuto subito due figlie e dopo due anni mi sono separata. Il cruccio della mia vita è stato il fatto di riuscire a fare la mamma separata e mantenerle con un certo reddito per poter fare le cose cui ero abituata prima, e nonostante questo ... tentare di mantenere il più vivo possibile il rapporto con le mie figlie. Adesso alla luce degli anni passati, le mie figlie hanno ormai 41 anni e 39 anni, mi sembra di esserci riuscita. Certo con molto sacrificio da parte mia e molti rimpianti adesso che forse valeva più la pena privilegiare meno le cose materiali, quindi dire: ahimè, se non ci possiamo permettere quella cosa lì, io lavoro due ore in meno al giorno, non ci permettiamo quella cosa lì, ma stiamo insieme ... Però è un senno di poi, invece se non avevamo quella cosa lì, magari il nostro rapporto non sarebbe stato bello com'è stato, chissà?
Interviewer	Aveva aiuti?
Signora Torrielli	Sì, sì, ma io sto proprio parlando del rapporto personale che è quello che conta, non è chi gli dà la minestra, chi gli dà la pastasciutta. Quello che io intendevo è proprio il tempo mancato della quotidianità, del minuto col minuto ... comunque tutte le donne che lavorano questo problema ce l'hanno, in più io avevo la colpa di essere separata, sentivo questa colpa qui. Ma qui tutte hanno i bambini e i bambini stanno a casa e la mamma li porta dalla nonna, li porta all'asilo nido, insomma, non ha importanza, ma per nove ore al giorno chi lavora non vede i figli. Adesso poi che uno sia una buona mamma, paziente, per tutte le 24 ore o che invece per il suo carattere è meglio che faccia la mamma tre ore al giorno piuttosto che 21 ore, io penso di appartenere a quel gruppo, preferisco vederli nel momento in cui

sono più disponibile piuttosto che averli tutto il giorno poi magari essere nervosa come vediamo in certe mamme in giro ...

Lei tiene molto alla famiglia, vero?	*The family means a lot to you, doesn't it?*
il cruccio	Difficult to translate in one word. *Lo Zingarelli 2004*: **tormento, afflizione, dolore morale; seccatura, fastidio.** Perhaps Signora Torrielli just means *anxiety*.
ahimè	*oh dear, alas.*
un senno di poi	**senno** is *wisdom, sense*, so can you guess? *Hindsight.*
chi gli dà la minestra, chi gli dà la pastasciutta.	**minestra** is *soup*, usually with pasta or rice in it. But it can also mean *first course* (pasta course) of a meal. **pastasciutta** is what we know as simply *pasta*. But Signora Torrielli means the children's food in general. An interesting sidelight on the centrality of *pasta* in the Italian diet.
la colpa	*guilt.* Don't forget separation was less common then. Indeed it would have been before divorce was possible in Italy, i.e. before 1970. But separated parents will possibly understand Signora Torrielli's feeling anyway.
qui tutte hanno bambini	Signora Torrielli is at her workplace: she is referring to her employees.
vederli nel momento in cui sono disponibile	Signora Torrielli is talking about 'quality time', time when the mother's attention is devoted entirely to the children.

Comprehension 3

1 Signora Torrielli says that as a mother separated from her husband she tried to do two things for her daughters, which

were very difficult to combine. What were they? And does she think she achieved her aims?

2 What was the cost to her personally? What does she wonder?
3 Signora Torrielli had help with the children of course. But what does she think is important for a mother?
4 What does she say of the women who work in the factory?
5 What does she feel made her situation particularly difficult?
6 What sort of mother does she think she was?

SESSION 7

The subjunctive after impersonal expressions

Signora Torrielli says:

> per il suo carattere è meglio che <u>faccia</u> la mamma tre ore al giorno piuttosto che 21 ore

A number of impersonal expressions are usually followed by a subjunctive. A list of common ones is provided in the **Reference grammar**. An element of judgment, of subjectivity, is always present. (Subjunctive – subjectivity, point of view, do you remember? See Unit 5.) For instance, in the example above, one might ask: **meglio** *better* according to what criteria? These impersonal expressions relate to judgments about necessity, importance, advisability, possibility and similar concepts.

Reading

Read this extract from an article from *La Stampa*.

Studio dell'Istat: 'Colpa del marito'
La donna sposata lavora
due ore in più al giorno

Sul posto di lavoro pubblico e privato resta la discriminazione contro le femmine

ROMA. E' colpa dei mariti: sono loro, infatti, a procurare alle donne due ore di fatica in più ogni giorno. Come se non bastassero le 60 ore settimanali di lavoro, dentro e fuori le pareti domestiche, che vengono svolte da oltre la metà di loro. Più di un terzo, poi, supera anche le 70 ore a settimana.

Il vantaggio di non avere un partner per le donne occupate e con figli è emerso da uno studio presentato ieri, nella sede dell'Istat, dal ministero delle Pari Opportunità ...

E i 'numeri' presentati dicono tanto. A scuola, per esempio, le donne riescono senz'altro di più degli uomini: su 1000 femmine con la licenza media, 160 arrivano alla laurea contro appena 107 maschi. Ma, poi, quando si tratta di trovare un lavoro, la musica cambia bruscamente: se nella categoria 'impiegati' sono più numerose dei colleghi maschi, nei luoghi dove si decide la presenza femminile è davvero ridotta.

Tra i dirigenti dei ministeri, le donne sono appena il 7,8 per cento, tra i primari ospedalieri il 6,9 per cento, tra i prefetti il 5,4 per cento. E, se nell'università raggiungono l'11,1 per cento dei professori ordinari, la carica di rettore si riduce ed è riservata appena al 3,1 per cento. Per non parlare delle istituzioni pubbliche: senza scomodare i 'record' stabiliti dalla Norvegia e dalla Svezia, dove la presenza femminile si aggira intorno al 40 per cento, ci sono più donne nei Parlamenti dell'Africa del Sud, del Portogallo e della Spagna che nel nostro.

Eppure qualcosa sta cambiando, anche se molto lentamente, è emerso dai dati elaborati dall'Istat. Le donne delle nuove generazioni – ha sottolineato il ministro Balbo – 'non sono più quelle delle campagne italiane di 50 anni fa'. Dal '93 al '98 sono aumentate le imprenditrici (da 54.000 a 83.000), le libere professioniste (da 125.000 a 200.000), le socie di cooperative (da 65.000 a 128.000), le donne quadro (da 240.000 a 324.000).

Il problema è che questa crescita procede disordinatamente, a macchia di leopardo, e perciò il tasso di disoccupazione femminile, ad esempio, oscilla in maniera vistosa tra Emilia Romagna (8,4 per cento) e Calabria (39 per cento) ...

(*La Stampa*, martedì 9 febbraio 1999)

Istat	Istituto Centrale di Statistica
licenza media	The *diploma* awarded to those who pass the final examinations at the end of middle school.
primari ospedalieri	*hospital consultants*
prefetti	*prefect*, senior civil servant who represents the government in a province
rettore	*rector*, the senior academic who presides over a university. English equivalent: *Vice-Chancellor*.
donne quadro	*women executives*
a macchia di leopardo	*in an uneven way*

Activity 9

Imagine you are the Minister for Equal Opportunities and you are reporting on the Istat findings to your colleagues. However, there is to your mind some doubt about the statistics. Transform the following statements inserting **sembra che** and changing the verbs to reflect your doubts, as in the example:

Example: Più di un terzo delle donne italiane supera le 70 ore di lavoro alla settimana.

More than a third of Italian women work over 70 hours a week.

In base ai dati Istat, **sembra che** più di un terzo delle donne italiane **superi** le 70 ore di lavoro alla settimana.

1 A scuola le donne riescono più degli uomini.
In base ai dati Istat, sembra che ...
2 Su 1000 femmine con la licenza media, 160 arrivano alla laurea contro appena 107 maschi.
In base ai dati Istat, sembra che ...
3 La presenza femminile è davvero ridotta nei luoghi in cui si decide.
In base ai dati Istat, sembra che ...
4 Nell'università, le donne raggiungono l'11,1 per cento dei professori ordinari.
In base ai dati Istat, sembra che ...
5 Il tasso di disoccupazione femminile oscilla in maniera vistosa tra il nord e il sud.
In base ai dati Istat, sembra che ...

Ce l'hanno: word order

In the following sentence, Signora Torrielli illustrates together two usages which are common in spoken Italian:

Tutte le donne che lavorano   *All working women have*
questo problema ce l'hanno.   *this problem.*

One usage is to put the object before the verb and then in effect to repeat it by using a pronoun which stands for it. Here the object is **questo problema** and the l' refers to it. It is a way of stressing, emphasizing the object. If you look back through the texts in the book you will find other examples. You had no difficulty in understanding, and once you are in Italy, with ears pricked, listening hard to the way people speak, you will find yourself doing exactly the same thing, although in English you would not dream of saying: *All working women this problem they have it.*

Sometimes, particularly in speech, the object comes after the verb but is emphasized by a pronoun standing for it being inserted before the verb. There is an example in the extract from Natalia Ginzburg's account of winter in the village where her husband was exiled: the peasants say to them:

'Ma quando ci tornate alle case vostre?'

It is useful to remember that in Italian word order is more flexible than in English. Look out for this and gradually try to imitate what Italians say.

Ce l'hanno: a peculiarity of the verb *avere*

It is common practice, in spoken Italian, to use **ci** with the verb **avere**. This is particularly so when there is an object pronoun, but not only then.

Activity 10

You are setting off on an important business trip. You will be away for a week. You are rather apprehensive about the trip. In the taxi taking you to the airport you check mentally that you have everything you need with you.

Example: Il passaporto: **Il passaporto, ce l'ho**? Sì, **ce l'ho**!
 Passport: Have I got my passport? Yes, I have.

1 Le chiavi di casa: ....
2 Gli appunti per il convegno: ....
3 L'indirizzo dell'albergo: ....
4 Il telefonino: ....
5 La patente: ....
6 Gli occhiali: ....
7 L'agendina: ....
8 Le pastiglie per il mal di testa: ....

SESSION 8

▶ Interview 4

We have looked a lot at the problems of working women. We must redress the balance of the sexes a little! Carlo's career, a very successful one, has presented rather different problems. Indeed, Carlo has an approach to life which means problems are simply a challenge. He is now Managing Director of an old established firm in Trieste but, as he told you in Unit 4, he came from humble origins in the countryside near Asti. His first job, immediately after his military service, was selling office furniture at shows. Here's how he describes his first moves up the career ladder.

Carlo   Guadagnavo molto poco, però all'epoca, era una cosa molto curiosa, c'era l'Ente Risi, che promuoveva il riso, e facevo tutte le fiere con l'Ente Risi, per coincidenza, e quindi mangiavo mattina, cena, a colazione, questi risi che erano offerti a prezzi di promozione quindi, ero pagato poco ma riuscivo a sbarcare il lunario. Dopo sei mesi, ho mandato il mio cv alla Nestlé e sono entrato alla Nestlé come amministrativo, usando il mio diploma. Ma non mi piaceva, non ero capace, allora ho chiesto di passare dalla parte commerciale e ho avuto fortuna perché mi hanno mandato in Val d'Aosta a sostituire un ispettore che c'era. Io ho sempre avuto veramente molta fortuna, sono sempre andato o in mercati facili o a sostituire degli incapaci o della gente che non erano granché lavoratori ecc. Allora in Nestlé ho avuto molta fortuna perché ho vinto vari premi come quello che aveva venduto le maggiori quantità o ottenuto il maggior numero di nuovi punti di vendita, e grazie a tutte queste piccole vittorie, sono passato alla Cinzano come ispettore nella filiale di Milano e poi direttore vendite. A 28 anni ero già dirigente, una cosa importante a quell'epoca.

He worked hard, improving his academic skills in evening classes.

E poi ho chiesto alla società di mandarmi all'estero perché capivo che era più facile fare carriera all'estero per la semplice ragione che c'era meno concorrenza. Mi avevano prospettato di andare in Inghilterra ed ero entusiasta. Pensavo: imparerò bene l'inglese, avrò la possibilità di confrontarmi con un mondo molto competitivo, molto professionale. E invece è saltata fuori un'opportunità in Brasile e io all'inizio non ero per niente interessato perché dicevo: vado in Brasile, mi sfrutteranno come un frutto e poi mi butteranno via. Invece ho imparato tantissimo in Sud America. Ho imparato a essere duro, a sporcarmi le mani, affrontare le responsabilità. In Brasile ho avuto anche dei buoni risultati grazie al fatto che era un mercato che stava sviluppandosi molto bene.

Poi ho lasciato la Cinzano, sono diventato direttore generale per la Moët et Chandon. La mia prima iniziativa imprenditoriale era aprire una fabbrica nel Rio Grande del Sud, una terra ricca di immigrati italiani e tedeschi e che produceva del vino buono ...

Poi la Cinzano mi ha richiamato e mi ha chiesto se non volevo fare il direttore generale su in Venezuela, una piccola società … e ho avuto delle soddisfazioni enormi, ho tirato su una società che aveva 50 dipendenti a 180 a distanza di un anno circa, lanciando tre prodotti che erano dei pilastri che poi si esportavano … poi sono diventato presidente nel Sud America.

Nel frattempo la famiglia, ho capito che si stava un po' troppo incentivando, perché lì fai la vita di club, golf club, con persone di servizio, ecc. E capivo che questo è bello se tu lo fai con umiltà, però se tu lo fai per troppo tempo, finisci che ti convinci che tu sei fra quei pochi privilegiati, che questa è la vita, e siccome né io, né Anne ci divertivamo a fare la vita dei ricchi, e specialmente temevamo un pochino per le implicazioni negative per i figli, ho deciso di fare ritorno in Europa.

In quel momento gli inglesi hanno comprato la Cinzano e mi hanno promosso, mi hanno offerto la direzione generale della Spagna e del Portogallo. Allora sono venuto in Spagna e anche lì ho avuto fortuna perché ho sostituito ancora una volta qualcuno pieno di arie ma poco lavoratore, poi erano anche gli anni che si preparavano i mondiali, gli Olympic Games, Madrid Capitale della Cultura, Siviglia Expo, quindi c'era tutto boom, è andato tanto bene però non avevo più la possibilità di fare l'imprenditore perché in una multinazionale tutto è già stabilito, tu ricevi solamente, la campagna pubblicitaria è già fatta, il prodotto c'è, e allora un headhunter mi ha cercato, e mi è stata offerta una posizione che era quella di una società a Trieste, la Stock, dove c'erano gli azionisti che erano litigiosi e che volevano mettere la società praticamente nelle mani non più della famiglia ma di qualcheduno che avesse un'esperienza diversa … Così ho accettato.

In fact, the family shareholders made Carlo's job impossible as they were hopelessly divided on policy. After six months he handed them his resignation. The shareholders' reaction was:

'Se tu dici che non possiamo gestire quest'azienda, allora l'unica prospettiva è quella di vendere.' In quel momento, l'azienda è stata venduta ai tedeschi e i tedeschi in questo momento sono i miei azionisti. Ho una esperienza molto bella perché ho degli azionisti molto intelligenti che mi hanno fatto delle proposte molto chiare: 'Il business è tuo. Se funziona, bene. Se non funziona, una fucilata al cuore e via.' E l'azienda nel frattempo stava andando molto male ed è lì che è cominciata quella triste storia di ristrutturazione che è cominciata esattamente al febbraio dell'anno '97 e mi ha obbligato a fare dei tagli di ben 107 persone. Era la prima volta che io avevo un bilancio negativo e che dovevo licenziare delle persone, tutte le mie esperienze erano affari positivi, ero sempre in crescita e in questo momento mi accingo a fare la seconda ristrutturazione per garantire un ulteriore sviluppo della nostra azienda.

le fiere	*trade fairs, shows* (e.g. agricultural shows). But a *funfair* in Italian is **luna park**.
sbarcare il lunario	*to make ends meet*
usando il mio diploma	You may remember, Carlo is a **ragioniere**.
direttore generale	*general manager*
iniziativa imprenditoriale	Carlo had managed established businesses. Now his work was more that of an entrepreneur, starting a new activity from scratch, even if he had Moët behind him.
su in Venezuela	*up in Venezuela.* Carlo was then in Brazil, so he sees a northward move as 'up'.
incentivando	An unusual use of the verb. It is normally used in the context of business meaning: *motivate*. Of course, what he means is he and his wife feared the children were getting too used to the artificially high standard of living of an expatriate **direttore generale**.
Anne	Carlo's (Scottish) wife.
pieno di arie	Carlo means: all appearance rather than substance. **Darsi delle arie** *to give oneself airs*.
i mondiali	*the World Cup* (1984 soccer – and Italy won!)
una fucilata al cuore	*a bullet through your heart* (**fucilata**: *(gun)shot*)

Comprehension 4

1 Carlo's first job was not well paid but he managed to get by. How?
2 Carlo reckons he has had a lot of luck in his career. What sort of luck?
3 He is proud of his early success. What does he say that reveals this?
4 Why did he not want to go to Brazil?
5 Why does he not regret going?
6 He enjoyed his job with Moët and the place he worked in. Why?
7 He also found his job in Venezuela satisfying. In what way?
8 What did he and his wife feel about their life style in South America?
9 Why did Carlo consider himself lucky when he came to work in Spain and Portugal?
10 Why does Carlo consider his German shareholders good to work for?
11 What experiences has he had with Stock which were new to him – and which he has not enjoyed?
12 What is your overall impression of Carlo?

SESSION 9

Carlo's interview was a long one, but the Italian was not very difficult. We thought you would enjoy a man's view. Now you should go over the various interviews and articles in this unit. You should find them easier. And we hope they will give you things to talk about to yourself – or others. Here are some suggestions.

Activity 11

Talking to yourself

1 Quanto conta la fortuna nella vita? Lei si considera fortunato/a? E quanto conta essere avventuroso, intraprendente? Quali altri fattori contribuiscono al successo nella vita, secondo Lei? Infatti, per Lei, che cosa è il successo nella vita?

2 Per una coppia che ha figli da educare, essere ricchi costituisce un problema nella Sua opinione? Quali sono le difficoltà? E per una famiglia povera, quali problemi esistono nell'educazione dei figli? Se Lei è di una generazione che ha educato figli qualche anno fa, secondo Lei, a parte le condizioni materiali personali, sarebbe più difficile oggi, nella società in cui ci troviamo ora?

3 La signora Torrielli ha sollevato la questione della qualità del tempo che la madre (e il padre, perché no?) passano con i figli. Secondo Lei, è meglio essere sempre con loro, ma magari squattrinati, stanchi, ecc. o avere un lavoro, migliori condizioni economiche – e dedicargli forse tre/quattro ore al giorno – tutte per loro?

4 Molti uomini vedono poco i loro figli, a causa delle ore lavorative che richiede la società. Nei paesi nordici, pare che ci siano leggi per combattere questo problema e infatti per dare ad ogni genitore la possibilità di partecipare pienamente all'educazione dei figli. E' una buona idea, secondo Lei?

5 E la gestione della famiglia e della casa? Quale dovrebbe essere il contributo di ogni coniuge alla casa e alla famiglia?

You can probably think of plenty more topics arising from the interviews in this unit. Don't get into any arguments! But keep thinking in Italian!

08
senza scopo di lucro

In this unit we shall
- learn about voluntary work in Italy
- meet some people who give some of their spare time to helping others
- learn how to say what you would do if ...
- meet the imperfect subjunctive
- look at some suffixes to produce shades of meaning
- meet the subjunctive after certain conjunctions
- meet the past definite

SESSION 1

Reading 1

The voluntary sector in Italy is flourishing. Here are some statistics:

Gli adulti italiani che si dedicano attualmente, o si sono dedicati in passato, ad attività di volontariato, sono quasi 9 milioni, il 18,1 per cento della popolazione che ha superato i 15 anni. E' questo il risultato di un sondaggio svolto dalla Doxa nel giugno scorso ... Secondo il sondaggio, 3.900.000 persone, l'8 per cento di tutti gli adulti sono i volontari 'certamente' attuali, in quanto hanno svolto qualche attività negli ultimi 12 mesi. Per il 57,8 per cento di loro si tratta di attività molto impegnative, perché svolte regolarmente, almeno una volta alla settimana. I tipi di attività più frequentemente citati dagli intervistati sono i seguenti: ecologiche, ambientali, 16,9 per cento; parrocchiali in genere, 15,5 per cento; sportive, ricreative, 11,9 per cento. Seguono le citazioni dei destinatari di attività di assistenza: i malati (11,8 per cento), gli anziani (10,1 per cento), i disabili (9,6 per cento), i bambini (3,5 per cento). Non mancano le citazioni della raccolta di indumenti, medicinali, ecc. (5 per cento) e donazione di sangue (5 per cento).

From the website of *Repubblica* (**www.repubblica.it**), 'Dall'ambiente alla parrocchia, sono 9 milioni i volontari.' 15 settembre 1998

The passage throws up a number of words which do not translate literally from Italian. We hope you haven't forgotten your false friend: **attuale, attualmente.**

il 18,1 per cento	Note the definite article: **il 18 per cento, l'8 per cento**
superato i 15 anni	Note the definite article.
Doxa	From the Greek **doxa** = opinion. It is the Italian institute for opinion polls and market research, founded in 1946.
3.900.000	Note that the decimal place is indicated in Italy by a comma (**virgola**) and the thousands by a full-stop (**punto**), i.e. the opposite of the Anglo-Saxon practice.
si tratta di	lit. *it is a question of.* Perhaps here it might translate: *this means.* Often in English it is appropriate to say: *it's about.*

impegnativo	**Un impegno** is *a commitment, an engagement,* **impegnarsi** *to commit oneself.* Here **impegnativo** might be translated *demanding, exacting, requiring commitment.*
assistenza	The main meanings of **assistere** are: 1 *to be present at* (a meeting, for instance); 2 *to look after* (a sick or injured person; or the interests of, say, a client). In other words, it has overtones not there in the English *assist.* Similarly, perhaps *assist,* with its Latin origins, has overtones in English not present in Italian. English words of Latin origin tend to be thought more formal, even learned: compare *assist* and *help.* **Assistenza**, the noun, relates solely to the second meaning of the verb (above). Here, as you can see from the context, it means *giving help* to the sick, the elderly, children, the handicapped. Simply *to help* is **aiutare**.
Non mancano le citazioni	*There is no shortage of mentions (of).* **Mancare** is *to be missing* or *lacking.* It conveys an idea which is usually put the other way round in English: **Manca un chiodo**. *There's a nail missing;* **Mi manca tanto Roberto**. *I miss Robert so much;* **Mancano tre giorni alla partenza**. *There are three days left before the departure / we leave.*

Reading 2

An earlier article gives slightly different statistics, gathered in a different way, with a different definition of **volontariato**, *but the basic message is the same:*

Gli italiani propensi all'altruismo? Sembrerebbe di sì. Sono infatti oltre cinque milioni le persone (per esattezza 5.397.000) che nel 1997 si sono impegnate in prima persona in attività di volontariato sociale e civile ...

Gli italiani, dunque, sono persone di cuore, capaci di prodigarsi gratuitamente per cinque ore e mezzo a settimana; se lo stesso tempo fosse regolarmente retribuito ci vorrebbero in un anno circa 750 mila lavoratori a tempo pieno. Di fatto il 12 per cento della popolazione adulta svolge attività di volontariato, un dato nella media con i paesi europei ...

From the website of *Repubblica*, 'Cinque ore alla settimana ecco l'Italia dei volontari.' 7 luglio 1998

in prima persona	*personally,* i.e. actually working, not just giving money.
ci vorrebbero	*would be needed,* conditional of **ci vuole**.

Comprehension: Readings 1 and 2

1 Can you detect the reason for the differences in the figures given in the two articles?
2 What might be the implication behind the words: **sociale** and **civile** when applied to **volontariato**?
3 Is Italy exceptional in the numbers of people involved in voluntary work?

i The voluntary sector is indeed lively in Italy today. Much of the work is done to high, even professional, standards. Serious training is often required of the volunteer. Some of the voluntary organizations are connected to the Catholic Church, catholicism being the traditional religion of Italy, but many are *secular* (**laico**). One often heard complaint is that volunteers do work that should be done by the state, filling the gaps in provision which arise from state inefficiency. We would add that there seems to be a great capacity in Italy for criticism of the Italian state and Italian institutions, linked to a conviction that things are better ordered in other countries. Which is not necessarily the case!

As an aside, however, it has to be said that Italy has suffered more than many advanced countries from poor government for much of the postwar period. This is not the place to examine the problem in any detail other than to say the blame lies partly in the fact that there was not, until very recently, what Italians call **alternanza**. In other words, the same group of political parties held power for a very long period, without the opposition ever coming to power. These parties governed in coalition governments which were often fragile and short-lived. When a government falls, so does the legislation it is trying to put through. What looked like political instability in fact led to too much stability. Reforms have not been made as in other countries. This has certainly contributed to the inefficiency of the state.

However, while Italians are sure every other country runs itself better than Italy, has a more efficient civil service, etc., when it comes to the fabric of everyday life – food, fashion, friendships and social life in those areas Italians know Italy is best!

Mention is made in the first article of being a blood donor. It may be of interest to know the blood donor service is run by a voluntary organization: **AVIS (Associazione Volontari Italiani del Sangue)** which, according to its website (**www.avis.it**), supplies 70% of the country's requirements for blood.

SESSION 2

Introducing the imperfect subjunctive

In the second article we read:

se lo stesso tempo fosse regolarmente retribuito ci vorrebbero in un anno circa 750 mila lavoratori a tempo pieno.	*if the same amount of time had been paid for (in wages) in a year about 750,000 full time workers would be needed.*

Look at the verbs. As we said in the Notes at the end of the passage, **ci vorrebbero** is a conditional. What about the other? You have seen it before but not had your attention drawn to it. It is the imperfect subjunctive of **essere**. This type of sentence is one we often use. *If this were the case, then we should ...* Here are some more examples:

Cosa faresti se vincessi il primo premio alla lotteria?	*What would you do if you won the first prize in the lottery?*
Se avessi tempo, andrei più spesso al cinema.	*If I had time, I'd go to the cinema more often.*
Se i bambini fossero più grandi, andremmo all'estero in vacanza.	*If the children were older, we'd go abroad for our holiday.*

If you look back to Unit 7 you will see that Emanuela several times said what she *would like to do, would do* – but she did not spell out the other part of the condition: **se potessi permettermi di non lavorare**, *if I could afford not to work*.

The form of the imperfect subjunctive

This is very easy: you need to think back to the imperfect. Take the same root as for the imperfect. Any verb which had a special root for the imperfect will have that same special root again in the imperfect subjunctive, with three exceptions.

passare	avere	pulire	fare
passassi	avessi	pulissi	facessi
passassi	avessi	pulissi	facessi
passasse	avesse	pulisse	facesse
passassimo	avessimo	pulissimo	facessimo
passaste	aveste	puliste	faceste
passassero	avessero	pulissero	facessero

Note: The stress is irregular in the first and third persons plural, falling on the characteristic vowel of the group in the antepenultimate syllable, not on the penultimate syllable.

The three exceptions are:

essere	dare	stare
fossi	dessi	stessi
fossi	dessi	stessi
fosse	desse	stesse
fossimo	dessimo	stessimo
foste	deste	steste
fossero	dessero	stessero

You can see the endings are always the same so, given the first person singular, you should be able to form all the parts.

Activity 1

Complete the sentences using the correct form of the imperfect subjuncive.

Example: Cosa faresti se (**vincere – tu**) .... il primo premio alla lotteria?
Cosa faresti se **vincessi** il primo premio alla lotteria?
What would you do if you won the first prize in the lottery?

1 Cosa faresti se (**essere – tu**) .... il Presidente della Repubblica Italiana?
2 Signora Rossi, cosa farebbe se (**avere – Lei**) .... più tempo libero?

3 Ragazzi, che cosa fareste se vi (**dire** – **io**) ....
che la settimana prossima la scuola sarà chiusa e sarete in
vacanza?

4 Cosa faresti se un tuo amico ti (**chiedere** – **lui**)
.... di occuparti del suo cane durante le
vacanze estive?

5 Signor Rossi, cosa farebbe se (**scoprire** – **Lei**)
.... che Sua moglie ha un amante?

6 Che cosa fareste se una persona vi (**passare** – **lei**)
.... davanti in una coda?

7 Che cosa faresti se (**essere** – **tu**) .... in una
coda al supermercato, (**avere** – **tu**) il
carrello strapieno di acquisti, e (**scoprire** – **tu**)
.... di avere dimenticato a casa il portafoglio?

8 Signor Bianchi, che cosa farebbe se (**essere** – **loro**)
.... le tre di mattina e il vostro vicino di casa
(**stare** – **lui**) .... ascoltando musica a tutto
volume?

9 Che cosa faresti se il tuo datore di lavoro ti (**dare** – **lui**)
.... una vacanza di tre mesi?

10 Che cosa faremmo se non (**avere** – **noi**) ....
tutte le comodità che abbiamo al giorno d'oggi e (**dovere** –
noi) .... vivere allo stesso modo in cui
vivevano i nostri nonni?

SESSION 3

▶ Interview 1

*Silvia Lena, whom you were introduced to briefly in Unit 2, is
not a trained volunteer worker but she has given much of her
time to helping others, particularly the victims of conflict. So we
asked her about some of her experiences.*

Silvia Non ho fatto volontariato sociale. In Italia il volontariato
sociale è diffusissimo, moltissimi giovani sono impegnati in
attività sociali, di aiuto a persone anziane, persone
handicappate, bambini. Ecco, questa cosa io l'ho fatta
solamente in un breve periodo all'università quando
andavamo ad aiutare i vecchietti di ringhiera. Si chiamano
così quei … quelle persone che vivono in delle case minime,
chiamate così 'case minime', case povere fatte di una sola
stanza, nella periferia di Milano. Eravamo universitari, e per
caso abbiamo incontrato dei vecchietti che ci chiedevano
aiuto per fare i loro documenti e abbiamo creato un gruppo

di studenti disponibili a fare tutte le pratiche – mediche, negli uffici, accompagnare queste persone anziane a comprare gli occhiali, dall'oculista, dall'ortopedico ... Per un breve periodo abbiamo fatto questa cosa, all'università, ma era più un divertimento, per stare insieme, infatti io ho conosciuto lì mio marito.

vecchietti di ringhiera	**case di ringhiera** are a type of housing typical of the late 19th century, with several floors and balconies along each floor, with metal balustrades (**ringhiere**); the doors of the individual dwellings open on to these balconies. Sometimes originally they shared **servizi igienici** *lavatories.* A possible translation is *tenement.*
case minime	*tiny houses.* **minimo** *piccolissimo* is the irregular form of the superlative. See **Reference grammar**. They would be flats/apartments, not individual houses. **Casa** is often used in this way.
disponibili	*available and willing*
fare tutte le pratiche	*carry out bureaucratic procedures.* It refers to filling in forms and going through procedures, often necessitating visits to offices, so as to take advantage of medical and other services, pensions etc.

Comprehension: Interview 1

1 What sort of thing did Silvia and her fellow students do for the old people they helped?
2 What was the students' main motivation?
3 What does Silvia cite to support this?

SESSION 4

Suffixes in Italian

Silvia says:

il volontariato sociale è diffusissimo

voluntary work is very widespread

| moltissimi giovani sono impegnati in attività sociali | *very many young people are committed to voluntary work* |
| aiutare i vecchietti | *to help old people* |

You will be familiar with -issimo added to adjectives, meaning *very*. And you will know -etto being added to nouns to form a diminutive (cf. English *piglet, lambkin*). In Unit 3 we referred to -one which means *big*. There is quite a range of suffixes which can be added to nouns, changing their meaning slightly. The Italian word for these slight changes in meaning is **sfumature**. Good guessers will note that this contains the word **fumo**, *smoke*. The word is used, as is the verb **sfumare**, in relation to gradual, subtle, imprecise changes of colour, tone, etc. In Italian the suffixes are traditionally classified as:

diminutivi (which indicate size smaller than usual)
accrescitivi (which indicate greater size than usual)
vezzeggiativi (adds an idea of being lovable)
spregiativi (which indicates the person or thing is despised; it can also hint at irony)

However, some cross boundaries or vary in meaning according to the sense of the noun they are attached to or even the context. So they are not easy to use and you are advised at first just to note examples you hear and their meaning. Gradually you will feel able to use at least some of them. Probably one needs to have grown up in Italy to feel really at home using them. A good Italian dictionary will tell you which suffixes you can add to any given word. Some are also more common than others.

-etto, -ino, -ello, -cello, -icello, -erello

These are usually considered diminutives, but affection often comes in too. Gabriella referred to her **mammina** and there affection came into play. Also in **vecchietti**.

ragazzo, ragazzino	*boy, little boy*
casa, casetta	*house, small house*
sorella, sorellina	*sister, little sister*
gatto, gattino	*cat, kitten*
vento, venticello	*wind, little breeze*

-**ino** can also be added to adjectives and adverbs:

carino	*pretty, sweet, cute*
piano, pianino	*softly, very softly*
bene, benino	*well, quite well*

Note also: **pian pianino** meaning *little by little, step by step*.

-one

This indicates large size (**accrescitivo**) and has the peculiarity that when it is added to a feminine noun, the noun becomes masculine. However a feminine ending also exists, **-ona**.

una donna, un donnone	*a woman, a large woman*
gatto, gattone	*cat, large cat*
una cena, un cenone	*supper, the usually huge meal traditionally eaten late on New Year's Eve, to welcome in the New Year.*
uomo, omone	*man, large man*

This suffix can also be added to **bene**.

'Come sta?' 'Benone.'	*'How are you?' 'Very well indeed.'*

The suffixes **-otto**, **-ozzo** are usually listed as **accrescitivi**. They can also have diminutive force and/or express contempt, the idea of the object being a bit of a joke! **Ragazzotto** can, for instance, mean *a stocky young boy* (**accrescitivo** – in size) or *not yet a full boy* (17–18 years) *but not a child* (**diminutivo** – in years). Not easy for the foreign learner!

-accio, -astro, -onzolo, -ciattolo, -ucolo, -ipolo

These usually indicate unpleasantness, nastiness (**peggiorativi**).

parola, parolaccia	*word, swear word*
tempo, tempaccio	*weather, dreadful weather*
verme, vermiciattolo	*worm, nasty little worm*
professore, professorucolo	*teacher, an ineffectual teacher (one not worthy of respect)*
vino, vinaccio	*wine, poor quality wine*
uomo, omaccio, omaccione	*man, nasty man, great big nasty man*

-icino, -olino, -uccio, -uzzo

These indicate affection (**vezzeggiativi**).

porta, porticina	*door, tiny little door*
corpo, corpicino	*body, poor thin little body*
cane, cagnolino	*dog, puppy*
tesoro, tesoruccio	*darling, dear sweet darling*

Note also: 1. Many words formed with the use of suffixes have become words in their own right: e.g. **violino, violoncello**. 2. In addition there are also words which look as though they are formed with a suffix but this is in fact the case, e.g. **mattone** *brick*; **padrone** *master, proprietor, boss*; **rubinetto** *tap*; **bottone** *button*.

Looking at the question of suffixes at another way, the word: **ragazzo** (*boy*) can be altered thus: **ragazzaccio** (*bad*); **ragazzetto** (*small*); **ragazzino** (*small*); **ragazzone** (*big*); **ragazzotto** (*big*); **ragazzuccio** (*small*); **ragazzuolo** (*small*). They have varying 'sfumature'. The important thing, as we have said, is to be aware, and not to worry! Just use words and suffixes you hear Italians using.

Activity 2

You almost certainly know the story of **Treccedoro e i tre Orsi**, *Goldilocks and the Three Bears*. So we won't tell it to you, but here are some illustrations. Can you put labels to them in a way which fits the story?

Example:

a orsone
b orsa
c orsino

Activity 3

Study the following words and, using a dictionary, decide which are words modified by suffixes and which are not:

1 cassetto
2 tacchino
3 giornataccia
4 filetto

5 cagnolino
6 cappuccio
7 focaccia
8 casetta

SESSION 5

▶ Interview 2

The motivation of 'stare insieme', which perhaps reflects an aspect of the Italian character, the enjoyment of being with a group of friends, was also at the origin of the **Gruppo Mio.** *You may remember we met three members of the group briefly in Unit 2: Antonella, Riccardo and Monica. Here, they tell us something about the group. They, again, are not volunteers of the sort referred to by Silvia in the phrase:* **volontariato sociale.**

This is a long extract from an even longer interview but you are becoming proficient now and we suggest you listen and try to pick out the main points, in particular: 1 how the group came into being 2 what its various activities are and 3 what motivates the speakers.

| Interviewer | Che cosa vuol dire MIO e che cosa è il Gruppo? |
| Riccardo | La sigla MIO vuol dire Moriondo Insieme Ovunque. E' un gruppo che è nato da un incontro di alcuni amici. |

Hanno passato una giornata di ritiro riflettendo insieme e hanno avuto un po' questa proposta e questa voglia di mettersi insieme e iniziare a lavorare per i poveri. Quindi lo scopo era di andare al di là, non trovarsi solo come amici per divertirsi o comunque per passare il tempo insieme ma fare anche qualcosa di utile, visto che c'erano queste opportunità e questa voglia dentro ognuno così di noi di creare qualcosa per gli altri, per chi ha bisogno, quindi per la realtà locale di Moriondo e anche per i più poveri. Quindi ovunque, insieme ovunque, insieme perché uniti in gruppo visto che l'unione di più forze dà frutti migliori, ovunque per tutti, quindi dove c'era maggior bisogno si è cercato di coinvolgere le nostre forze.

Interviewer Ma lo stare insieme fa parte anche della motivazione del Gruppo, no?

Antonella Sì, diciamo che il nostro gruppo è un gruppo un po' strano, no? Perché è un gruppo parrocchiale, perché si occupa della realtà della parrocchia, con tutte le attività di animazione ai più giovani, ai bambini, ai ragazzi, e tutte le attività che ci sono nella parrocchia, tipo animazione della messa ecc. E' anche un gruppo missionario, e come gruppo missionario, facciamo parte dell'Operazione Mato Grosso, dalla quale poi siamo nati e ci occupiamo in particolar modo del Brasile e di un lebbrosario in Brasile. E poi siamo un gruppo di amici, infatti la caratteristica del nostro gruppo è che raggruppa un po' gente di tutte le età, no? Abbiamo i genitori, i neo-genitori, cioè ragazzi che hanno fondato 15 anni fa Il Gruppo, che adesso hanno formato una loro famiglia ma abbiamo anche ragazzi giovani, 14, 15, 16 anni, no? E quello che ci raggruppa è questa voglia di stare insieme, no? Quest'amicizia che è nata fra di noi.

Interviewer E vi incontrate, dunque, una volta alla settimana?

Monica Noi c'incontriamo generalmente il lunedì sera. Noi abbiamo avuto la possibilità di avere come nostra sede la vecchia chiesa di Moriondo, che veniva utilizzata per la messa prima che venisse costruita l'attuale chiesa. Noi ci raduniamo lunedì sera appunto intorno alle nove così e, niente, programmiamo un pochino le attività che normalmente facciamo. Sosteniamo appunto questo lebbrosario in Campo Grande in Mato Grosso e poi al di là di quest'attività, che comunque ha portato alcuni nostri amici a stare giù per un po' di tempo, no? proprio per testimoniare in modo più concreto, no? questo voler aiutare il prossimo, abbiamo comunque anche attività che svolgiamo nell'ambito della parrocchia. Facciamo animazione liturgica alla messa la domenica ...

E poi ci occupiamo dei ragazzini per i quali, insomma, organizziamo nel periodo estivo l'Estate Ragazzi, per i bimbi più piccolini e poi anche perfino i ragazzi delle medie ...

Interviewer Che cos'è Estate Ragazzi?
Monica Estate Ragazzi è un periodo di circa 15 giorni dove, utilizzando l'Oratorio, diamo la possibilità ai ragazzini tutti i pomeriggi di, insomma, restare insieme. Organizziamo ogni anno generalmente un Estate Ragazzi a tema, nel senso che fissiamo magari un tema particolare da portare avanti durante tutto il periodo, per esempio quest'anno abbiamo scelto come tema il Circo e ai ragazzi appunto presenteremo delle attività, dei lavoretti manuali, dei giochi, ecc. sul tema del circo e verranno ogni giorno a trovarci in persona, qui da noi, i personaggi del circo, quindi verrà a trovarci un domatore di animali, verrà un giocoliere ... Normalmente i ragazzi accorrono abbastanza volentieri, i genitori ce li portano, ce li mandano ... hanno fiducia e così cerchiamo di dare il nostro contributo.

Oltre a questo Estate Ragazzi, facciamo anche i Campi Scuola che sono periodi di circa una settimana che facciamo fuori parrocchia, facciamo esattamente in Val Varaita, a Sampeyre, dove appunto i ragazzini delle elementari, poi successivamente, in un secondo turno, i ragazzi delle medie e delle prime superiori, hanno la possibilità di riflettere su dei temi stabiliti. Quest'anno abbiamo proposto le Gemme di Hazan, un racconto, che è un sussidio estivo che viene preparato dalla diocesi e offerto alle parrocchie per poter proprio animare, gestire sia i Campi Scuola o eventualmente l'Estate Ragazzi qualora i Campi Scuola non venissero fatti ... E' centrato sul tema dello Spirito Santo ... E legato a questo, si fanno attività, si fanno giochi, è un modo per riuscire comunque ad aggregare questi ragazzi ... si cerca di trasmettere i valori che sono quelli che abbiamo ricevuto a nostra volta dai più grandi.

E durante l'anno, Don Giacomo ci lascia l'Oratorio per i ragazzini, la domenica pomeriggio dalle tre fino intorno alle sei e mezza e quest'anno abbiamo tentato anche una cosa un po' diversa, abbiamo utilizzato l'Oratorio anche il sabato. Il sabato, dividendo in due parti: c'era la possibilità di iscriversi ad una squadra di pallavolo o di calcio, e poi la possibilità di fare attività di laboratorio, attività manuali, si è insegnato a fare gli aquiloni, a fare le magliette,

Antonella   la telecamera, abbiamo insegnato a riprendere, la fotografia,

Monica   Esatto … Un sacco di cose e poi la possibilità anche di far parte di queste squadrette di calcio e di pallavolo che sono nate così come una prova l'anno scorso … tra l'altro funziona abbastanza bene perché quest'anno le nostre ragazzine in pallavolo sono arrivate seconde al torneo della zona, invece i ragazzini l'anno scorso si sono beccati il primo posto.

Interviewer   Se non facevano questo, questi ragazzi …?

Riccardo   Innanzitutto l'Oratorio è stato per un lungo tempo chiuso, quindi è stata una conquista anche riaprire l'Oratorio, perché non c'era nessuno che lavorasse coi ragazzini, invece noi abbiamo cercato di riaprire l'Oratorio proprio per dare poi possibilità ai ragazzini di fare qualcosa d'utile per gli altri, quindi cominciare ad aggregarsi e non passare soltanto il tempo sulle panchine perché l'alternativa è quella, sui seggiolini della piazza coi motorini …

Interviewer   E come aiutate il lebbrosario in Brasile, a parte quelli di voi che sono andati a lavorare lì?

Antonella   Noi innanzitutto organizziamo delle attività, ad esempio la raccolta carta, ferro e stracci, che facciamo per il ricavato; organizziamo delle mostre artigianali, dei lavoretti in legno, in cuoio, in stoffa e li andiamo a vendere nelle scuole, cercando proprio di non mettere solo il banchetto e vendere, ma anche facciamo vedere delle diapositive, dei filmati, portando la testimonianza di persone che ci sono state, persone che vivono questa realtà … E poi c'è anche un discorso di farmaci, che vengono inviati, essendo un ospedale comunque ha bisogno, di medicinali …

Riccardo	Vorrei aggiungere che c'è un altro tipo di missionarietà vissuta molto più vicino, ad esempio, è stata forse una delle prime attività che abbiamo portato avanti e tuttora continuiamo a portare avanti ed è appunto andare a trovare delle nonnine alla Piccola Casa di Trofarello, che è un ospizio, molto piccolo quando abbiamo iniziato 15 anni fa, adesso si è ingrandito molto ma l'abbiamo sempre seguito, visto passare tutti i nonnini … L'attività nostra consiste nell'andare a trovarli il sabato pomeriggio e non fare nulla di particolare se non stare con loro, parlare con loro, cantare, far passare due ore di allegria a queste persone che spesso sono sole, tristi, quindi hanno proprio la necessità di avere qualcuno che vada a sorridere, a parlare con loro, che si metta a cantare con loro, quindi … Sappiamo a memoria tutto il repertorio delle canzoncine …
Antonella	un po' vecchie …
Riccardo	Poi distribuiamo tè, caffè, biscotti, è un momento di incontro …
Antonella	Festeggiamo una volta al mese i loro compleanni, cioè festeggiamo tutti i compleanni del mese, facendoli soffiare delle candeline, portando delle torte … Loro ci tengono a vederci …
Interviewer	Dalle vostre facce vedo che prendete grande piacere … c'è gioia …
Antonella	Sì.

Moriondo	Moriondo is a **frazione** of Moncalieri, a town of about 60,000 inhabitants just on the southern edge of Turin. Moriondo is on the fringe of Moncalieri, adjacent to Trofarello, the neighbouring **comune**, mentioned later.
una giornata di ritiro	*a day spent in retreat.* The group is a church group.
andare al di là	lit. *to go beyond*; perhaps *to go a bit further*
tipo animazione della messa	*such as helping with mass.* This use of the word **tipo** is common in spoken Italian. More formal usage would say: **per esempio**.
la vecchia chiesa … che veniva utilizzata	Note the use of **venire** to form a passive: *was used.*

stare giù per un tempo	to *stay down there for a while*. Down there: at the leper hospital in Brazil.
Estate Ragazzi: Campi Scuola	Often organised by local authorities but also by churches in Italy, between the end of the school year and the start of the main summer holiday period. It is probably useful for working parents, but in these days of small families and urban living, children miss the mixing with others they get at school, are often not able to go out and play in the streets, etc.
Val Varaita	In the Southern Alps, south-west of Turin. Sampeyre is at about 950 metres above sea level.
Oratorio	This can mean a place for prayer. But it is also commonly used for the building most churches have available for use by children and young people in the afternoons. Italian schools usually finish their day around 13.30 hours. The idea originated with the Salesian Order, founded by Don Bosco.
tra l'altro	Common in spoken Italian, adding little to meaning: *furthermore, moreover.*
li andiamo a vendere	*we go and sell them*. You can also say: **andiamo a venderli.**
un sacco di cose	*lots, loads of things.*
si sono beccati il primo posto	*they won / walked off with first place.* The expression is however more vivid than the translation we give: **beccarsi** is related to **becco**, the *beak* of a bird.
facciamo vedere	*we show*. The usual way of expressing the idea of *showing*.
hanno ... la necessità di avere qualcuno che vada a ... che si metta a cantare ...	Note the subjunctives (**vada, con loro si metta**), following the indefinite antecedent.

Comprehension: Interview 2

These are the points we suggested you try to listen out for. Don't forget you can listen to the interview again and again, as often as you like.

1 How did the group come into being?
2 What are its various activities?
3 What motivates the speakers?

SESSION 6

Study of words and their use

The interviews throw up a number of interesting points to do with use of words:

a   suffixes: notice the frequency of diminutives, often used affectionately: i **bimbi più piccolini**, le **nonnine**, i **nonnini**, **canzoncine**, un **pochino**, **lavoretti**, etc.

b   some words which are difficult to translate although the meaning is clear: 1) **realtà** as in **la realtà locale**, and **la realtà della parrocchia**. **Realtà** means, of course, *reality*, but might perhaps be better translated here by *community*. Dictionaries define it as **il complesso dei fatti**. 2) **animazione**: *bringing to life*, making events lively and meaningful by an organizational contribution. In the context of the summer camp etc. **animare** is really just *leading, organizing*.

c   **frutto, fruttificare**: you will know **la frutta**, a collective noun, in the way *fruit* can be in English. *I must buy some fruit. We eat a lot of fruit.* A single fruit is **un frutto**, also used in the figurative sense. The plural is **frutti**. The verb **fruttificare** means *to bear fruit*.

d   **un discorso di farmaci**: **discorso** is often used when in English we might use *matter, subject*. (See Unit 3, Interview 2, Notes.)

Activity 4

The spoken language

The three representatives of the Gruppo Mio were excited about being interviewed and full of enthusiasm for their group. Whether this affected the way they spoke, we can't judge, but it was very much **lingua parlata**, spoken language, with, in particular, words slipped in as props which contributed little to the meaning but perhaps helped them 'keep their balance', so to speak. Can you pick some of these out in the first speech of each of the three participants?

The subjunctive after certain conjunctions

Monica says:

> la vecchia chiesa di Moriondo, che veniva utilizzata per la
> messa <u>prima che venisse</u> costruita l'attuale chiesa.
> *the old church of Moriondo which was used for mass before
> the present church was built.*

> un racconto, che è un sussidio estivo che viene preparato
> dalla diocesi e offerto alle parrocchie per poter proprio
> animare, gestire sia i Campi Scuola o eventualmente l'Estate
> Ragazzi <u>qualora</u> i Campi Scuola non <u>venissero</u> fatti.
> *a story, which is a summer (teaching) aid which is prepared
> by the diocese and offered to parishes precisely to help lead,
> organize, either the School Camps or Summer for Children
> if the School Camps are not held.*

You will notice the imperfect subjunctive. But why the
subjunctive? Because certain conjunctions require the verb in the
clause they introduce to be a subjunctive. See the list in the
Reference grammar. Note however **prima che** *before* needs the
subjunctive but **prima di** is followed by an infinitive. You can
use **prima di** only if the subject of both verbs is the same:

> Prima che arrivi Giorgio, cerchiamo di mettere in ordine il
> soggiorno.
> *Before George arrives, let's try to tidy the living room.*
> (George is arriving but we are doing the tidying.)

> Prima di uscire, devo finire di scrivere questa lettera.
> *Before I go out, I must finish writing this letter.*
> (I am both writing the letter and going out.)

> Prima di partire, telefona alla nonna.
> *Before you leave, phone grandma.*
> (You are going out and the speaker wants you to telephone
> grandma.)

The conjunctions requiring the subjunctive are always
subordinating conjunctions. A moment's reflection will confirm
that sentences with conjunctions are fairly complex. We tend to
keep to relatively simple structure when speaking. So this use of
the subjunctive is more common in written language and you
will normally be recognizing subjunctives after conjunctions
rather than having to produce them.

Activity 5

The following sentences are based on an article 'Il **volontariato non seduce più**' (*La Stampa*, 12 febbraio 1999), printed at the end of this unit. It is not necessary to have read the article to do this exercise. We found it interesting however and put it in for you, hoping you do too. Complete the sentences using the correct form of the subjunctive.

Example: Sebbene molti volontari (fare) **facciano** lavori faticosi e difficili, come scavare nel fango o assistere i malati, senza ricevere nessuna ricompensa, non si considerano degli eroi ma delle persone normali.

1 Sebbene i volontari (essere) .... sia uomini che donne, le donne volontarie sono in numero leggermente più alto degli uomini.

2 Nonostante il numero dei volontari che si impegnano attivamente all'interno delle associazioni (sembrare) .... essere in calo, le associazioni volontarie continuano a prosperare perché molti italiani versano loro dei soldi affinché (potere) .... proseguire la loro attività.

3 Benché il volontariato (avere) .... successo ovunque in Italia, la maggior parte delle organizzazioni opera nelle regioni settentrionali piuttosto che nelle regioni meridionali.

4 Sebbene (esistere) .... ancora molti gruppi volontari senza alcuno scopo di lucro, molti di loro si sono 'professionalizzati' e sono diventati cooperative sociali, che danno lavoro e reddito.

5 Benché la Chiesa Cattolica (giocare) .... un ruolo molto importante nella società italiana e all'interno del volontariato, in Italia esistono anche molti gruppi volontari aconfessionali.

6 Affinché le statistiche sul lavoro volontario in Italia (risultare) .... affidabili, bisogna escludere dal conteggio i semplici simpatizzanti, come per esempio i donatori di sangue.

The subjunctive after a negative antecedent

Riccardo says:

non c'era nessuno che lavorasse   *there was no one working*
    coi ragazzini   *with the children*

This is similar to the use we saw in Unit 5, Session 5, with an indefinite antecedent. Here we have a negative antecedent, **nessuno**. The subjunctive would also be required after **niente**:

Non c'è niente che faccia più
paura che ...

*There is nothing which
frightens more than ...*

Look for another example of **niente che** + subjunctive in the next Interview.

SESSION 7

▶ Interview 3

Some of Silvia Lena's work has been with single individuals whose cause she has embraced. We asked her to tell us one particular story again. It involved helping a Kurdish refugee from Turkey who had been living in Switzerland with his wife and small daughter.

Silvia Sì ma questa è stata un'esperienza molto particolare. Sono stata coinvolta con i curdi, ma questa è una cosa personale, cioè io non ho mai fatto niente che non passasse attraverso l'amicizia. Cioè tutte le cose che ho fatto, le ho fatte perché avevo degli amici e che avevano bisogno di essere aiutati. La storia è così, molto sinteticamente: io conosco la causa dei curdi perché ho un'amica in Svizzera che ha fondato un'associazione Suisse-Kurdistan perché in Svizzera ci sono tantissimi immigrati curdi e lei, avendoli conosciuti nella loro vita sciagurata, nella loro disperazione, abitanti di cantine, perseguitati, accusati da turchi immigrati in Svizzera di cose non commesse, quest'amica si è dedicata alla loro causa e un giorno mi ha telefonato se potevo muovere l'amministrazione comunale di Bologna in aiuto di un curdo che era stato accusato di avere commesso un omicidio ed era stato poi assolto perché l'accusa veniva da un turco a lui ostile. La cosa è stata smascherata quindi lui doveva essere rilasciato dal carcere ma, in base alle leggi svizzere, messo su un aereo e inviato in Turchia dove lo aspettava una condanna a morte. Lui aveva una moglie bambina con una piccola di pochi mesi e quest'amica non si rassegnava a pensare che lui morisse e si è data da fare finché ha saputo che se c'era uno stato che avesse accolto questo curdo avrebbe potuto essere inviato e salvato. Io andai direttamente dal sindaco di Bologna che fu di una disponibilità meravigliosa. Mise a disposizione un'automobile con un autista e uno psicologo, perché pensava che questa persona sarebbe stata molto male, e ha preso contatto con il carcere svizzero dove lui si trovava, e lo ha mandato a prendere. Poi dovevo interessarmene io, perché il comune non poteva assumersi questa persona, quindi questo curdo è stato qua a casa mia; la moglie e la bambina lo hanno raggiunto, sono arrivate di notte, con un taxi svizzero ... E io li ho ospitati in un istituto di suore che non avevano mai ospitato un uomo ma, commosse da questa storia, le suore sono diventate delle grandi sostenitrici del popolo curdo.

niente che non passasse attraverso l'amicizia	*Nothing which didn't happen through friendship.* Subjunctive after **niente** again.
mi ha telefonato se potevo muovere l'amministrazione comunale di Bologna ...	*she telephoned me (to ask) if I could stir the Bologna city authorities ...*
smascherata	*unmasked.* Another example of **s** negating a word.
una moglie bambina	*a very young wife.*
se c'era uno stato che avesse accolto	This is a subjunctive after an indefinite antecedent. *If there were a state which would accept him.* The tense is the pluperfect subjunctive and the usage is similar to the use in reported speech which we met in Unit 5. This is quite complex. But you understand, surely, without the explanation! And that is what matters.
un istituto di suore	*a convent*

Comprehension: Interview 3

1 Why did Silvia's Swiss friend found the Switzerland Kurdistan Association?
2 She telephoned Silvia seeking her help and that of the Bolognese city administration for a Kurdish man. What was he accused of?
3 Who was his accuser?
4 Injustice apart, why did Silvia's friend find it impossible to accept that the man should be returned to Turkey?

5 What did the mayor of Bologna do to help?
6 Once the man arrived, what did Silvia have to do?
7 Who gave the man and his wife shelter and what effect did his story have on them?

The end of the story

The stay in the convent for the Kurdish family was short term and Silvia was able to move them to a small hostel for immigrants that she had started together with a young priest in response to another need – another story. And how did the story of the Kurdish family end? Silvia wrote in response to the question:

Ora Imam vive con Aynur e quattro bambine in una banlieue (*suburb*) di Parigi, fa il giardiniere comunale, guadagna abbastanza, si sente ricco e felice. Lo andrò a trovare in ottobre con la mia amica svizzera Jacqueline che si occupava dei curdi.

And this in reply to a question about the mayor at the time:

Renzo Imbeni era il sindaco di Bologna. L'amministrazione comunista era allora molto aperta ai problemi internazionali. Imbeni ora è parlamentare europeo. Certamente è stata un'iniziativa esemplare ed eccezionale, ne parlò la stampa.

It should perhaps be added that Bologna had a Communist administration for some 50 years after the war. Bologna was indeed the Italian Communist Party's showpiece.

SESSION 8

Talking about the past: the past definite

When Silvia started to tell what she did on receiving her Swiss friend's call for help, she used some verbs you may not have met before:

Io <u>andai</u> direttamente dal sindaco di Bologna che <u>fu</u> di una disponibilità meravigliosa. <u>Mise</u> a disposizione un'automobile con un autista e uno psicologo.

I went straight to the mayor of Bologna who was marvellously willing to help. He made available a car with a chauffeur and a psychologist.

This single word past tense is known as the *past definite*, in Italian **passato remoto**. It is used when recounting events in the past, as is the perfect. The classic rule, based on Tuscan Italian, is that it is used for a past which is viewed as no longer having any link with the present, not necessarily very remote in time, but no longer having a relationship to today. But Tuscan Italian is no longer viewed as the model all must follow. Other regional varieties are equally acceptable. Notice that Silvia, who is not Tuscan, uses it in story-telling mode, as it were. She used it again in the message about the mayor of Bologna: **ne parlò la stampa** *the press reported it.*

The use varies from one part of Italy to another so that a hard and fast rule cannot be given. It is rarely used in speech in Northern Italy. In Central and even more so in Southern Italy you will hear it. And it is more widely used in writing. Writing necessarily distances events from us. But it does depend on the type of writing. It will be used particularly in academic writing, in novels written in 'classic' Italian. For instance, Natalia Ginzburg normally used it in her novels, but in *Caro Michele*, which consists largely of letters interspersed with some narrative, the narrative is in the **passato remoto**, and the letters in the **passato prossimo**.

As a student of Italian, at first you need only learn to recognize it. Indeed you might never need to use it yourself. You will find the meaning very guessable. The form is as follows:

firmare	**vendere**	**partire**
firmai	vendei (-etti)	partii
firmasti	vendesti	partisti
firmò	vendè (-ette)	partì
firmammo	vendemmo	partimmo
firmaste	vendeste	partiste
firmarono	venderono (-ettero)	partirono

The forms in brackets are alternative forms which exist for Group 2 verbs. You may meet them. The underlining indicates irregular stress.

Many verbs in Group 2 are irregular in this tense. You met **mise** (**mettere**) above. However, they are irregular in the first and third person singular and in the third person plural only. In the second person singular and first and second person plural they are regular. Here are some examples:

avere	chiedere	decidere	leggere	prendere	scrivere
ebbi	chiesi	decisi	lessi	presi	scrissi
avesti	chiedesti	decidesti	leggesti	prendesti	scrivesti
ebbe	chiese	decise	lesse	prese	scrisse
avemmo	chiedemmo	decidemmo	leggemmo	prendemmo	scrivemmo
aveste	chiedeste	decideste	leggeste	prendeste	scriveste
ebbero	chiesero	decisero	lessero	presero	scrissero

If you are given the first person singular of the past definite of an irregular verb, you should, consulting this table, be able to work out the whole pattern, given that the second person singular will be regular. This is not true of **essere** which has the following forms: **fui, fosti, fu, fummo, foste, furono**. **Dare** and **stare** are also irregular in all persons. There is a list of common irregular past definites in the **Reference grammar**.

Activity 6

Look back to the story in Unit 4, Activity 5, about the three Rossi girls during the war. Imagine you are rewriting it for publication and decide the past historic would be a more suitable tense. Make the necessary changes.

SESSION 9

Reading 3

Gli 'Angeli del Fango'

A remarkable phenomenon in recent years has been the way people, particularly young people, have helped in the event of natural disasters, of which there have been many. The following article recalls, 30 years afterwards, the flooding of the city of Florence in 1966, an event which, in addition to loss of life and damage to buildings, caused widespread damage to art treasures. Note that it is recounted in the past definite.

L'Arno smise di tagliare in due la città e diventò Firenze. Tutto era fiume alle 7,26 del 4 novembre 1966. In quell'istante l'Arno aveva rotto gli argini e l'onda di piena (4.100 metri cubi al secondo) raggiunse, travolse e invase botteghe, case, musei e qualsiasi cosa incontrasse sul suo cammino. Si trattò di un evento tragico, frutto insieme delle precipitazioni eccezionali e soprattutto del dissesto idrogeologico che tuttora, in misura sempre maggiore, interessa l'intero bacino dell'Arno e non solo quello. Un evento che ferì gravemente un patrimonio d'arte e cultura di valore inestimabile e di appartenenza universale.

Eppure quell'alluvione fu contemporaneamente l'occasione di una straordinaria mobilitazione civile che coinvolse migliaia di giovani provenienti da ogni parte d'Europa: i cosiddetti 'Angeli del Fango', che per giorni prestarono la loro opera contribuendo a liberare dall'acqua, dalla mota e dalla nafta le strade del capoluogo toscano, le centinaia di migliaia di volumi della Biblioteca Nazionale, decine e decine di tele, i reperti del museo archeologico, i monumenti cittadini. Una identica molla spinse centinaia e centinaia di ragazze e ragazzi a raggiungere Firenze nei giorni successivi all'alluvione, ed a lavorare instancabilmente per ridare splendore alle opere ferite dalla melma: un sentimento comune, un voler bene all'Italia ed al suo patrimonio artistico, considerato a ragione patrimonio del mondo.

In questo numero di 'Legambiente Notizie' troverete un ampio servizio dedicato alla settimana di manifestazioni che la nostra associazione ha voluto dedicare – nel trentennale dell'alluvione di Firenze – agli 'Angeli del Fango': il loro impegno è un simbolo, un invito ad impegnarsi in prima persona che non va dimenticato. Così come non va dimenticata l'alluvione di Firenze e le tante, troppe, che l'hanno seguita, che hanno dimostrato come l'incuria, la cementificazione selvaggia e spesso abusiva del territorio, il conseguente dissesto idrogeologico rendano estremamente fragile il tesoro d'arte e natura che possediamo.

Ermete Realacci, Presidente Nazionale Legambiente, *Legambiente Notizie*, 30 ottobre 1996

| **... diventò Firenze** | i.e. the Arno no longer flowed between its banks, but through the whole city. The Arno is the river which in normal circumstances flows through the centre of Florence. |
| **qualsiasi cosa incontrasse** | imperfect subjunctive after an indefinite antecedent. |

dalla mota e dalla nafta	**nafta** is a word commonly used for the oil burned in central heating boilers, traces of which could be clearly seen on some buildings in Florence long after most signs of the flood had gone, at a height of up to two metres. It indicated the level the water reached. **Mota** is *mud*, as is **fango**: earth mixed with water to a paste.
... del capoluogo toscano	Florence is the capital of the region of Tuscany. **Capo** *head, main*, **luogo** *place*; C.F. **capostazione** *station master*, **capolavoro** *masterpiece*, **capolinea** *terminus* (of a bus route, for instance), etc.
melma	is the word for the *mud* at the bottom of a river, or in a marsh, or indeed left by a flood when the water subsides.
che non va dimenticato	*which should not be forgotten*. The passive with **andare** (see Unit 6, Session 4).

Comprehension: Reading 3

1 What did the 'Angeli del Fango' do?
2 The writer sees their commitment as constituting an invitation. To do what?
3 The writer seems to be pessimistic. Pick out the words which indicate this.

i The mention of **dissesto idrogeologico** is not infrequent in discussions of environmental issues in Italy today. **Dissesto** is difficult to translate: *confusion, disorder, imbalance*. It is the opposite of **sesto**: *the normal position or state*, used in phrases like **sentirsi fuori sesto** *not to feel right*; **rimettersi in sesto** *to get back to normal*. The expression **dissesto idrogeologico** refers to the set of environmental problems which make flooding and landslides likely. First it must be remembered that much of Italy is mountainous or hilly, so that heavy precipitation leads inevitably to fast-flowing rivers and streams. Add to that centuries, not to say millennia, of deforestation; much more recently the flight from the land, land that is tough to farm and doesn't give as good a living as a factory job, usually in hilly areas which are then left in a state of neglect (**l'incuria**) – for instance drainage ditches become clogged up and the water flows elsewhere; then, lower down the rivers, building on land known to flood, and building, sometimes without permission, without making any – or adequate – provision for possible flood water (**la cementificazione selvaggia e spesso abusiva del territorio**). Thus land which was once like a natural sponge can no longer cope with heavy rainfall. As we said in Unit 3, Session 4, the problems are now being taken more seriously. Current law requires a geological report on any building site before permission to build is granted. And, in some areas at least, prevention is beginning to be considered.

On a historical note, it should be added that another great art city of Italy, Venice, also suffered exceptionally bad flooding in November 1966. But of course it is sadly no stranger to flooding. And the causes are perhaps more complex. The exceptionally heavy rain was common to both events.

SESSION 10

Here are your last pieces of practice in *Improve Your Italian*. Silvia talks about another project she has been involved with over the years. It is still not classic **volontariato sociale** but we hope you'll find it interesting. And an article in *La Stampa* questions whether the **volontariato** picture is perhaps changing. We hope these passages will show you what a lot of progress you have made since Unit 1.

▶ Interview 4

Silvia Mah è difficile parlare di volontariato veramente perché io ho solamente fatto delle … cioè m'interessava essere viva e partecipare, fare qualche tipo di intervento … fare qualche tipo di intervento in politica internazionale, delle donne. E' molto ambizioso, questo termine, però è un po' così. Non ho fatto volontariato sociale.

Invece dopo anni di lavoro per la famiglia, anni in cui non ho fatto nulla di particolare per gli altri, quando sono venuta ad abitare a Bologna era molto vivo un centro di documentazione della donna. All'inizio ero un po' ostile su queste … Perché c'erano delle donne molto femministe e io non sentivo di condividere molto con loro. Poi, c'è stato un viaggio importantissimo nella mia vita, 1990, quando andai

Italy: physical geography

a Gerusalemme con loro in una marcia della pace attorno alle mura di Gerusalemme. Mi sembrava una cosa molto bella e infatti è stata un'esperienza che praticamente ha cambiato la direzione della mia vita. Perché era una marcia internazionale e io ho conosciuto tantissime donne e soprattutto ho conosciuto delle donne palestinesi e israeliane che manifestavano insieme con una metodologia particolare che è quella delle Donne in Nero, una forma di protesta silenziosa che ogni giorno nella piazza principale di Gerusalemme mettevano in pratica, cioè stando in piedi, vestite di nero in segno di lutto per le morti di palestinesi che ci sono state in questi anni ... Questa manifestazione è iniziata da delle donne israeliane molto aperte alla causa palestinese e a loro si sono associate delle donne palestinesi. Per anni hanno manifestato così coperte di insulti e di sputi. Noi ci siamo unite a loro e loro ci hanno chiesto di portare questa pratica in giro per il mondo. E noi l'abbiamo fatto. Ero con altre quattordici donne di Bologna. Appena siamo tornate a Bologna abbiamo deciso di fare come loro. E poi abbiamo deciso un'altra cosa: di organizzare un campo di pace con ragazzini italiani, palestinesi e israeliani. Questa è una tradizione che è iniziata nel '91 e che è ancora in piedi con solamente un anno di interruzione nel momento più drammatico degli scontri fra gli israeliani e i palestinesi, ma anche quest'anno ci sarà un campo di pace, un'iniziativa molto bella nella quale mi sono impegnata con passione anche perché allora, all'inzio, erano coinvolti parecchi amici di Amnesty International di cui io sono sempre stata socia.

un campo di pace	The group had help again from the local authorities; for instance they made available premises at Cattolica, on the coast of Emilia Romagna, for the peace camp.
quest'anno	The interview was given in July 1998.

Reading 4

Uno studio rivela: 'Si riducono i gruppi cattolici, ma le organizzazioni raccolgono maggiori risorse'

Il volontariato non seduce più
In calo chi si impegna per gli altri

Roma. Scavano nel fango, assistono i malati, spengono gli incendi, difendono il patrimonio artistico. C'è chi diventa un eroe, chi si fa fratello di chi assiste, chi trasforma quell'anelito ad aiutare gli altri in una professione. Ma il volontario è soprattutto una persona normale. E' un adulto (il 31,5% ha tra i 30 e i 45 anni, anche se uno su tre ha meno di 29 anni), può essere uomo o donna (con leggera prevalenza di quest'ultime, il 50,3%), ha una occupazione (il 45%) o comunque l'ha avuta (il 18,7% sono pensionati), ha un diploma di scuola superiore (4 su 10, mentre il 14,1% è laureato), si impegna in modo costante: fino a tre ore la settimana (36,4%), da 4 a 5 ore (18,2%), da 6 a 8 (25,6%) ma anche più di 8 ore (19,8%).

La fotografia del volontario-tipo, più nitida e meno enfatica che nel passato, viene dal secondo rapporto della Fivol – la Fondazione Italiana del Volontariato, una delle centrali più importanti del settore, nata dalla Banca di Roma, presentata ieri a Roma.

La prima indagine fu nel '93, questa si ferma al '97, ed è la più aggiornata. Che cos'è cambiato in quattro anni? La 'sorpresa' dello studio, curato dai ricercatori Fivol Renato Frisanco e Costanzo Ranci, arriva a pagina 40: 'Assistiamo ad una riduzione del lavoro volontario e ad un aumento delle risorse finanziarie utilizzate'. In pratica ci sono meno italiani disposti ad impegnarsi per gli altri, ma più persone che si mettono a posto la coscienza versando qualche soldo. Ecco le cifre: il 41% delle associazioni ha avuto dal '93 al '97 un calo del numero di volontari superiore al 20% (e il 29% è stabile), mentre una su due segnala un incremento delle entrate annue. Cambia anche la matrice ideologica: quelle aconfessionali (sono la maggioranza) crescono dal 67,5% al 61,2, mentre le cattoliche calano dal 40,4 al 36,3.

Nel '93 la Fivol aveva azzardato una stima di 3 milioni e 700 mila volontari. Nel rapporto presentato ieri questa cifra invece non si trova, ci si ferma a quota 400 mila, censiti. Perché? 'In quel dato – spiega Renato Frisanco – erano compresi i simpatizzanti, come i donatori di sangue o quanti partecipavano saltuariamente all'attività della loro associazione. Ora abbiamo individuato 12.909 gruppi, con gli effettivi aderenti.'

Ma quello che colpisce di più non è il calo della partecipazione – tocca soprattutto le associazioni più tradizionali come la San Vincenzo o i gruppi parrocchiali, bensì l'aumentato divario tra Nord e Sud. Oltre metà delle organizzazioni opera nelle regioni settentrionali, mentre nel Mezzogiorno è presente solo il 29% dei gruppi.'

(Gigi Padovani, *La Stampa*, 12 febbraio1999)

si mettono a posto la coscienza	*they soothe their consciences* (lit: they put their consciences straight)
crescono dal 67,5% al 61,2	There seems to be some mistake here; probably the first figure should be 57.5% but this was how it appeared in the newspaper and we have been unable to get a correction.
censiti	counted carefully, as in a census
San Vincenzo	A Roman Catholic organization which helps the poor, in the footsteps of Saint Vincent de Paul.

🛈 Il divario tra Nord e Sud

This is an aspect of Italy today we have not touched on. It is something for your future studies! Suffice it to say here that whatever measure of economic well-being, often of social well-being, you take, the North is ahead, often a long way ahead, of the South. The North is often referred to as the Centro-Nord, which means Tuscany and Umbria are being included, even Rome. Tuscany and Umbria certainly belong with the North in terms of economic prosperity.

SESSION 11

Talking to yourself

We hope this is a real habit by now. Unit 8 should have provided plenty of subjects to think about. Here are some:

1 Lei fa un lavoro volontario di qualche tipo? In che cosa consiste? Quanto L'impegna? Perché lo fa?

2 Forse non ha il tempo di svolgere lavoro volontario, ma sostiene opere di carità, o associazioni volontarie, facendo donazioni e offerte. Che tipo di associazione e attività aiuta? Perché? Di che cosa si occupano?

3 Lei pensa che il lavoro volontario debba essere un complimento o un sostituto dello stato? Quanto dobbiamo aspettarci di diritto dallo stato in cambio del nostro voto e delle tasse che paghiamo?

4 Conflitti e guerre nel mondo: quali conosce? Di quali segue le vicende? Come sono iniziati? Che conseguenze hanno portato?

5 Disastri naturali: Lei è mai stato colpito da un disastro naturale? Saprebbe parlare di un disastro naturale che ha colpito il Suo Paese? o qualche altro paese?

LANGUAGE LEARNING TIP You will have noticed that this unit did not contain many exercises. What it did contain was lots of authentic Italian. As you become more proficient, that is the way to learn. So what you need to do now is get practice. We made some suggestions in Unit 1.

One very useful source of material is the Internet. A good search engine is **www.google.it**. You will gradually find the sites that interest you but the following may be a useful start. They also provide useful web links to other interesting sites.

www.corriere.it **www.lastampa.it** } **www.repubblica.it**	three leading newspapers
www.supergiornale.it	summaries of selected articles from the day's press with links to individual newspapers. Some have unfortunately become subscription only but at the time of writing you can consult them via their direct website.
www.legambiente.it	the website of the environmental group
www.fivol.it	Federazione Italiana Volontari
www.avis.it	the blood donor service
www.slowfood.it	the Slow Food movement, started in Italy
www.italmensa.net	another site for lovers of Italian food
www.embitaly.org.uk	the Italian Embassy in London, a site which offers many links

You can also explore Italy this way. You will find some sites are in English or offer a choice of languages. The vocabulary for the web is English, e.g. **server, provider, link,** or derived from English, e.g. **cliccare.** Sites do to some extent come and go, so we apologize if something proves unavailable. Have fun surfing Italy.

Even better: go to Italy!

We hope you have enjoyed working through *Improve Your Italian*. We wish you much enjoyment as you learn more Italian – and many happy visits to Italy!

grammar ... ■

The technical jargon explained

Many people find the study of a language off-putting because of references to adverbs, conjunctions, subordinate clauses, etc., terms which they are unfamiliar with. They speak and write their own language perfectly well without knowing the words for analyzing it. Why does learning a foreign language have to involve learning all these grammatical terms? Well, of course, it doesn't. However, if they are used, they enable us to make generalizations about patterns: instruction and learning can become more efficient. And, in fact, people subconsciously understand grammar; it is just the terminology that foxes them. You don't think you understand grammar? Well, look at this:

'Twas brillig, and the slithy toves
  Did gyre and gimble in the wabe:
All mimsy were the borogoves,
  And the mome raths outgrabe.

'Beware the Jabberwock, my son!
  The jaws that bite, the claws that catch!
Beware the Jubjub bird, and shun
  The frumious Bandersnatch!'

He took his vorpal sword in hand:
  Long time the manxome foe he sought –
So rested he by the Tumtum tree,
  And stood awhile in thought.
        'Twas brillig ...

And, as in uffish thought he stood,
  The Jabberwock, with eyes of flame,
Came whiffling through the tulgey wood,
  And burbled as it came!

One, two! One, two! And through and through
  The vorpal blade went snicker-snack!
He left it dead, and with its head
  He went galumphing back.

'And hast thou slain the Jabberwock?
  Come to my arms, my beamish boy!
O frabjous day! Callooh! Callay!'
  He chortled in his joy.

JABBERWOCKY by Lewis Carroll

It's nonsense. And yet, we feel it's English. It conjures up images in our imagination, we can give it meaning even though among ourselves we might disagree about that meaning. We recognize it as acceptable as English. And yet many of the words are unknown to us and indeed to any dictionary we might consult.

Think about what happens in your mind when you read *Jabberwocky*. At least three things go on:

1 You use the words you understand as springboards for guessing what the ones you don't understand might mean. e.g. *'Twas* is understandable as *it was*, and you know that in a sentence of the sort the poem starts with, *it was* usually introduces information about the weather, the conditions.

2 You give meaning to the nonsense words by comparing them to words which are similar in sound, e.g. *brillig – brilliant, bright*. You assume *brillig* is related to the quality of the light.

3 Most importantly, you can give a role, a function to the words in the sentences even when they are unknown to you, for instance, you know that the ... *toves* can be completed by the addition of a word such as *little, ugly, blue, fascinating* and you accept *slithy* as a word of that type. You know that it would not work to insert a word like: *here, now, tomorrow*; nor would *have, sing, are, think* be suitable. You have an instinctive ability to attribute a role to words in sentences. You know that *little, ugly, blue, fascinating*, all have the same function, they describe the word that follows them: in *blue moon, blue* describes *moon* and *slithy* must describe *toves*.

So you see, you have a feeling for English grammar, you know what sort of word is needed in any given slot – even if the sentence is full of nonsense words. Really all you need to do is to learn the names of the technical words used for talking about language. For instance *little, ugly, blue, fascinating* are all examples of adjectives.

Definitions of grammatical terms can be tortuous and hedged around with provisos. Intuition is often a more effective way of understanding them. Of course, dictionaries contain definitions and this may help but we have tried to provide a way for you to understand the terms we use intuitively, taking our examples, as far as possible, from *Jabberwocky* and supplementing that with some ordinary, straightforward words.

The definitions which follow are arranged as far as possible logically. When we use another grammatical word in an explanation we have tried to deal with that next or soon afterwards.

Sentence Probably not a problem for you. A chunk starting with a capital letter and ending with a full stop, question mark or exclamation mark and containing a verb. (Carroll also makes use of the colon and technically that is not a sentence boundary. It ends a clause.) A sentence will have at least one **main clause** and may have **subordinate clauses**. Examples: *He chortled in his joy. The sun was setting behind the hill. Napoleon was finally defeated at the Battle of Waterloo.*

Main clause *And ... The Jabberwock ... came whiffling through the tulgey wood ...* As its name suggests, the main frame of the sentence, which could stand alone. You can have parallel main clauses, as is the case here where the sentence continues: *and burbled as it came!*

Subordinate clause *as in uffish thought he stood* – effectively another sentence inserted into the main clause; it could not stand alone.

MAIN CLAUSE

|I eat apples.|

MAIN CLAUSE   MAIN CLAUSE

|I eat apples| and |I drink coffee.| } Coordination

↑
Coordinating conjunction

MAIN CLAUSE

|I eat apples|

Subordinate clause   } Subordination

|because it is healthy|

↑
Subordinating conjunction

MAIN CLAUSE

|I eat apples|

Subordinate clause   Sub clause   Sub clause

|because it is healthy| and |the doctor says| |I should.|

MAIN CLAUSE   MAIN CLAUSE

|I eat apples| and |I drink coffee|

Subordinate clause   Subordinate clause

|because it is healthy| |because I like it.|

Phrase *the jaws that bite; by the Tumtum tree; with eyes of flame.* A group of words that together make a chunk of meaning. The difference between a phrase and a **clause** is that in a phrase there is no **verb**. (*that bite* is a subordinate clause).

Noun *The Jabberwock, toves, wabe, son, jaws ... thought.* (The word *thought* can of course also be used as a **verb**.) If it can have *the* or *a* in front of it, it is probably a noun, or being used as one: the *world*, a *hope*, a *grandfather*. A noun is a word used as the name of a person, place, quality, state or thing.

Adjective *brillig, slithy, mimsy, frumious, frabjous,* etc. from the poem. As we said above: *little, ugly, blue, fascinating* are adjectives. An adjective tells you more about a noun. The technical term for that is **qualify**. The adjective qualifies the noun. More examples: *long, futile, extraordinary, fictitious ...*

Verb *was, did gyre, (did) gimble, beware, catch, shun, took, rested,* etc. The heart of the sentence. A verb expresses action, being or occurrence. Note: *beware* is unusual in English in the way it works: you cannot say *I beware, he bewares.* You normally can with a verb: your innate grammatical sense tells you that it is possible to say *I gimble, he gimbles.* You also know: *I am, he is, I catch, he catches, I take, he takes,* etc. Other non-nonsense verbs are: *to try, to sneeze, to decide, to hope.*

Verbs have a variety of technical terms associated with them which it is helpful gradually to become familiar with:

Infinitive: this is the part of the verb you find in dictionaries: *to gimble, to be, to catch, to take,* etc.

Finite verb: the verb in use with a **subject**: *I gimble, I used to gimble, The slithy toves **will gimble** tomorrow.*

Non-finite: certain parts of the verb are non-finite: *to gimble, gimbling, gimbled* (see below). There is no **noun** or **pronoun**. In English, words like *gimbled*, the past participle, can also have another function: simple past tense. The Italian equivalent cannot.

Transitive, intransitive: finite verbs can be **transitive** or **intransitive**. A transitive verb can have a direct **object**: *He slew the Jabberwock. Mary had a little lamb.* Intransitive verbs cannot have a direct object. *I went to London. They despaired. The King reigned for 40 years. To go, to despair, to reign* are intransitive verbs.

Conjugate, conjugation: when you go through person by person, *I am, you are, he is,* you are conjugating the verb. In our text we have used this word in particular to say that in compound tenses some verbs use **avere** and others **essere**: they are *conjugated with* avere or essere. We have also called the different types of verb Group 1, Group 2, etc. These groups are often referred to as *first conjugation, second conjugation,* etc.

Root: this is used to refer to the unchanging part of the verb to which all the endings are added. It can also apply to other words (**nouns, adjectives,** etc.), especially when you are looking at how the word came into being and/or acquired its current meaning. The use is a simple analogy with plants, the root being the basis.

Tense: verbs have tenses: present, past, future.

Mood, mode: Italian categorizes **finite verbs** into four moods:

1 **indicative:** the form you will already be used to: present, past, future. It is for factual statements rather than the hypothetical (see conditional below) or actions viewed as being the wish, fear, belief etc. of the speaker (subjunctive – see below and units).

2 **conditional:** this is the equivalent of the English: *I would (do).* You almost certainly know **vorrei** *I would/should like.* The conditional is subject to a condition: *if this were the case then B* <u>*would*</u> ...

3 **subjunctive:** this has almost disappeared from English but some people still use it in sentences like: *I wish it* **were** *true.* The subjunctive is not about fact, but rather uncertainty, wishes, etc. It is more fully explained in the text. Note: we tend to say that certain conditions **require** the subjunctive.

4 **imperative:** for telling people what to do, orders, instructions, advice: *Come to my arms* ...; *Beware the Jabberwock ... and* **shun** *the frumious Bandersnatch!*

It is also usual for Italian grammarians to talk about **non-finite moods** which are:

1 **the infinitive** (see above): *to be, to laugh, to hide, to surmize.*

2 **the participles** (see Units): *being, been; hiding, hidden; laughing, laughed; surmizing, surmized.* You may perhaps see that some can act as adjectives.

3 **the gerund** (see Units): it ends in *-ing,* i.e. it has the same form as the present participle in English: *hiding, laughing, being, surmizing.*

Pronoun *'Twas brillig* ('T' is really *'it'*); *He took his vorpal sword*; *He left it dead*; *And hast **thou** slain*. All these are **personal pronouns**; they stand for nouns which the writer does not want or need to repeat. *Jabberwocky* does not give much scope for illustrating other types of pronoun. In *The jaws **that** bite*, *that* is a **relative pronoun**: it relates what follows to the preceding noun. In fact it stands for the noun. The word the relative pronoun stands for is called the **antecedent**. So *jaws* is the antecedent of *that*.

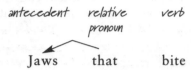

antecedent	relative pronoun	verb
Jaws	that	bite

This particular clause is an **adjectival clause** because it acts as an adjective. It tells you more about the *jaws* in just the same way as *huge* or *strong* would. There are other types of pronoun: **interrogative** (for asking questions): *who? which?*; **demonstrative** (for pointing out): *those*, etc.

Subject A **noun** or a **pronoun** showing who is doing the action of the **verb**: e.g. *I* or *the slithy toves*. It is subject of both the **verb** and the **clause**.

Object A **noun** or **pronoun** on which the action of the **verb** is performed. *He took his vorpal **sword** in hand; He left **it**; And hast thou slain the **Jabberwock**?* The words in bold print are the **direct object** of the verb. *Come to **my arms***: in this case, *my arms* is the **indirect object**. The **preposition** *to* is a clue but English does not always need the preposition. (*He gave me chocolates: He* – subject, *gave* – verb, *me* – indirect object, *chocolates* – direct object. It is clumsy to analyze in words, but you might say *chocolates* underwent the action of the verb directly – they were given; *me* benefitted. Your intuition probably seizes the idea better.)

S.	V.	D.O.	I.O.
I	sent	a letter	to my love.

Subject	Verb	Direct Object
The sudden thunderstorm	ruined	the concert.

Adverb *Jabberwocky* doesn't contain a good example. But most adverbs are easy. In English they usually end in *-ly*: *silently, quickly, fearlessly, he slew the Jabberwock. She sings **well**, beautifully, loudly*. They are said to **modify** the **verb** they go with. They can also modify **adjectives**. *That coat looks* *beautifully warm. His work is* **incredibly** *interesting. I like my coffee* **very** *strong.* Less easy to identify are adverbs like: *And stood* **awhile** *in thought. Awhile* is an adverb. *In thought* is an adverbial **phrase** (i.e. a phrase doing what an adverb does).

Preposition *in the wave; He took his ... sword* **in** *hand;* **by** *the Tumtum tree; The Jabberwock,* **with** *eyes of flame, came whiffling* **through** *the tulgey wood; Come* **to** *my arms.* Other English prepositions include: *under, on, beside, at,* etc. and phrases such as: *next to, at the side of* etc. They mark the relationship between a **noun** or **pronoun** and another word.

Conjunction Just as a junction is where roads or railway lines meet and so connect, so a conjunction connects words, **phrases**, **clauses**. The most common are *and* and *but* called **coordinating conjunctions** because they simply join or relate two clauses or two words to each other. However in studying a language the ones you need to look out for are the **subordinating conjunctions** which introduce a subordinate clause. These are words like: *because, although, while, if, when,* and phrases like *in spite of the fact that.* They introduce a clause which is inserted into the main clause. See diagrams above (page 211) which illustrate coordination and subordination.

Prefix This is simply a group of letters which can be put before the beginning of a word to make a new word. An example might in fact be *pre* which placed before *fix* forms another word. Others are: *dis-: appear, disappear; approve, disapprove; in-: appropriate, inappropriate; hospitable, inhospitable.*

Suffix This is similar except that the group of letters is placed at the end of the word: *pig, piglet.* Many adverbs are formed by adding the suffix *-ly* to an adjective: *slow, slowly.*

Interjections This is what you would call the exclamations *callooh! callay!* in Lewis Carroll's poem.

We hope the above was helpful – and that it doesn't ruin *Jabberwocky* for you for ever! It has a magic which we would be loath to destroy.

reference grammar

This section contains lists for reference and help with certain points not covered in the text. For students who want to perfect their Italian, a book devoted exclusively to Italian grammar is recommended. Particularly helpful are:

Derek Aust with Mike Zollo, **Azione Grammatica**, Hodder & Stoughton, new edition 2000. A full, clear and concise treatment of the main points of the grammar of Italian, with plenty of help for those not used to studying grammar and well thought-out exercises to practise the various points.

Denise De Rôme, consultant Paola Tite, **Soluzioni!: A Practical Guide to Italian Grammar**, Hodder Arnold, 2003. A clearly laid out and fairly full guide to Italian grammar for the learner wanting to know more; intended to be useful to beginners and accessible to readers unused to grammatical terminology, it will also be valuable for the more sophisticated and advanced student. Includes exercises.

Martin Maiden and Cecilia Robustelli, **A Reference Grammar of Modern Italian**, Arnold, 2000. A comprehensive work of reference but written with the intention of being accessible to learners of Italian of all levels of competence. Recommended for those who want to know all the details and for more advanced learners becoming aware of points not covered by course books.

Nicola Zingarelli, **Lo Zingarelli 2004 – Vocabolario della lingua italiana**, Zanichelli Editore, Bologna. Readers wanting to buy an Italian monolingual dictionary may like to consider the one used for our definitions. It is updated annually and is available with a CD-ROM.

Comparative and superlative of adjectives

interessante *interesting*	più interessante *more interesting*		il più interessante *the most interesting*		interessantissimo *very interesting*
allegro *happy*	più allegro *happier*		il più allegro *the happiest*		allegrissimo *very happy*

Common irregular forms are:

buono	*good*	migliore also più buono	*better*	il migliore	*the best*	ottimo	*very good*
cattivo	*bad*	peggiore	*worse*	il peggiore	*the worst*	pessimo	*very bad*
piccolo	*small*	minore	*smaller*	il minore	*the smallest*	minimo il minimo	*very small* *the least*
grande	*big*	maggiore	*bigger*	il maggiore	*the biggest*	massimo il massimo	*very big* *the utmost*
alto	*high*	più alto, superiore	*higher*	il più alto	*the highest*	altissimo	*very high*
basso	*low*	più basso, inferiore	*lower*	il più basso	*the lowest*	bassissimo/ infimo	*very low*

Comparative and superlative of adverbs

lentamente *slowly*	più lentamente *more slowly*	il più lentamente possibile *as slowly as possible*	molto lentamente lentissimamente *very slowly*

Note: bene, meglio *well, better*   male, peggio *badly, worse*
      molto, più *much, more*   poco, meno *little, less*

Personal pronouns

Subject		Direct object (unstressed)		Indirect object (unstressed)		Reflexive		Strong (stressed)	
io	*I*	**mi**	*me*	**mi**	*to me*	**mi**	*(to) myself*	**me**	*me*
tu	*you*	**ti**	*you*	**ti**	*to you*	**ti**	*(to) yourself*	**te**	*you*
lui	*he*	**lo**	*him*	**gli**	*to him*	**si**	*(to) himself*	**lui**	*him*
lei	*she*	**la**	*her*	**le**	*to her*	**si**	*(to) herself*	**lei**	*her*
Lei*	*you*	**La***	*you*	**Le***	*to you*	**Si***	*(to) yourself*	**Lei***	*you*
noi	*we*	**ci**	*us*	**ci**	*to us*	**ci**	*(to) ourselves*	**noi**	*us*
voi	*you*	**vi**	*you*	**vi**	*to you*	**vi**	*(to) yourselves*	**voi**	*you*
loro	*they*	**li**	*them*	**gli**	*to them*	**si**	*(to) themselves*	**loro**	*them*

*The formal *you*, singular. The usual plural is **voi**. Only in very formal speech/circumstances is **Loro** used as a plural formal *you*. Its form is as **loro** *they* given above.

Notes:

1 You may also meet the subject forms **egli**, **ella** (*he*, *she*), but usually in elegant, written style rather than in speech. Similarly **esso**, **essa** (*it*), **essi**, **esse** (*they*). Also in more elegant speech or writing, *to them* is **loro** and it follows the verb.

Informal speech: **Gli parla.** *He's talking to them.*   Formal speech: **Parla loro.** *He's talking to them.*

2 Strong or stressed pronouns are used:

(a) after a preposition: **Viene con me?**   *Are you coming with me?*
(b) for emphasis: **Cerca lui, non te.**   *He's looking for him, not you.*

3 The direct and indirect object pronouns usually come before the verb but are added to the infinitive, the imperative (**tu** and **voi** forms), the past participle standing alone, and the gerund.

Combining pronouns

When both direct and indirect object pronouns are used, they are combined in this order:

1 the indirect pronouns **mi, ti, si, ci, vi** become **me, te, se, ce, ve** and are followed by **lo, la, li, le, ne.**

2 the indirect pronouns **gli, le** and the plural **gli,** all become **glie** and precede and are joined to **lo, la, li, le, ne.**

TIP: Rather than try to learn that as a rule, learn examples as you come across them:

Glielo dico.	*I'll say it to him/her/ them –* or *you* (formal)
Me lo dai?	*Are you giving it to me?* (Often: *will you give it to me?*)
Non me ne parla.	*He/she doesn't talk to me about it.*

	lo	**la**	**li**	**le**	**ne**
mi	me lo	me la	me li	me le	me ne
ti	te lo	te la	te li	te le	te ne
gli	glielo	gliela	glieli	gliele	gliene
le	glielo	gliela	glieli	gliele	gliene
Le	Glielo	Gliela	Glieli	Gliele	Gliene
ci	ce lo	ce la	ce li	ce le	ce ne
vi	ve lo	ve la	ve li	ve le	ve ne
loro	glielo	gliela	glieli	gliele	gliene
si	se lo	se la	se li	se le	se ne

Negatives

Simple: **non** before verb. Non abito qui. *I don't live here.*

Strong negatives:

non ... mica	non ... per niente
non ... affatto	non ... per nulla

Non sono mica un suo amico. *I'm definitely not a friend of his/hers.*

non ... nessuno	*no one*	non ... più	*no longer, not anymore*
non ... niente	} *nothing*		
non ... nulla		non ... neppure	}
non ... ancora	*not yet*	non ... nemmeno	} *not even*
non ... mai	*never*	non ... neanche	}

Prepositions

Warning: The use of prepositions, particularly the commonest (**a, di, da, su**), is often tricky. Some meanings have been dealt with in the text. Further help is available in dictionaries or books such as *Azione Grammatica* (above). The list below is not exhaustive.

a	*to, at*	invece di	*instead of*
accanto a	*next to*	lontano da	*far from*
attraverso	*across*	lungo	*along*
circa	*about*	malgrado	*in spite of*
con	*with*	nonostante	*in spite of*
contro	*against*	per	*for, through*
da	*from, by*	presso	*near*
davanti a	*in front of*	prima di	*before*
dentro	*inside*	quanto a	*as for, as regards*
di	*of, from*	rispetto a	*compared to*
di fronte a	*opposite*	secondo	*according to*
dietro	*behind*	senza	*without*
eccetto	*except*	sopra	*above*
fino a	*as far as, until*	sotto	*under*
fra	*between, within*	su	*on*
in	*to, in*	tra	*between, within*
in fondo a	*at the bottom of, at the end of*	tramite	*by means of*
		tranne	*except*
in mezzo a	*in the middle of*	verso	*towards*
intorno a	*around*	vicino a	*near*

Interrogative pronouns and adjectives

che cosa? cosa? che?	*what?*
chi?	*who? whom?*
come?	*how?*
come mai?	*how come? how (can it) possibly (be so)?*
dove?	*where?*
perché?	*why?*
quando?	*when?*
quanto? quanti?	*how much? how many?*
quale?	*which? which one?*
quali?	*which? which ones?*

Cases where the subjunctive is required

1 After verbs expressing:

   a *an opinion or casting doubt*: **pensare che, credere che,**
      (which, in the negative, both imply doubt), **dubitare che,
      non essere sicuro/certo che,** etc.
   b *an order, a request, a wish that something be done or
      not done*: **comandare che, ordinare che, insistere che,
      desiderare che, volere che, proibire che, suggerire che,
      aspettarsi che,** etc.
   c *necessity* – see list of impersonal expressions below.
   d *fear, pleasure, and other emotions*: **avere paura che,
      temere che, essere contento/a che, essere felice che, essere
      triste che, stupirsi che, essere deluso che,** etc.

2 The subjunctive is also used after certain common impersonal
   expressions:

basta che	*it is sufficient that*
bisogna che	
è necessario che	*it is necessary that*
occorre che	
è importante che	*it is important that*
importa che	*it matters that*
è probabile che	*it is likely that*
è bene che	*it's a good thing that*
è meglio che	*it's better that*
è possibile che	*it's possible that*
può darsi che	
sembra che	*it seems that*
pare che	
è un peccato che	*it is a pity that*

3 The subjunctive is used after certain subordinating conjunctions. Common, or fairly common, are:

benché, sebbene, quantunque	*although*
perché, affinché, in modo che	*so that*
nonostante (che), malgrado (che)	*in spite of the fact that*
qualora, nel caso che, caso mai	*in the event that, in case*
purché, a condizione che	*provided that, on condition that*
a meno che	*unless*
prima che	*before*
finché non	*until*

Note: When **perché** means *because*, it does not require the subjunctive.

Imperative

Tu form
Group 1 (**are**) verbs end in **a**.

All other verbs (including all irregular verbs), end in **i** (the **tu** form of the present indicative.)

e.g. Group 1   **scusa, guarda, mangia**
e.g. All others   **senti, finisci, vieni**

Exceptions: verbs which do not use the **tu** form of the present indicative:

essere	→ sii		sapere	→ sappi
avere	→ abbi		dire	→ di'

Some common verbs have two possible forms, one abbreviated, the other regular:

andare	→ va'/vai		dare	→ da'/dai
stare	→ sta'/stai		fare	→ fa'/fai

Voi form (plural *you*)
Use the **voi** form of the present indicative:

scusate, guardate, decidete, finite, sentite, venite

Noi form (*Let's …*)
Use the **noi** form of the present indicative:

andiamo, mangiamo, decidiamo, finiamo

Lei **form**

This uses the present subjunctive:

-**are** verbs end in i: **scusi, guardi, mangi, s'accomodi**
All others end in a: **decida, senta, finisca, dica, venga**

Verbs which are irregular in the present subjunctive have that form in the imperative (**dica, venga**). Here are some other common ones:

essere	→ sia	fare	→ faccia
avere	→ abbia	sapere	→ sappia
andare	→ vada	stare	→ stia
dare	→ dia		

Note: Object (and reflexive) pronouns are attached to the end of the **tu** and **voi** forms, but precede the **Lei** form. This gives you:

tu form: scusami   dimmi*   ascoltami   accomodati
voi form: scusateci   diteci   ascoltateci   accomodatevi
BUT
    Lei form: mi scusi   mi dica   mi ascolti   s'accomodi

*When pronouns other than **gli** are attached to the abbreviated **tu** forms listed above, the first consonant of the pronoun is doubled: e.g. **dimmi**.

TIP: Use these or other commonly heard verbs as models to help you remember.

The negative imperative

It is formed by putting **non** in front of the positive imperative, EXCEPT in the **tu** form, which uses **non** before the infinitive:

voi form: non venite
Lei form: non venga
BUT **tu** form: non venire

Common irregular past participles and past definites

Since there is sometimes a link between the past participle and the past definite, it may be useful to have them listed together. Given the first and second persons singular of the past definite, it is possible to form the complete tense. Compounds of these verbs behave in the same way: e.g. **coinvolgere** behaves like **volgere**, **sorprendere** like **prendere**.

Infinitive meaning	Past participle	Past definite
essere *to be*	stato	fui, fosti, fu, fummo, foste, furono
avere *to have*	avuto	ebbi, avesti
assumere *to take on (staff)*	assunto	assunsi, assumesti
bere *to drink*	bevuto	bevvi, bevesti
chiedere *to ask*	chiesto	chiesi, chiedesti
chiudere *to close*	chiuso	chiusi, chiudesti
conoscere *to know (person)*	conosciuto	conobbi, conoscesti
correre *to run*	corso	corsi, corresti
dare *to give*	dato	diedi/detti, desti
decidere *to decide*	deciso	decisi, decidesti
dire *to say*	detto	dissi, dicesti
dirigere *to direct*	diretto	diressi, dirigesti
discutere *to discuss*	discusso	discussi, discutesti
escludere *to exclude*	escluso	esclusi, escludesti
fare *to do, to make*	fatto	feci, facesti
includere *to include*	incluso	inclusi, includesti
leggere *to read*	letto	lessi, leggesti
mettere *to put*	messo	misi, mettesti
nascere *to be born*	nato	nacqui, nascesti
perdere *to lose*	perso/perduto	persi/perdetti, perdesti
persuadere *to persuade*	persuaso	persuasi, persuadesti
prendere *to take*	preso	presi, prendesti
ridere *to laugh*	riso	risi, ridesti
rimanere *to remain*	rimasto	rimasi, rimanesti
rispondere *to answer*	risposto	risposi, rispondesti
rompere *to break*	rotto	ruppi, rompesti
sapere *to know (fact)*	saputo	seppi, sapesti
scegliere *to choose*	scelto	scelsi, scegliesti
scendere *to go down*	sceso	scesi, scendesti
scrivere *to write*	scritto	scrissi, scrivesti
spegnere *to extinguish*	spento	spensi, spegnesti
stare *to remain, stay*	stato	stetti, stesti
stringere *to grasp, squeeze*	stretto	strinsi, stringesti
succedere *to happen*	successo	successi, succedesti
uccidere *to kill*	ucciso	uccisi, uccidesti
vedere *to see*	visto, veduto	vidi, vedesti
venire *to come*	venuto	venni, venisti
vincere *to win*	vinto	vinsi, vincesti
vivere *to live*	vissuto	vissi, vivesti
volere *to want*	voluto	volli, volesti
volgere *to turn*	volto	volsi, volgesti

Common verbs followed by the infinitive without a preposition

amare	to love	interessare*	to be interesting
bastare*	to be enough	lasciare	to allow
bisognare*	to be necessary	occorrere*	to be necessary
convenire*	to be advisable	odiare	to hate
desiderare	to desire, to want	osare	to dare
detestare	to detest	piacere*	to be pleasing
dispiacere*	to be displeasing	potere	to be able
dovere	to have to	preferire	to prefer
fare	to make, to have done	vedere	to see
		volere	to want
importare*	to matter		

*Usually used impersonally.

Devo uscire.	*I have to go out.*
Fammi vedere la foto.	*Show me the photo.*
Faccio costruire una casa.	*I am having a house built.*
Lascia fare a me.	*Leave me to do it, let me do it.*
Mi piace andare al cinema.	*I like going to the cinema.* (see treament of **piacere** in Unit 1)
Posso aiutare?	*Can I help?*
Preferisco partire presto.	*I prefer to set off early.*
Basta telefonare.	*All you need to do is telephone.*
Bisogna telefonare.	*It is necessary to telephone (You/we need to telephone).*
Conviene comprare qui.	*It is advisable to buy (it) here.*

Common verbs requiring *a*, *ad* or *di* before an infinitive

Many speakers use **ad** before a verb beginning with a vowel, especially when the vowel is **a**, e.g. **aiutami ad alzare questo pianoforte** *help me lift this piano*.

Note: Verbs with similar meanings tend to work the same way, e.g.
chiedere and domandare; avere vergogna di and vergognarsi di.

accettare di	to accept to	mettersi a	to start to, to start ...ing
aiutare a	to help to		
andare a	to go to, to go and	minacciare di	to threaten to
avere intenzione di	to intend to	non vedere l'ora di	to look forward to ...ing
avere paura di	to be afraid of ...ing		
avere ragione a	to be right to	parlare di	to talk of ...ing
avere torto a	to be wrong to	permettere (a qualcuno) di	to permit/allow (someone) to
avere vergogna di	to be ashamed of ...ing	pregare di	to beg/ask to
avere voglia di	to want to	promettere di	to promise to
cercare di	to try to	rendersi conto di	to realize
chiedere (a qualcuno) di	to ask (someone) to	ricordare/ ricordarsi di	to remember to
cominciare a	to begin to, to begin ...ing	rifiutare di	to refuse to
		rinunciare a	to give up ...ing
consigliare (a qualcuno) di	to advise (someone) to	riprendere a	to start again ...ing
convincere a	to persuade to	riuscire a	to succeed in ...ing, to manage to
costringere a	to force to		
credere di	to believe	sapere di	to know
decidere di	to decide to	scegliere di	to choose to
dimenticare/ dimenticarsi di	to forget to	scusarsi di	to apologize for ...ing
		servire a	to be used for ...ing
domandare (a qualcuno) di	to ask (someone) to	smettere di	to stop ...ing
finire di	to finish ...ing	sopportare di	to stand/put up with/bear ...ing
impedire (a qualcuno) di	to prevent (someone) from ...ing	sperare di	to hope to
		tentare di	to try to
insegnare a	to teach to	venire a	to come to
mancare di	to fail to	vergognarsi di	to be ashamed of ...ing
meritare di	to deserve to		
		vietare (a qualcuno) di	to forbid (someone) to

Common verbs which take a direct object in one language and an indirect in the other

ascoltare qualcuno/qualcosa	to listen to someone/something
assomigliare a qualcuno	to resemble someone
cercare qualcuno/qualcosa	to look for someone/something

chiedere qualcosa a qualcuno	*to ask someone something*
credere a qualcuno, qualcosa	*to believe someone/something*
but credere in qualcuno/qualcosa	*to believe in someone/something*
dare qualcosa a qualcuno	*to give someone something*
dire qualcosa a qualcuno	*to tell someone something*
entrare in un luogo	*to enter a place*
guardare qualcuno	*to look at someone*
occuparsi di qualcosa	*to look after something*
pensare a qualcuno	*to think about someone*
piacere a qualcuno	*to please someone*
rinunciare a qualcosa	*to give something up, to go without something*
rispondere a qualcuno/qualcosa	*to answer someone/something*
(ad una domanda, al telefono)	*(a question, the telephone)*
telefonare a qualcuno	*to telephone/call someone*
volere bene a qualcuno	*to love someone, be fond of someone*

Note also other differences between common verbs in the two languages. Collect others as you learn!

dipendere da	*to depend on*
leggere sul giornale che ...	*to read in the newpaper that ...*
parlare con qualcuno	*to talk to someone*
sognare qualcosa	*to dream about something*
sposarsi con qualcuno	*to marry someone*
vedere qualcosa alla tv	*to see something on TV*

Notes on pronunciation

The purpose of this section is not to take you through all the sounds of Italian, but to help you with the problem areas which English speakers encounter. Italian is, for English speakers, fairly straightforward to pronounce. And the language has the bonus that it is, by and large, written phonetically. In other words, the spelling reflects the sound. There are however a few areas which can cause difficulty.

Double consonants

These must be pronounced differently from single ones, otherwise there is a risk of misunderstanding – or of sounding silly! You don't after all want people hearing the word *anus*, **ano**, when what you meant to say was *year*, **anno**! Try to linger on the two consonants, saying one and then the other before moving on. Of course, the preceding vowel is affected: it is shorter before a double consonant. Just practise saying:

> babbo; cotto; cappa; mamma; ninna nanna; freddo; terra; ecco; cappuccino; stesso.

Pronunciation of *r*

The spelling reflects what is said, so try to pronounce each consonant including **r**. This is particularly difficult for speakers of certain varieties of English. By now, you surely know about the trap of saying **cane** (*dog*) when you mean **carne** (*meat*). The **r** is the difference between them. Always pronounce **r** if it is there in the spelling. And twice if there are two as in: **birra** (*beer*). If you have difficulty with a rolled **r**, you could try a guttural **r**. Some Italians do use this, it's called **erre moscia** (*soft r*). But you must say the **r**. If you practise hard, you will probably find you can learn to do a rolled **r**. We advise perseverance!

Stress

The problem here is irregular stress. Stress in Italian words, as you probably know, generally falls on the syllable before the last, the penultimate syllable:

andi<u>a</u>mo; rom<u>a</u>no; ferrov<u>i</u>a; generalm<u>e</u>nte.

If it falls on the last syllable there is no problem because an accent (grave – i.e. backward leaning) is put on the vowel to show this:

città; più; possibilità; tivù; mercoledì.

The difficulty comes where the stress falls earlier in the word. And if you have not heard the word spoken, you have no means of knowing where to put the stress, except to guess 'penultimate', which in some cases will be wrong. We advise you to get into the habit when you write words down for learning purposes of marking irregular stresses in by some system of your own – we use underlining in this book. You can check stress in a dictionary if you are unsure. They will have some way of showing where the stress falls. There are also words where stress changes meaning, for example:

t<u>e</u>ndine (m.s.) *tendon* and tend<u>i</u>ne (f.pl.) *curtains*
princ<u>i</u>pi (pl. of princ<u>i</u>pio) *principles* and pr<u>i</u>ncipi (pl. of pr<u>i</u>ncipe) *princes*
s<u>u</u>bito *immediately* and sub<u>i</u>to *endured, suffered*.

You could argue that the context usually leads the mind to the correct meaning but in practice the wrong stress can obscure meaning. In fact it can create more problems in communicating than a bad Italian 'accent'. It may help to know there are certain groups of words which all work the same way i.e. the stress falls on the antepenultimate syllable:

a   the adjectives ending in -<u>a</u>bile, -<u>i</u>bile, -<u>e</u>vole, or simply -ile. These often correspond to English words ending in *-ble*.

am<u>a</u>bile *amiable, lovable*; fless<u>i</u>bile *flexible*; poss<u>i</u>bile *possible*; soci<u>e</u>vole *sociable*; <u>u</u>mile *humble*; diff<u>i</u>cile *difficult*

b   nouns ending in -<u>a</u>gine, -<u>a</u>ggine, -<u>i</u>gine, -<u>i</u>ggine, -<u>u</u>dine (which are all feminine)

imm<u>a</u>gine *image*; testard<u>a</u>ggine *obstinacy*; or<u>i</u>gine *origin*; vert<u>i</u>gine *giddiness, dizziness*; ful<u>i</u>ggine *soot*; abit<u>u</u>dine *habit*

c   the third person plural of the verb in all single-word tenses except the future:
present: **pensano**, conditional: **farebbero**, imperfect: **imparavano**, past definite: **mangiarono**, present subjunctive: **capiscano**, imperfect subjunctive: **andassero**.

English/Italian spelling conflict

The fact that, for a limited number of sounds, the English spelling conventions conflict with those of Italian is an area of difficulty until the learner gets used to the Italian rules. This happens within the areas of the sounds *k, g, ch, j, sh, gl, gn* (English spelling). The rules of Italian apply consistently and just have to be learned. Imitating Italians speaking will help you. Try also fixing sounds in your mind by reference to words you know well. Try learning one word for each case.

gli   The letters **gli** represent a sound which is similar to the middle of the English word *million*.

       figlio; **Gigli** (the legendary tenor); **aglio** *garlic*; **foglia** *leaf*; **dirgli** *to tell him*

       In a few words **gli** is pronounds as in *glee*: **glicine** *wisteria*, **anglicano**, **glicemia**, **glicerina** and other chemistry words.

       In front of other vowels **gl** is pronounced as in *glue*: **gloria**, **gladiolo**, **glucosio**.

gn   These letters represent a sound similar to the middle of the word *onion*.

       ogni *every*; **Mascagni** (the composer); **giugno** *June*; **gnocchi**.

sc(i)   This is the Italian spelling convention for the sound spelt in English *sh*. The **i** is necessary before **a, o, u,** but not before **e**:

       sciarpa *scarf*; **sciopero** (stress on **o**) *strike*; **sciupare** *to spoil*; **scendere** *to go down*; **sci** *ski*

sc   + **a, o, u** is pronounced as in English (sk):

       scala *staircase*; **scopo** *purpose, aim*; **scultore** *sculptor*.
       sch is the way to write the English sound *sk* before **e** or **i**: **scherzo** *joke*, **schifo** *disgust*.

English sounds **ch, j**

In Italian these are written:

before **e** or **i** → **c** **cento, violoncello, San Francesco, Puccini**

→ **g** **gelato** *ice-cream*; **gente** *people*; **gita** *excursion*; **Gina.**

before **a, o, u** → **ci** **ciao, Luciano; socio** *member*; **ciò** *that*; **ciuffo** *tuft of hair*

→ **gi** **giallo, Gianni, giorno, Giotto, giù, Giulia, Giuseppe** (often mis-spelt and mis-pronounced by English speakers).

English sounds **k, g**

In Italian these are written:

before **a, o, u** → **c** **casa, Canada, cosa, Como, curioso, Cuneo** (a town in Piemonte, stressed on **u**)

→ **g** **galleria, Garda, gondola, gorgonzola, guardare, Guttuso** (20th century painter), **Guido, Gucci.**

before **e** or **i** → **ch** **orchestra** (stressed on **e**, not on first syllable as in English); **Cherubino, Michelangelo, chilo, Chianti**

→ **gh** **spaghetti, ghetto, ghiro** *dormouse*; **Lamborghini, Ghiberti, Ghirlandaio.**

key

Unit 1

Comprehension 1 1 Most of all she enjoys reading. 2 She feels she doesn't organize it. 3 Contemporary fiction. 4 Translations (of books written in English). She likes to read in the original language. 5 Because she wanted to brush up on those two languages. 6 She likes walking and cycling. 7 Pasta and puddings. 8 She most enjoys eating the pasta courses, more than meat. (You will probably have learned that the pasta course is the first course of an Italian meal, followed by the meat course and then the pudding.) 9 She likes chatting, spending time with girlfriends and talking. 10 Going to the cinema. She and her husband go with another couple approximately once a week in the winter. Perhaps every ten days, taking an average. 11 She would like to know Tuscany better because, surprising as it may seem, there are lots of little villages she hasn't yet seen, especially in the northern part. 12 She needs a 'fix' of news. She always wants to be up-to-date with the latest news. She turns on the radio or the television. She can't survive if she doesn't know what has happened (in the wider world).

Activity 1 Mi piace ... 1 ballare 2 andare a teatro 3 viaggiare 4 navigare su Internet 5 lavorare in giardino 6 guardare la televisione 7 ascoltare la musica classica 8 andare in discoteca 9 guidare la mia nuova macchina 10 parlare italiano.

Activity 2 1 Le piace andare al cinema? 2 Le piace viaggiare in macchina? 3 Ti piace cucinare? 4 Che cosa ti piace cucinare? 5 Ti piace lavorare in giardino?

Activity 3

Group 1: comprare camminare cucinare mangiare chiacchierare parlare visitare
Group 2: leggere riprendere scegliere rivedere conoscere accendere resistere
Irregular: dire andare essere fare stare sapere

You will have noted that Angioletta didn't actually use any third group verbs. This was just chance.

Activity 4 1 Subject pronouns: **Lui ama il teatro ... Io non capisco niente di musica ... Lui ama i musei, e io ci vado con sforzo. ... Lui ama le biblioteche, e io le odio. Lui ama i viaggi, ... Io resterei sempre a casa ...** She uses the pronoun when she is contrasting their tastes which seem to be diametrically opposed. Once it is clear who she is referring to, in Paragraphs 4 and 5, she omits the pronoun. In the last paragraph of the extract: **a lui piacciono ... A me piace ...** These are <u>strong</u> pronouns used after the preposition **a**. In the case of **lui**, the form is the same as the subject pronoun.
2 She uses **piacere** when referring to food and **amare** for everthing else: the cultural pursuits, travel, etc. You may care to note that she seems to like simple country food. Her husband's tastes are perhaps more middle class.
3 A lei piace (mangiare) **il minestrone, il pancotto, la frittata, gli erbaggi. A me non piacciono queste cose. Preferisco le tagliatelle, l'abbacchio, le ciliege, il vino rosso.** The verb in the first sentence could equally be plural: A lei piacciono **il minestrone, il pancotto, ecc.** It would have to be plural if you had no single nouns in the list, just, perhaps, **gli erbaggi.**

Activity 5 1 I bambini amano / Ai bambini piace (molto) nuotare / il nuoto. 2 Ci piace camminare nei dintorni / nella campagna intorno. 3 A mio marito piace cucinare e ognuno prepara una parte del pasto. 4 Lui preferisce cucinare la carne. 5 Io sono brava a cucinare dolci. 6 A mio marito piace leggere. Io preferisco / A me piace di più suonare il pianoforte. 7 A mia figlia piace cantare. E' molto brava. 8 Ci piace visitare i musei, andare al cinema e qualche volta ai concerti. 9 Non ci piace la televisione.

Activity 6 1 Al mio compagno / Alla mia compagna piace andare in palestra la sera. Io preferirei rimanere / stare a casa. Leggerei, guarderei la TV o forse ascolterei un po' di musica. 2 Il mio compagno / La mia compagna passerebbe le vacanze/ferie a casa. Andrebbe in giro/farebbe delle passeggiate nei dintorni, giocherebbe a tennis e andrebbe al cinema. Io preferirei andare all'estero. Mi piace viaggiare/Amo i viaggi. Vorrei visitare l'America/gli Stati Uniti. Visiterei New York. Vedrei il Metropolitan, andrei al Met e sarebbe interessante visitare il museo dell'immigrazione a Ellis Island. M'interessa l'emigrazione italiana in America.

Activity 7 1 'Things of all kinds, sorts': a possible link is **genus**, pl. **genera**. It refers to kinds of plants, animals, etc. Or maybe literary *genre*, again, *type, kind*. 2 'I refuse, don't allow myself': surely, very like *refuse*. Using it reflexively stresses determination. 3 'A good point or a failing, a virtue or a weakness': **difetto** is easier to work out, *defect, fault*. The context indicates **pregio** is an opposite. 4 'A couple': surely the sound gives this one away. 5 'Places': here it is probably a case of guessing from the context. 'Visiting new ... seeing old ... again'. 6 'Up-to-date': **aggiornata** contains the word **giorno,** *day.* That should be the clue. 7 'What has happened': as a noun, **successo** is *success,* but here we have a past participle. Perhaps there is no obvious clue, and one is having to guess from the context. Why would someone who is really interested in politics switch on the radio or TV first thing in the morning? In Italy you will find **succedere** is very frequently used: **Cosa succede?** *What's happening?*

Activity 8 Expressions Angioletta uses which are common in speech and which seem to give thinking time are: *Mah; no?; E poi; Ecco; voglio dire; non so.*

Comprehension 2 You may not have picked out everything, depending on your way of interpreting what Angioletta said. 1 You can learn a lot (outside school) if you want. (In your case: outside the book) 2 Seek opportunities to learn. 3 Read the ingredients on biscuit packets to see if you can learn new words. Here Angioletta was effectively saying: every time you see something in the language you are trying to learn, make the most of it, see what you can learn from it. 4 When you hear the language being spoken, see if you can't get a little practice by initiating a conversation with the speaker. 5 Listen to recordings in the language. 6 Try to talk to yourself in the language. 7 Think in the language. Think out how you might describe someone you can see, for example, on a bus. 8 Try to find ways of remembering which work for you. 9 Adopt a determined mental approach, the approach of *wanting* to learn.

Unit 2

Comprehension 1 1 (a) Antonella. (b) Renata. (c) Mario Rotondale. He says he is 30, but then explains he will be 30, on 17th August, his birthday. (d) Riccardo. (e) Silvia. (f) Silvia again. (g) Monica. 2 Nicola and Mario Rotondale are father and son, respectively. The first Mario we heard is 30 and could not be the father of a man with an adult man's voice. Nicola refers to another Mario, his father.

Activity 1 1 (Io) sono *or* (io) mi chiamo. 2 (Io) sono *or* faccio il/la ... 3 Sono laureato/a in ... 4 (Io) ho (from avere, *to have*) + the number of years. 5 Sono nato/a ... 6 Faccio parte del Gruppo Mio da parecchi anni. Abito a Bologna da circa 20 anni. 7 Ho insegnato nelle scuole medie per parecchi anni.

Comprehension 2 1 Both focus largely on family, in Gabriella's case her parents and siblings, in Piera's case her sons and grandson. This is probably because of the importance of their families in their lives. Piera tries to describe her physical appearance but keeps to very obvious aspects: height, weight, hair colour, eye colour.

2 Gabriella: Italian father = English mother

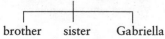

brother   sister   Gabriella

She tells you about her parents and that her brother and sister are older than she. She also says her brother was born in France and that at the outbreak of war her parents left France and came to Italy. One can deduce therefore that the sister was born in Italy as well as Gabriella and therefore the brother is the oldest.

Piera: Piera = husband (*we assume*)

```
                    ┌───────────┴───────────┐
          son aged 30                      son aged 25
               grandson (Thibaut) aged 1
```

We can't deduce which son is the father of Thibaut from what Piera says – you may say it is likely to be the older one. We know Thibaut lives in France, in Brittany.

Activity 3   **1** I miei amici (if we know they are all female: le mie amiche). **2** La nostra famiglia. **3** Il suo libro. **4** Il suo libro. **5** Il loro fratello. **6** I loro fratelli. **7** Il mio amico/la mia amica – depending on gender. **8** La sua amica. **9** La sua amica. **10** Nostra madre.

Activity 4   **1** Mi chiamo/Sono Jonathan. Sono insegnante/faccio l'insegnante di lingue straniere. Insegno da tre anni. **2** Mia sorella si chiama Olimpia. È medico. Lavora in un ospedale. Lavora nell'ospedale da sei anni. **3** George ha trentadue anni e lavora per una grossa società. Fanno/fabbricano accessori per l'industria automobilistica. George lavora nella società da diciotto mesi. **4** Mio figlio studia medicina. È studente all'università di Southampton. Studia medicina da due anni. **5** Mio fratello è psichiatra. Lavora a Boston. Gli piace moltissimo Boston. È nato a Cambridge, in Inghilterra, e ora vive/abita a Cambridge, nel Massachusetts. Vive/abita a Cambridge da otto anni. **6** Mia moglie si chiama Jane. È scrittrice. Sua madre è un'attrice famosa. Suo padre è americano. Abbiamo tre figli. Il nostro figlio maggiore ha otto anni, nostra figlia ne ha sei e il nostro secondo figlio maschio ne ha quattro. **7** Studio italiano/imparo l'italiano da nove mesi. **8** Capiamo il gallese. Abbiamo abitato per ventiquattro anni nel Galles. Ora/adesso abitiamo a Londra. **9** Parlo francese da vent'anni. **10** Leggo spesso una rivista italiana che si chiama **Panorama**.

Comprehension 3   **1** He is tall (**alto**) and **longilineo**, which means that he is long-limbed with a relatively slight torso. He doesn't consider himself handsome: **non sono un bell' uomo**. But at the same time he doesn't think he is in any way unpleasant-looking **sgraziato** means lacking in grace and could apply to appearance, way of moving, or even manners. **Aggraziato** is its opposite. **2** As for his character, he says perhaps defensively that he is 'very normal' and easy-going, **bonaccione**. **3** He appears to be referring to intelligence, to what is in the **testa**. This is gathered from the two sentences which follow.

Activity 5   Definitions from *Lo Zingarelli* Italian dictionary. The full entry gives examples of usage too. We have made quite a wide range of suggestions, many of which we would not expect you to know but which you may want to adopt.

STATURA E CORPORATURA (*height and build*):

alto, grande *tall*

basso (di statura), piccolo *short*

grande can be *tall, large*

grasso *fat*, referring to excessive fat (Zingarelli: 'Che presenta
abbondante sviluppo del tessuto (*tissue*) adiposo')

grosso usually *fat, large* (Zingarelli: 'Che supera la misura ordinaria
per massa, per volume')

longilineo *long-limbed*

magro *thin*

robusto *sturdy, strong*

snello *slim, agile, active, quick* (Zingarelli: '1. Agile, svelto, leggero,
nei movimenti; 2. Che ha forma slanciata, sottile ed elegante. CONTR.
Tarchiato, tozzo')

svelto *slender, lively, quick-witted* (Zingarelli gives four meanings: 1.
Che si muove, agisce ... con prontezza ...; 2. Lesto, sollecito ... 3.
Sottile e slanciato, agile ... 4. Sveglio, vivace ...) So svelto can refer
to quickness of mind; it is also associated with quickness of
movement. Whereas snello is more usually used to describe
slimness, i.e. size, shape. But as you can see, the meanings overlap

tarchiato *thickset* (Zingarelli: 'Di persona dalla corporatura robusta
e massiccia') So it indicates a person with a sturdy or bulky
frame. Zingarelli gives an opposite: *slanciato*.

tozzo *stocky*; (Zingarelli: 'Di cosa o persona eccessivamente grossa
rispetto all'altezza') Is our translation a good one? It is standard in
translating dictionaries.

TESTA E FACCIA (*head and face*):

capelli neri / bruni / biondi / rossi / castani

occhi bruni / azzuri / castani; bocca carnosa (*fleshy*) / piena (*full*) /
sottile (*thin*, the opposite of *full*)

naso curvo / aquilino / greco / all'insù or nasino alla francese
(*turned up*); camuso (*flat*) / a patata (*big and shapeless, like a
potato!* You may also be amused to learn ficcanaso someone who
pokes their nose into other people's business, *nosy*)

sopracciglia (*eyebrows*) folte (*bushy*) / ben disegnate / disordinate /
sottili

una mascella quadrata *a square jaw*

un mento pronunciato *a prominent chin* opposite: un mento
sfuggente *a receding chin*; doppio mento *double chin*;

orecchie a sventola *ears that stick out*

guance scavate *hollow cheeks*

zigomi pronunciati *prominent cheekbones*.

Activity 8 assomigliare a; rossa di capelli; avere un carattere ...
inglese; allegro opp: triste; posato opp: impulsivo; serio opp: leggero;
ligio al dovere; spensierato opp: serio, prudente, sollecito, premuroso,
riflessivo; disubbidiente opp: ubbidiente; felice opp: infelice, triste;
contento opp: scontento; avere doti.

Comprehension 4   1 His strong will to win any battle he decides to take on. And to win hands down – Deaglio considers this latter a vice (**un vizio**). 2 The art of compromise. He is not worried about what people think of him. 3 Less fierce than he is painted. 4 (a) **concreto**, (b) **pragmatico** 5 She had only just started the job and she had no money to pay the wages. It was the 250th anniversary of the opera house. She asked for sponsorship from Fiat. Romiti telephoned her immediately and said he had signed a cheque for one thousand million lire. Her explanation was that, yes, he cared about music, but he also cared that workers should get their wages. 6 (a) **antipatico**, (b) **chiuso**.

Comprehension 5   1 She clarifies the custom – and law – concerning a married woman's surname. Italian women, for official purposes, do not change surname when they marry. Socially, however, many do use their husband's surname. 2 They thought Emanuela and John were not married, since Emanuela was still using her maiden name.

Unit 3

Comprehension 1 and 2   1 She went to England for the last two years of high school, did an International Baccalaureate (rather than the **maturità**) and she then took her degree and Master's – presumably an MSc. – at the London School of Economics, University of London. 2 Because she felt poorly prepared for working in an Italian business environment, having been away from Italy for so long. 3 There is no link except insofar as that management of all businesses has things in common no matter what the end product. 4 Because it owns restaurants and since she likes eating and cooking, she finds it more fun than construction, building. 5 He had trained in bookkeeping, accountancy but he felt he would be very bad at it and was unsuited to working in a bank. He doesn't add that he loves sport but that must have been a factor. 6 Because in any other European country students doing courses similar to the one he completed get degrees. 7 At the time he graduated recruitment of teachers was at a standstill. No jobs were being made available. 8 He has been there since November 1994. 9 A swimming pool and probably new gyms.

Activity 1   Marina: ho studiato, ho fatto, sono stata, sono tornata, ho cominciato, sono stata, sono andata, mi sono trovata, sono andata, mi ha ... introdotto, sono uscita, sono andata, ho lavorato, sono arrivata.

Mario: ho fatto, sono passato, ho fatto, mi sono accorto, ho proseguito, mi sono lanciato, ho cominciato, mi si è presentata, mi sono tuffato, è successo, è iniziata, abbiamo aperto, abbiamo cominciato, (abbiamo) ripreso.

Activity 2 1 andato *gone*; 2 uscito *gone out*; 3 tornato *returned*; 4 lanciato *thrown*; 5 saputo *known*; 6 conosciuto* *known*; 7 capito *understood*; 8 caduto *fallen*

*Note an *i* is needed after the *sc* to indicate you use a <u>sh</u> sound, not a hard <u>k</u>. As in the present, verbs in the second group usually keep the sound throughout.

Activity 3 **Marina:** fatto (fare); stata (stare – note this could be the past participle of **essere** too); introdotto (introdurre)

Mario: fatto (fare); accorto (accorgersi – a reflexive verb); successo (succedere); aperto (aprire); ripreso (riprendere)

Activity 4 The two auxiliary verbs are **avere** and **essere**. Using **avere: Marina:** ho studiato, ho fatto, ho cominciato, mi ha introdotto, ho lavorato, **Mario:** ho fatto (twice), ho proseguito, ho cominciato, abbiamo aperto, abbiamo cominciato, abbiamo ripreso.
Using **essere: Marina:** sono stata (twice), sono tornata, sono andata (three times), mi sono trovata, sono uscita, sono arrivata. **Mario:** sono passato, mi sono accorto, mi sono lanciato, mi si è presentata, mi sono tuffato, è successo, è iniziata.

Comprehension – **Passage 1** 1 In the southern part (zone) of the crater. 2 A fire broke out in the vegetation on the ridge (nearby presumably). 3 It put out the fire. 4 In case they needed to help possible injured tourists. 5 The village, which can be reached only by sea, had been cut off for two days by bad sea conditions.

Passage 2 1 One. 2 15 million lire. 3 Possibly because the man had not covered his face. Had he been wearing a mask he would have been more noticeable! 4 They set up road blocks. But to no avail.

Passage 3 1 In a lift which stalled 1m.70 from the first floor in the Club Med tower at Sestriere. The tower is not used in summer. 2 To collect faxes, presumably from an office in it. He is the caretaker. 3 She felt that he had been missing for too long, she was afraid something had happened to him.

Passage 4 1 The father of the young Tunisian who was arrested in Sicily. 2 Because he had entered Italy clandestinely – and illegally, since he had no permit to stay. 3 He rushed to Rome. 4 The documents needed to prove the young man was his son.

Activity 5

Passage 1: due boati hanno annunciato; che ha provocato; Le fiamme sono state domate ...

Passage 2: l'assalto è avvenuto; un bandito ha fatto irruzione; il rapinatore ha varcato; (il rapinatore) si è diretto; Li ha minacciati; li ha costretti; il colpo è stato messo a segno; nessuno si è accorto; il bandito è riuscito; (i carabinieri) sono accorsi; hanno istituito.

Passage 3: L'hanno trovato; l'ascensore s'è bloccato; lui è rimasto; una barista ha dato.

Passage 4: È arrivato; le forze di polizia lo hanno sorpreso; T.A. Karim, che ha appena compiuto; ha lasciato; i militari ... sono riusciti; il padre che si è precipitato.

The passive form: The other passive was: il colpo è **stato messo** a segno (Passage 2).

Activity 6 (*Possible answers*) 1 (Oh, Maria, sai che cosa?) Ieri ho visto (sono stato/a testimone di) un incidente stradale (automobilistico). Una macchina non si è fermata al semaforo rosso ed è finita dentro un'altra che traversava con il verde. 2 Mi scusi, signorina. Ieri sera ho lasciato il mio portafoglio nel bar dell'albergo. E' stato ritrovato, per caso? 3 Cara Mamma, ieri ho fatto una passeggiata bellissima con Paolo e Marco. Abbiamo preso il sentiero vicino alla stazione di servizio. Siamo saliti per la collina (abbiamo salito la collina) e siamo entrati nei boschi. Abbiamo seguito il sentiero fino a Castiglione. 4 Mario, ho telefonato a Anna ieri sera. Sua madre si è rotta il braccio. E' caduta per strada. Anna mi ha chiesto di salutarti.

Guessable words

Il **bancone** is the word ending in -**one**. It is the word for the kind of counter used in banks and other offices where the staff are separated from the public. It is based on the word **banco** which is also the basis for the word **banca**. Note: some banks are actually called **banco**, e.g. Banco di Napoli, Banco di Santo Spirito. The word **bancone** is in fact more usually used for counter in shops and bars. In a bank, more commonly one talks of **gli sportelli**.

Activity 7

(*Possible answer*) Mi chiamo Arturo Marullo. (Many Italians would say: Marullo, Arturo, putting the family name first.) Sono nato il 6 febbraio 1958. Sono nato a Terni e poi sono andato a fare le scuole medie superiori a Perugia. Ho fatto il liceo scientifico di Perugia. Poi ho fatto l'università, sempre a Perugia. Mi sono laureato in economia e commercio nel 1984. Poi sono andato a lavorare per dei commercianti in vino, i Fratelli Alberti, a Orvieto. Sono stato lì tre anni. Quindi mi sono trasferito a Milano e ho lavorato 7 anni per i Supermercati Gatti. E poi sono entrato nella ditta Pasta Bastoni, come direttore di marketing.

Unit 4

Comprehension 1 1 In a convent, because her parents thought that was the right place for a girl living away from home. 2 Because her husband worked there. 3 Because she had nearly finished and it wasn't advisable. 4 She missed people. She was used to living with others and she was alone. 5 Because they say in Tuscany that it is difficult to be accepted by the Florentines. 6 Her one close friend, who was a fellow-student. 7 No. She gave private lessons and she studied. 8 By cooking

– you remember it is one of her favourite activities – and by cleaning the house, polishing everything. 9 Two, two and a half years. 10 They moved to Arezzo, which happened to be near Angioletta's parents, family and friends, so, although the interview doesn't say so, the unhappy period was over.

Activity 1 1 I moved to the outskirts of Florence where I found great difficulties getting to know/making friends with the neighbours. I had a very good friend who was also at university with me and so I spent/used to spend a lot of time with her. (Apart from the suggestion *I used to spend*, it is difficult to convey in English the underlying sense of the imperfect as used here.) 2 I made/used to make/would make lots to eat. I used to cook a lot (meaning possibly *frequently*, possibly *large quantities of food*, probably both), I liked experimenting ... and I used to clean the house, I was a very careful housewife, I polished/used to polish everything, I even waxed/used to wax the kitchen floor. (Note: this would have been of ceramic tiles which do not need polish!) 3 Annalisa was born in Florence and then we moved when she was six or seven years old.

Activity 2 You should have been able to group the verbs thus:
Group 1: **io** stavo, passavo, lavoravo, studiavo, cucinavo, lucidavo, davo; **tu** lavoravi; **lui/lei** stava, lavorava; **loro** si sentivano.
Group 2: **io** avevo, facevo; piaceva.
Group 3: **io** soffrivo, pulivo.
And you will have found: **ero** and **era**. You will have quickly spotted that each of the three types of verbs has its characteristic vowel throughout the imperfect and, that apart, the endings for all verbs are the same.
You found the 1st, 2nd and 3rd person singular and the 3rd person plural in the text. You may well have felt confident enough to deduce the following:
Group 2: (tu) avevi, facevi; (lui/lei) aveva, faceva; (loro) avevano, facevano. Group 3: (tu) soffrivi; pulivi; (lui/lei) soffriva, puliva; (loro) soffrivano, pulivano.
More than that by yourself you can't really do. For ease of reference the form is given in the text. (Note: in the above answer we treated **dare** and **stare** as regular verbs since they behave regularly in the imperfect.) For **fare**, see text.

Comprehension 2 1 They were peasant farmers (**contadini**). 2 They wanted to do better than their parents, get out of their agricultural background (**emergere**). 3 They set up a small business, probably a shop. It was a great struggle and things were very tight (financially) but they were hard workers. 4 He went to school in Asti. It meant travelling 15–20 km daily by bus. 5 He (and his friends) went birdnesting, they fished in the rivers for eels, he learned to swim in streams, he went collecting truffles.

Activity 3 Passato prossimo: Sono nato; hanno cominciato; hanno permesso; mi sono formato; ho imparato. If you reflect, you will realize all these are 'one-off' events; and they are (long) finished.

Imperfetto: *describing*: erano figli di contadini; era gente; Quelli erano praticamente; *habitual, repeated actions*: Si andava ad Asti; si tornava la sera; si andava per nidi; si andava a pescare (*twice*); Si andava per tartufi; *background*: cercavano di emergere; c'era sempre un vecchio che conosceva.

You can argue about the way the imperfects are classified, but the point of view, the aspect of the action which the speaker has in mind, is different from that in the **passato prossimo** verbs, which definitely view actions as past and completed.

Comprehension 3
1 He used to say his mother was the enemy. His father decided to send him away to school. 2 That people wouldn't give them food. 3 She went to milk a ewe to get milk for her children and she was fired at. 4 No, she was very young (born at the end of 1940, Unit 2, Interview 2).

Activity 4

Passato prossimo: mio papà l'ha dovuto (meaning not just *he had to*, but viewing the necessity as a finished action – he had to do it once – and did it); sono venuti fuori; Hanno perso, han perso (Gabriella uses **perso; perduto** is also possible); si è alzata; è andata; hanno sparato (notice this series of verbs is preceded by **una volta** – Gabriella's mother did this once); ha sempre girato; abbiamo sempre visto (here you might almost have expected an imperfect, seeing **sempre** and knowing it meant the action was repeated. But those times are over, Gabriella is seeing the actions as finished).

Imperfetto: *describing*: era (molto piccolino); era il nemico; mamma era; *habitual, repeated actions*: diceva; scappavano; (perhaps) eravamo sfollati; voleva darci da mangiare; *background*: mio fratello ... non voleva, temeva.
Other verbs: ricordo (present); dicesse (imperfect subjunctive – we'll come to that later); possa (present subjunctive – we'll come to that later too).

Activity 5
1 splendeva; 2 sono tornate; 3 hanno deciso; 4 era; 5 combattevano; 6 sapevano; 7 dovevano; 8 erano; 9 pascolavano; 10 giocavano; 11 hanno sentito; 12 si sono buttate; 13 sono arrivati; 14 avevano; 15 volevano; 16 ha detto; 17 sparavano; 18 sparavano; 19 erano; 20 hanno preso; 21 è finita; 22 sono andati; 23 era; 24 sono uscite; 25 erano; 26 sono tornate; 27 hanno deciso

Here is a part translation to help you grasp the meaning: *It was a lovely spring day. The sun was shining. The three little girls came home from school and decided to take the geese to graze on the other side of the river. The other bank of the river was dangerous. Often the partisans used to fight the German army there. The three little girls knew that they ought not to go there but they were curious about it. While the geese were grazing the three girls played in the meadow. Suddenly the three girls heard gunshots. They threw themselves into a ditch with the geese. Shortly afterwards the partisans arrived.*

Comprehension 4 1 How well educated her mother was. (Note: istruito *educated*; educato *well-behaved*; maleducato *rude*. Educazione refers to *behaviour, upbringing*. Note also il **Ministero dell'Istruzione, dell'Università e della Ricerca**.) 2 What high standards her mother adhered to in her personal life, dress, habits etc. 3 She liked to have a cigarette and a coffee and do crosswords. 4 Very much the same as her own: they had all to be dressed and come to breakfast together even if they had no reason to be up and about. No lying in bed! 5 Once she had organized the supper, at about 4.30 p.m., she used to wash and change as though getting ready to go out. 6 She appears to have been a person with high standards, devoted to her family, always finding time to attend to their needs and to be with them.

Activity 6 In this interview there are very few perfects: **Mi sono accorta quando mamma è mancata** *I realized when mother passed away* – both events, completed. **Quando poi sono andata in Inghilterra mi sono accorta.** Another completed event: Gabriella went to England and there she realized … Otherwise the imperfect is used, since every verb is expressing either a repeated action, or describing or filling in background. Except in a case dealt with next: the pluperfect.

Activity 7 You are right to say that the **trapassato** is formed using the imperfect of **avere** (**avevo, avevi, aveva, avevamo, avevate, avevano**) and the past participle of the verb, on the same lines as the perfect. It expresses one stage back in time, rather as in English *he had finished*. Question: If this is the case, what do you think might happen in the pluperfect to verbs which use **essere** to form the perfect? Answer: They use the imperfect of **essere** (**ero, eri, era, eravamo, eravate, erano**) plus the past participle.

Activity 8 You need not change any of the verbs which were in the imperfect in Activity 5. So that leaves: 2 erano tornate; 3 avevano deciso; 11 avevano sentito; 12 si erano buttate; 13 erano arrivati; 16 aveva detto; 20 avevano preso; 21 era finita; 22 erano andati; 24 erano uscite; 26 erano tornate; 27 avevano deciso

Here is a partial translation to help you understand the way we have changed the text. *It was a lovely spring day. The sun was shining. The three little girls had come home from school and had decided to take the geese to graze on the other side of the river. … Suddenly the three girls had heard gunshots. They had thrown themselves into a ditch with the geese. Shortly afterwards the partisans had arrived.*

Activity 9 1 era; 2 piacevano (remember how **piacere** works); 3 scherzava; 4 organizzava; 5 piaceva; 6 portava; 7 avevamo (subject: **noi**); 8 uscivamo; 9 ho mai capito (yes, that is the perfect – it was understanding that Gabriella has never achieved. If you like, an event which has not happened! However, if you suggested a future (capirò), that is also acceptable); 10 si dedicava; 11 facevamo; 12 piaceva; 13 era; 14 aiutavano; 15 faceva; 16 piaceva; 17 piaceva.

Activity 10 1 tornavo; ho visto/veduto. 2 abitava; vedevamo; l'abbiamo incontrato. Usciva. 3 era; l'abbiamo ristrutturata; avevano; l'abbiamo trasformata. 4 cucinavano; riuscivano (subject: piatti)

Activity 11 1 John stava finendo una lettera. 2 Il treno stava entrando nella stazione. 3 Papà stava leggendo il giornale. 4 Mamma stava facendo la doccia.

Comprehension 5 1 She obviously missed the city she had left behind; and all it offered, particularly books, friends, and the many and varied happenings of city life. 2 The house seems to have been small. The housing stock of a small village in the Abruzzo is likely to have been limited. But it may have been that only one room was heated and this is why they all crowded into it. 3 The eagle was painted on the ceiling of the main room and for her it came to symbolize her exile. 4 The women wore black shawls and had red faces. The black was typical of villages since mourning was taken seriously and lasted some time. The red faces occurred presumably because of the cold. 5 They consulted him about the best time to have teeth extracted, about subsidies available from the local authority and about various taxes. In other words about anything they did not understand.

Unit 5

Comprehension 1 1 There are 15 at present and a 16th is about to be opened in Rome. 2 Marina mentions that there are two other establishments of a different sort but she doesn't say what they are and doesn't consider them part of the core business. 3 The self-service restaurants it runs are a little more luxurious than self-service restaurants usually are, in the surroundings they offer as well as the quality of the food. 4 The costs of setting up one of the restaurants are very high, as are the running costs and therefore they need to be sited so as to have what she calls 'a certain level' of business. In other words they need to generate a high turnover. 5 So far she has opened one or one and a half a year and that seems to her about right. 6 No, she feels the formula works quite well. 7 One is that the head office of the company is near Venice and she lives in Milan. She has a small office in Milan but needs to spend at least a couple of days each week in the head office. And secondly, she spends a lot of time going to see possible sites for new restaurants, scattered throughout Italy and occasionally abroad. 8 Looking at possible sites for new restaurants.

Activity 1 You will probably have found the vocabulary very guessable. Did you list the following, or most of them? (The English expression Marina used is *core business*.)

una società	*company*
gestire (*NB like*: capire)	*manage*
una catena	*a chain* (literal or figurative)
un locale	*premises*
il filone principale	*the core business* (filone: lit. (*coarse*) *thread*)
il prodotto	*the product*
allestimento	*the fitting out* (This word refers to the preparation for a performance, a party, a meal. It can be used for the fitting out of a ship.)
arredo	*furnishings*
formula	*a formula*
funzionare	*to work* (in the sense of *to function*)
un investimento	*an investment*
un costo	*a cost*
gestione (f) (*cf.* gestire)	*management*
garantire (*also like*: capire)	*to guarantee*
livello	*level*
attività	*activity, business*
originare	*to generate*
prestarsi	*to lend itself*
uno sviluppo a tappeto	*blanket development (blanket coverage)*
espandersi	*to expand*
sede (f) (linked to: sedere – to sit)	*head office*
amministratore delegato	*managing director*
strategico (cf. strategia (n))	*strategic*
aspetto	*aspect*
operativo	*related to the day-to-day running*
ricerca	here *search*; can mean *research*
controparte (f)	*counterpart*
verifica (cf. verificare)	*check, inspection (verification)*
insediamento (cf. sede)	*siting*

You may have picked out fewer or more words, depending really on where you see the world of business beginning and ending! But you must agree that, with a little thought, many of these words are guessable. Can you see also the value of making links between, say, nouns and verbs (**gestione, gestire**) and a word and its root (**insediamento** from **sede; la Santa Sede** is, incidentally, the *Holy See*). When guessing meanings, a very literal approach helps. For instance, you remember that **-one** is a suffix indicating that something or someone is large. **Un filo** is a thread, **un filone** might be the main strand.

Activity 2 Nouns: the corresponding verbs are: produrre (pp prodotto); allestire; costare; livellare; sviluppare; amministrare; ricercare; insediare.

Verbs: the corresponding nouns are: garanzia; fondazione (f); istituzione (f); prestito; espansione (f); investimento; verifica; valutazione (f).

(Note that most nouns ending in -ione are feminine. Note also that the importance of this exercise was less in getting it right than in thinking about the connections between words, so that your stock becomes ever larger.)

Activity 3 1 Ci stiamo espandendo. *We are expanding*, underlining that it is a process happening even now! 2a quello che prepariamo **da** mangiare (*what we prepare to eat, the food we prepare*); 2b un certo livello di attività che è difficile **da** originare (*a certain level of business which is difficult to generate*). 3 Beh, insomma, cioè, comunque, quindi.

Activity 4 1 una volta alla settimana; 2 tre volte al giorno; 3 due volte al mese.

Activity 5 We don't know what your answers were, but here are some recommendations: Bisognerebbe camminare almeno trenta minuti tutti i giorni, per esempio andare o tornare dal lavoro a piedi. Bisognerebbe praticare uno sport almeno una volta alla settimana. Bisognerebbe andare a dormire prima di mezzanotte tutti i giorni lavorativi, quindi almeno cinque volte alla settimana. Bisognerebbe mangiare frutta e/o verdura fresca almeno tre volte al giorno. Bisognerebbe fare una lunga e rilassante passeggiata una volta alla settimana.

Activity 6 1 Tra un anno (dodici mesi); 2 Tra un mese (tre/quattro settimane); 3 tra nove mesi; tra solo cinque/sei mesi (note: **Fra** is also correct)

Activity 7 You are free to write the postcard as you like, picking the places and sights that interest you most. The important point is that you use: **in** Veneto, Lombardia and Emilia Romagna; and **a** Venezia, Verona, Padova, Parma, Ferrara, Cremona, Milano, Mantova and any other town you mention. Use **a** also for the islands of Murano and Burano – they are small. If you were to go to a large island you would say: **in Sicilia, in Sardegna**. Here is a possible text:

Cari Anna e Andrea, Sono appena tornata da un viaggio bellissimo. Sono andata a Venezia in aereo e lì ho raggiunto una motonave che poi ci ha portati a fare una crociera lungo il Po. In Veneto, a Venezia, Padova e Verona abbiamo potuto fare visite guidate, molto interessanti. A Verona abbiamo anche visto l'Aida di Verdi all'Arena – magnifica! Poi abbiamo raggiunto la Lombardia dove siamo andati a vedere Mantova. Dopo, abbiamo potuto visitare Parma in Emilia Romagna e la crociera è finita a Cremona in Lombardia, da dove siamo andati in treno a Milano – poi ritorno a casa. Tanti cari saluti.

Activity 8   1 Non lo so ... credo una trentina. 2 Non lo so ... credo una cinquantina. 3 Non ne sono sicuro/a ... forse una trentina di milioni. 4 Non ne sono sicuro/a ... forse una decina di milioni. 5 Mah ... mi sembra un paio. 6 Mah ... mi sembra una quindicina. 7 Almeno un migliaio. 8 Almeno un centinaio. (Note: an Italian might also say 7 **mille**; 8 **cento**. It is not unusual to use both **cento** and **mille** when in English we might say: *hundreds, thousands*. The context will make it clear.)

Activity 9   Il cantante d'opera è la persona che canta l'opera nei teatri. Lo scrittore è la persona che scrive libri. L'amministratore delegato è la persona che amministra l'azienda. Il cuoco è la persona che cucina i pasti in un ristorante. Il controllore è la persona che controlla i biglietti sul treno. Il calciatore è la persona che gioca in una squadra di calcio. Il dentista è la persona che cura i denti dei suoi pazienti.

Activity 10   1 Manda un fax alla dottoressa Paolini **da cui** devo sapere se i lavori procedono regolarmente a Torino. 2 Telefona all'Avvocato Franceschi **con cui** devo discutere riguardo al nuovo contratto per il Brek di Monaco. 3 Scrivi una lettera di sollecito al Ragionier Barbato **da cui** devo ricevere i preventivi per i lavori al Brek di Vicenza entro la fine del mese. 4 Telefona all'Architetto Cappelli **cui/a cui** devo restituire i disegni e i progetti per il Brek di Roma con le correzioni al più presto.

Activity 11   Chi tardi arriva male alloggia. (Lit. *the person who arrives late gets the worst place, worst bed*. Obviously going back to days when late arrival in a town might mean there was nowhere left to sleep. It is often used to chide any lateness.)

Chi va all'osto perde il posto. (The Italians asked did not know what osto meant although they knew and used the saying. Children use it meaning: *If you give up your place, you can't expect to have it back when you come back*. It derives from **hostis**, the Latin word for enemy. So the idea is: *if you go and fraternize with the enemy, you can't expect a warm welcome on your return!*)

Chi va piano va sano e va lontano. (*The person who proceeds slowly, travels safely and goes a long way*. If you do things slowly and calmly, you'll get a lot done and done well.)

Chi la fa l'aspetti. (*Those who do harm to others should expect others to harm them*.)

Chi va al mulino s'infarina. (*You can't go to the mill without getting flour on you*. In other words, you can't undertake certain activities without them leaving their trace – often meaning a moral or character trace.)

Chi semina vento raccoglie tempesta. (*If you sow wind, you reap storms*. In other words, if you create negative situations, you'll get the consequences.) Chi la dura la vince. (*The person who keeps to his plans and pursues them with determination succeeds*.)

Chi di spada ferisce di spada perisce. (*The person who injures with a sword, will die by the sword*. If you hurt others, you can expect them to do the same to you. The meaning is really the same as: Chi la fa l'aspetti.)

Activity 12   1 Quella che indossa una minigonna è mia sorella, Anna. 2 Quella che indossa un vestito a fiori è la mamma (è Mamma). 3 Quello che fuma la pipa è Papà. 4 Quello che porta gli occhiali è mio cugino, Fausto. 5 Quello con i capelli lunghi è Antonio, il ragazzo di Anna.

Activity 13   1 quello che; 2 che; 3 cui; 4 che; 5 che; 6 quello che (ciò che); 7 alla quale (a cui); 8 chi; 9 quello che (ciò che); 10 quello che (ciò che); 11 dove (in cui); 12 che.

Activity 14   1 Il nostro gruppo garantisce sia cibo di ottima qualità sia un ambiente elegante. 2 offre sia servizio veloce sia salette da pranzo tranquille e silenziose. 3 ha sia costi di gestione alti sia investimenti alti. 4 vuole espandersi sia nel Nord Italia sia nel Centro-Sud.

Activity 15   1 La società gestisce dei ristoranti/ una (piccola) catena di ristoranti. 2 Ci sono 15 ristoranti. 3 Sono dei ristoranti self-service. 4 Cercano di offrire di più di un self-service classico. Cercano di offrire un ambiente un po' più di lusso, curato, e un menù un po' migliore. 5 I ristoranti hanno dei costi piuttosto alti sia di investimenti sia di gestione. Dunque, funzionano solo se garantiscono un certo livello di attività. 6 Il primo ristorante è stato aperto a Trieste. 7 Marina abita a Milano, perché suo marito è lì, ma la sede del Brek è nel Veneto. Lei ha un piccolo ufficio a Milano, ma deve andare in sede ogni settimana. 8 Si occupa soprattutto della gestione strategica della società, dello sviluppo. 9 Perché deve andare a studiare ogni possibilità ma è difficile trovare un posto adatto, che garantisca il livello di attività necessaria. A possible summary might be: Marina è amministratore delegato di una società che si chiama Ristoranti Brek. La società gestisce una catena di ristoranti self-service, un po' più di lusso del self-service classico sia nell'arredo sia in quello che offrono da mangiare. I costi di investimento e di gestione sono piuttosto alti per cui ogni ristorante deve garantire un certo livello di attività. Il primo ristorante è stato aperto a Trieste ma la sede del gruppo è vicino a Venezia. Marina abita con il marito a Milano dove ha un piccolo ufficio ma fa la pendolare tra Milano e il Veneto dove ogni settimana deve andare in sede. Si occupa soprattutto della gestione strategica e passa molto tempo a visitare posizioni possibili per nuovi ristoranti Brek.

Comprehension 2   1 Five including her. 2 Because she is not being paid the salary which should go with her job. 3 No, there is another but she is much older and has a high level qualification (which, by implication, it seems Emanuela does not have). 4 No, in both cases. (a) She says there are three other young people, all men, in her situation, doing the job of bank manager and not paid the correct salary. (b) She doesn't feel the banks discriminate provided the women in question are prepared to give the commitment required, which seems to be hours beyond the normal working day. 5 They expect a bank manager to be old, grey and male.

Activity 16   1 Emanuela works in a bank. She has a position of some responsibility and she would expect to receive a fairly high salary.

In fact her salary is rather low. 2 The reason for this state of things is that she has only recently been promoted to this level and so at the moment she is not yet paid as the law provides. In the future, however, she will be paid more. 3 As regards her credibility, as a woman, with male customers, Emanuela thinks that the current position of working women in Italy is better than in the past and she doesn't feel she has been the object of discrimination. 4 Nevertheless, in spite of the fact that Emanuela is optimistic on this count, sex discrimination in the work place is actually a live issue. Moreover, she herself says that many men who come into her bank are amazed to find a woman manager. (You will notice from the above that translation can be tricky! We have tried not to distort the English and yet render the flavour of the Italian.)

Activity 17   1 Group 1 verbs have an -i- in the ending of the 1st, 2nd, 3rd person singular and the 3rd person plural, all the other verbs have -a-. Irregular verbs also have -a, as you will see. 2 The **noi** form. This is true of <u>all</u> verbs. 3 Because the forms for 1st, 2nd and 3rd person singular are identical and therefore the pronoun is often needed to avoid ambiguity. 4 **Noi** and **voi**.

Activity 18

potere: possa, possa, possa, possiamo, possiate, possano
sapere: sappia, sappia, sappia, sappiamo, sappiate, sappiano
tenere: tenga, tenga, tenga, teniamo, teniate, tengano
volere: voglia, voglia, voglia, vogliamo, vogliate, vogliano
uscire: esca, esca, esca, usciamo, usciate, escano
dovere: debba, debba, debba, dobbiamo, dobbiate, debbano
produrre: produca, produca, produca, produciamo, produciate, producano
piacere: piaccia, piaccia, piaccia, piacciamo, piacciate, piacciano

Activity 19   1 sia; 2 è (it is a fact); 3 dimostra (we are referring to Marta specifically, not to a type of person in general); 4 abbia (here we are describing the type of person who is needed); 5 sia; 6 è; 7 abbia; 8 dice; 9 faccia (you might possibly feel it should be plural because the idea is plural – facciano); 10 voglia.

Activity 20   1 Mi hanno detto che questa direttrice ha (indicative: **dire che** does not imply doubt) ... 2 Credo che le donne siano ... 3 Però so anche che ad alti livelli le donne non ricevono ... 4 Ho paura che una donna non abbia abbastanza ...; 5 Spero che non sia vero ma temo che un direttore donna non garantisca ...

Activity 21   1 è; 2 sia; 3 sappia; 4 sa; 5 garantisca; 6 garantisce.

Activity 22   1 Non sono d'accordo! Penso che funzioni benissimo, che faccia caldo in inverno e che sia fresco in estate. 2 Non sono d'accordo! Penso che dia sempre ascolto alle nostre richieste. Penso che faccia attenzione ai problemi di tutti. 3 Non sono d'accordo! Penso che loro sappiano fare il loro lavoro. Penso che vengano a chiedere aiuto per imparare. 4 Non sono d'accordo! Non penso che debbano lavorare di più. Penso che tengano gli uffici molto puliti e che escano all'ora prevista dal loro contratto di lavoro.

Comprehension 3 1 25 years; 30 people. 2 She had no training at all in anything but what she enjoyed most was sewing, making clothes. 3 Firstly although she was still young she was no longer a girl, in other words, she was older that the usual students; secondly she didn't want any diplomas, she wanted to understand the techniques, rather than practise doing each until she was expert at it. She wanted an understanding of the whole process rather than a high level of skill in performing any one technique. 4 She made some model clothes and then telephoned round all her friend to say she was in business. 5 She found dressmaking for individual customers too personal, she didn't like it and wanted to produce in quantity. 6 That her first two employees are still with her, in her twenty-fifth year. 7 She had planned to make high quality ready-to-wear but has found it impossible to compete with the famous name designer labels, even though her garments were less expensive, better quality fabric, etc. People want the name, the designer label.

Activity 23 1 La nostra nicchia è andata **esaurendo**si; 2 **Fatto** questo tipo di scuola; 3 ho detto alla mie amiche che io **avevo aperto** ... una sartoria; 4 ho detto alla direttrice che **avrei** seguito i suoi corsi ... non **avrei** proseguito per settimane a fare gonne, **sarei** passata all'altra aula.

Activity 24 1 Le stoffe stanno/vanno rincarando. 2 La concorrenza sta/va crescendo. 3 Il mercato (si) sta/va saturando/saturandosi. 4 Il campo della moda sta/va cambiando. 5 La produzione sta/va rallentando. 6 Le grandi firme stanno/vanno invadendo il mercato del prêt-à-porter. 7 I guadagni stanno/vanno diminuendo. 8 La situazione sta/va peggiorando. (Note: You can use either **stare** or **andare**. **Stare** indicates that the action is going on. **Andare** underlines that it is a gradual process. In English you might use the continuous tense + *gradually* or *continually*.)

Activity 25 1 Una volta prese le misure, disegna il modello della gonna su carta. 2 Una volta disegnato il modello, riporta il modello / riportalo su stoffa. 3 Una volta riportato il modello su stoffa, taglia la stoffa. 4 Una volta tagliata la stoffa, cuci la gonna a mano. 5 Una volta cucita / imbastita la gonna a mano, indossala per controllare che vada bene. 6 Una volta controllata, cuci la gonna a macchina. 7 Una volta cucita a macchina stirala.

Activity 26 Ho chiesto al rappresentante per quando **avrebbe voluto** il prodotto finito. Io gli ho fatto notare che in quel caso noi **avremmo avuto bisogno** (1) della stoffa in maggio, che **avremmo dovuto cominciare** (2) a lavorarla entro fine maggio. Gli ho detto che rispettando queste date, **avremmo potuto garantire** (3) un primo lotto di capi finiti per fine luglio e che **saremmo stati in grado** (4) di consegnare il resto entro metà agosto. Per le consegne il rappresentante ha detto che **si sarebbero rivolti** (5) sempre allo stesso corriere, così noi **avremmo dovuto risolvere** (6) solo i problemi logistici. Gli ho spiegato che **sarebbe stato** (7) più pratico dare al corriere il numero di telefono del magazzino così il responsabile del magazzino **si sarebbe occupato** (8) di tutto.

Unit 6

Comprehension 1 1 Because competition is becoming fiercer as European banks start operating in Italy; the introduction of the Euro means many changes; and Italian banks will have to modernise their practices. All this will mean hard work for the staff. 2 Because she works hard, she knows she is appreciated and salary is the way value is measured for an employee. Professionally, she wants the salary due to her level. Personally, she wants it to provide her daughter with an easier future (easier, she means, than her own life), with a lovely house etc.

Activity 1 In the first person plural form, where the only difference between the two tenses is that the future has one **m** and the conditional a double **m**:

Future: capiremo *we shall understand*; saremo *we shall be*; potremo *we shall be able to.*

Conditional: capiremmo *we should understand*; saremmo *we should be*; potremmo *we should be able to.*

Activity 2 1 saranno; 2 modernizzerà; 3 Introdurrà; 4 Stabilirà; 5 lascerà; 6 riuscirà; 7 riceverà; 8 piacerà; 9 mancherà.

Note that with **lasciare** the -i- after sc is no longer necessary to indicate the soft sound in lascerò, etc. Similarly, in **mancare** the h after the c is necessary to indicate the hard c in mancherò etc. This applies to all verbs of this sort in Group 1 when forming the future.

A Of course, with a new managing director, there will be changes.

B Yes. We already know he will modernize the management system. He will introduce a system of targets to achieve. He will set his targets with each director and then he will leave him a wide freedom for decision-making. If the director is successful, he will get a bonus at the end of the year. If not …

A Of course this will please some but others will miss the present structure.

Activity 3 1 A Strano, c'è una luce da Gianni. (Lui) è andato negli Stati Uniti. B Sarà tornato. A Non penso. Saranno dei ladri. 2 A Guarda. Non è Pietro in quella Mercedes al semaforo? B Sì. Avrà vinto la lotteria. A Oppure sarà la macchina dello zio americano. E' in Italia in questo momento.

Activity 4 You should have found: 1 anni in **cui** dovranno cambiare tantissime cose. 2 lo stupido parametro con **cui** misuriamo il nostro valore.

Comprehension 2 1 There are two, possibly related, areas. One is the legal situation, with numerous often unclear, regulations, requirements for permits etc. The other is employment practices in the restaurant business which make it difficult for Brek to compete for staff and which add to the high costs of running the company. 2 According to Marina, most operators in the restaurant and bar business are small family enterprises and their management practices are not good: they pay staff cash in hand, thus avoiding the considerable costs due to the Italian state in taxes and social security payments, they fail to issue receipts, thus avoiding VAT and other taxes. They also tend to pay high wages, probably to tempt staff to accept the illegal deal. Brek finds it difficult to compete since they are doing things legally and, because of the costs involved, they cannot pay the same wage level. 3 The business is a family one and Marina sometimes finds it difficult to be working with family members with whom she has a relationship which is not primarily professional.

Activity 5 We hope you picked out 'tipicamente il bar e la trattoria **sono gestiti** a livello familiare; il personale che lavora nel settore è **abituato*** ad **essere pagato** in nero e **essere pagato** con delle cifre molto alte ...' *You may think this is just the verb **essere** + adjective; this is an acceptable analysis. Past participles are used as adjectives. We included it because the passive analysis is also possible.

Activity 6 1 Il padre del giovane è stato rintracciato da volontari. 2 Il problema di Emanuela è stato risolto dalla banca. 3 Il livello del suo lavoro è stato cambiato e il suo stipendio è stato aumentato di conseguenza. 4 Un incendio nei boschi è stato provocato da un'eruzione dello Stromboli. 5 La frazione Ginostra è stata isolata per due giorni dalle cattive condizioni del mare.

Do you think you understand the passive better? You are likely to choose the passive when the person or thing mentioned first in the above sentences (i.e. the subject) is what you want to emphasize. You would choose the active, as in the original sentences, if you consider the subject of those (the agent above) is the important item. For instance in number 1, it will depend on whether you consider it important that someone has managed to find the young man's father; or alternatively that the father was found by volunteers rather than by professionals. You will have recognized some of the items as being related to the reading passages in Unit 3, Session 4. If you read all five again, you will find they contain a number of passives – which we are sure did not bother you at the time!

Activity 7 1 Allora va isolato al più presto. *Then he must be isolated as soon as possible.* 2 Allora va liberato al più presto. *Then he must be freed as soon as possible.* 3 Allora va firmato al più presto. *Then it must be signed as soon as possible.* 4 Allora va dato al più presto. *Then it must be given as soon as possible.*

Activity 8 There are several examples of **che** as a relative pronoun: leggi poco chiare **che** vanno ... interpretate; operatori **che** sono ... molto piccoli; il bar e la trattoria .... **che** tendono a ignorare ...; il personale **che** lavora ...; i costi per l'azienda **che** sono molto alti ...; un intreccio di rapporti personali e professionali del lavoro **che** può essere ...; il rispetto **che** avrei se fossi ... Towards the end of the interview you should have found: persone ... con **cui** c'è un rapporto personale; un'estranea con **cui** c'è un rapporto ...

You can see in this interview that **che** is singular or plural, it can refer to people, objects or concepts and also that not every **che** is a relative pronoun: for instance, nel senso **che**; è evidente **che** ... .

Comprehension 3 1 The fashion house delivers to her the jacket – possibly a sample garment – the roll of fabric, the roll of paper patterns, the threads and the buttons. Her workers have 100 minutes to transform this into a jacket, on a coat-hanger, wrapped and ready for despatch. This would seem to imply that the price her firm is paid for their work allows 100 minutes of labour input, no more. 2 The craftsman's skill. They want her to perform like a factory (**l'industria**) but they still expect high craftsmanship in the finished product (**il risultato dell'artigiano**). 3 The customers have less money to spend but they want the designer clothes which are constantly promoted in advertising, newspaper articles etc. So the firms bring their prices down, to the detriment of the quality of the fabric and of the tailoring (**confezione**). 4 The customers get their designer label garments but they no longer have the value that the designer label once had, since the garments are no longer made as they ought to be. 5 High fashion, haute couture: **l'alta moda**. Presumably those who can afford to buy at this price scarcely need to look at the label!

Activity 9 You will find two passives with **essere**: **saranno sollecitati**; **come dovrebbe essere fatto** *as it ought to be made*. In the second case Signora Torrielli could have said **andrebbe fatto**, but it probably doesn't express sufficiently strongly the contrast she wants to make.

You will also find a number of passives made not with **essere**, nor indeed **andare**, but with **venire**: **non viene più pagata l'idea, non viene pagato più niente, ma viene solo pagato il minuto/lavoro** *the idea is no longer paid for, nothing is paid for any more, but the only thing that is paid for is the 'working minute'*; **non ci vengono più riconosciute le nostre ... bravure** *our exceptional skills are no longer recognized*; **il capo non viene più fatto** *the garment is no longer made*. Turn back to Unit 6 for an explanation.

Activity 10 1 Ecco il caffè. È caldo. Va bevuto subito. 2 La situazione è difficile. Va detto che John è una persona testarda. 3 Di solito in Italia i pasti sono/vengono accompagnati dal vino. 4 La lunga giornata lavorativa è/viene riconosciuta nella nostra remunerazione. 5 Il nostro lavoro è stimato. 6 Il prezzo va aumentato.

Activity 11 1 Future: tutti **avranno** sempre meno soldi, **potranno** sempre spendere meno, però **saranno** sempre più **sollecitati** (a passive in the future); quelle firme ... **continueranno** a discapito della qualità; la gente, sì, **metterà** un capo firmato ma non **avrà** più il valore ... 2 Present subjunctive: non vedo quale **possa** essere la soluzione. 3 Impersonal si: **si pretende** da noi l'industria; Non **si può**; Se **si parla** di (twice).

Comprehension 4 1 Most levels really, although she specifically mentions the girls who model the clothes and the photographic services which produce the publicity photos. But she says the only place savings can really be made is in the production of the garment itself and in the quality of the fabric. 2 From 'emerging markets' (third-world countries or countries of the former Soviet bloc) which she says don't at the moment produce good work, but very soon will. 3 Moving their production abroad. 4 They have closed, gone out of business. 5 Problems with the trades unions, legal requirements, and the USSL. These would include contracts, health and safety at work legislation, the level of social security payments employers have to make (cf. Marina) and possibly other constraints. 6 She is indeed proud of the business she has created but she no longer derives satisfaction from the work. The word **gratificata** implies the satisfaction bringing peace of mind, professional satisfaction. She is not happy that she is able to produce the quality of work she considers her hallmark within the constraints she now works with. 7 She has difficulty finding staff. The job demands concentration and she implies women may prefer to work in a situation where they just press buttons and don't have to think. She also feels that there is no longer the relationship between employer and employee which there used to be. Working hours are strictly adhered to whereas years ago, we understand, staff would be willing to do a little extra if they were behind on a contract.

Activity 12 1 Relatives pronouns:...una cosa <u>che</u> è in escalation; dell'ultimo che è <u>quello che</u> produce; a discapito dell'ultimo <u>che</u> mette insieme il capo; <u>che</u> è <u>quello che</u> non può difendersi; i mercati emergenti <u>che</u> producono ... ma <u>che</u> produrranno ...; <u>Tutti quelli che</u> hanno potuto; <u>tutti quelli che</u> avevano la potenza; Difficilissimo ... trovare ragazze <u>che</u> hanno voglia di fare questo lavoro; non è una fabbrica <u>dove</u> uno schiaccia un bottone; i contratti <u>che</u> hanno i dipendenti; è solo sull'ultimo gradino <u>che</u> è la produzione; quindi <u>chi</u> vede quello crede ...

2 Subjunctive: **credo che a Torino nel giro di quest'anno <u>abbiano chiuso</u> cinque o sei laboratori** (this is a perfect subjunctive: five or six factories have closed. But the reason for the subjunctive rather than the indicative is **credo che**. Signora Torriellli is not sure, she does not want to be categorical); **non è che la gente <u>capisca</u> la differenza** (the subjunctive here is required by the negative impersonal expression, again casting doubt); **chi vede quello crede che <u>sia</u> già stato fatto tutto dentro quel marchio** (in fact, this is passive, and a perfect subjunctive again. *Those who see this believe that everything has been made inside that company* – i.e. the company whose label is on the garment). Note the contrast with what follows: è **stato fatto tutto** – here Signora Torrielli is giving as fact that everything has been done (to save money for the profits of the company) not saying it is someone's belief – note it is another passive. Did you perhaps wonder why there was no subjunctive in the sentence **Difficilissimo già trovare ragazze che hanno voglia di fare questo lavoro?** You might say: this is a 'type' of girl, shouldn't it be subjunctive? Possibly another speaker would have used the subjunctive. An example of the dying subjunctive almost certainly.

3 Passive: we have already pointed out two passives in Activity 9. A third: le loro linee più basse <u>sono</u> già <u>state portate</u> ... fuori Italia a fare.

4 Future: i mercati emergenti ... che <u>produrranno</u>; <u>perderà</u> ; le persone <u>perderanno</u> i posti perché non ci <u>sarà</u> più il mercato.

Comprehension 5   1 (Sa) che il suo mestiere è quello di scrivere. 2 (Dice di non sapere nulla) sul valore di quello che può scrivere/di quello che scrive. 3 (Si sente) straordinariamente a suo agio. 4 Degli strumenti che le sono noti e familiari. 5 Soffre e si chiede di continuo come gli altri facciano queste cose. 6 Dice che può scrivere soltanto delle storie. 7 A scrivere articoli per un giornale, ma solo un po'. Fa fatica a farlo. 8 (a) si sente in esilio. (b) si sente come uno che è in patria. 9 Dice che farà questo mestiere fino alla morte, che è molto contenta di questo mestiere e che non lo cambierebbe per niente al mondo.

Unit 7

Comprehension 1   1 Firstly, Marina's choice of the verb **arrangiarsi**, with its implications of the solutions not being ideal, but the best one can do in the circumstances. Then the fact that although her husband is good at running the household, he's not pleased to have to do it. 2 Yes. She thinks they are making progress, changing – and in the last resort, as she says at the end, they simply have to get involved in the domestic arrangements if their wife is working, 'non c'è scelta'. As you probably thought when we mentioned stereotypes, many men of earlier generations did nothing in the house, indeed would have thought it demeaning. 3 His parents were separated so that he had quite a tough upbringing and had to look after himself at home more than is usual. He didn't have a mother to do everything for him. 4 The stereotype Italian **mamma** thinks for her children, takes care of everything for them, particularly perhaps for her sons.

Activity 1   (1) continua a; (2) prova a; (3) si accorge di; (4) si rifiuta di; (5) è abituato a; (6) farei finta di; (7) sarei contenta di; (8) comincerà a; (9) sono stufa di.

Activity 2   1 Martedì mattina avevo intenzione di comperare un regalo per il compleanno di mia figlia ma non sono riuscito a trovarlo. Ho dimenticato (avevo dimenticato) di chiedere a mia moglie in che negozio lo vendevano. 2 Mercoledì sera avevo intenzione di andare allo stadio con gli amici per vedere insieme la partita di calcio ma non sono riuscito a organizzare la serata. Mi sono dimenticato di comperare i biglietti. 3 Giovedì mattina avevo intenzione di andare alla Posta per pagare la bolletta del telefono ma non sono riuscito a pagarla. Mi sono accorto troppo tardi di non avere abbastanza contanti nel portafoglio. 4 Venerdì pomeriggio avevo intenzione di prenotare le vacanze per l'estate ma non sono riuscito ad andare all'agenzia di viaggi. Ho cominciato a leggere un libro molto interessante e mi sono dimenticato di uscire.

Comprehension 2   1 She is ambivalent about it. Sometimes she thinks she would enjoy it, but often she wishes she didn't work. This happens particularly when her daughter seems to be needing her a lot.

2 That by working she is missing the best years of her family life. She means, really, of her daughter. **3** They all find it difficult to combine work and family. Work makes big demands on them and yet their families too have needs they cannot ignore. **4** Because while recognizing that he shares all the household tasks, she feels this is only right, it is the duty of any married person. **5 Non c'è scelta.** *There is no choice.* In other words: they have to share in the household tasks. **6** They do the shopping, they leave the bathroom tidy, they look after the children, take them to the park, fetch them from swimming (lessons), etc. **7** Her sister does not work outside the home and therefore takes on all aspects of running the house and family. Her brother-in-law does nothing at all at home. But he works very hard – and clearly earns enough to have the luxury of a wife who doesn't work. **8** She herself never worked outside the home but she seems to feel regret. She certainly considers economic independence very important. **9** It seems to be one long round of trying to organize the household (meals for instance) and her daughter's activities. The reference to **la piscina** is a reminder that Italian children tend to have all sorts of lessons and activities outside school. Most schools operate in the mornings only and the afternoons can therefore be devoted to these activities. **10** She would like to 'go back to nature'. Not see anyone, not even wash, certainly not put on make-up, smart suit, high-heeled shoes … She would go cycling, eat simply and just do nothing all day long!

Activity 3   **1** Certe mattine Emanuela non vorrebbe andare a lavorare, <u>sapendo che</u> sua figlia sentirà la sua mancanza. **2** La vita di Emanuela è al momento molto faticosa, <u>dovendo</u> abbinare famiglia e lavoro. **3** <u>Condividendo</u> tutti i lavori domestici con lei, il marito di Emanuela le è di grande aiuto. **4** Certi mariti non si rendono conto che <u>non aiutando</u> in casa danneggiano l'armonia familiare e rendono la vita difficile a sé stessi prima ancora che alla moglie. **5** La maggior parte dei giovani mariti italiani è di sostegno alla moglie <u>lasciando</u> il bagno in ordine, <u>facendo</u> la spesa, <u>guardando</u> i bambini, <u>portandoli</u> al parco, <u>andando</u> a prenderli in piscina. *or* <u>andandoli</u> a prendere in piscina. **6** <u>Non dovendo</u> lavorare fuori casa, mia sorella ha molto più tempo di me per badare alla casa e alla famiglia.

Activity 4   **1** resistente **2** assordante **3** pesante **4** attaccante **5** aderente **6** deludente **7** trafficante **8** presidente.

Activity 5   **1** Che cosa fa il giornalista? **2** Chi è il fruttivendolo? **3** Chi è l'idraulico? **4** Che cosa fa il pianista? **5** Che cosa fa un pittore?

Activity 6   **1** Non preoccuparti. La porto io. **2** Non preoccuparti. La preparo io. **3** Non preoccuparti. (Te) le spedisco io. **4** Non preoccuparti. Ci vado io. (La faccio io).

Activity 7   (Note: a hyphen indicates the pronoun is attached to the preceding word) **A** (1) lei (2) le (3) le (4) loro (5) lui (6) -le (7) lei (8) -la **B** (1) la (2) lei (3) -le (4) -le (5) lui (6) -la (7) lui (8) lei (9) lui (10) -la. **C** (1) Si (2) si (3) si (4) si (5) loro (6) si

Activity 8   Here is a possible letter. Gentile Direttore, Ho letto recentemente un articolo pubblicato sul Suo quotidiano, in cui si diceva che gli uomini italiani della nuova generazione non sono più come i loro padri e i loro nonni, e che le giovani mogli italiane hanno di fronte a loro un futuro molto più roseo di quello che potevano aspettarsi le loro madri (e le loro nonne). Fosse vero! Sono una donna di quarant'anni, sposata da dodici e con figli adolescenti. Ho scelto di rinunciare alla mia carriera per occuparmi della famiglia, e per evitare di lavorare otto ore fuori casa e altrettante in casa tutti i giorni della settimana ... Io **non penso che** gli uomini italiani **stiano** cambiando, anzi. **Credo che** i giovani uomini italiani **crescano** ancora più viziati e coccolati di una volta, perché spesso sono figli unigeniti. **Ho l'impressione che** i loro genitori (e in particolare le madri) non li **educhino** per nulla all'indipendenza e all'autosufficienza, e che anzi li **proteggano** e li **aiutino** in maniera quasi ridicola. **Dubito che** le madri dei giovani uomini italiani **abbiano insegnato** loro a stirare, a lavare i piatti, a cucinare e a passare l'aspirapolvere. E sono sicura che quelli più 'avventurosi' che hanno scelto di lasciare la famiglia e di andare a vivere da soli ... sono sicura che il sabato e la domenica portano alla mamma la biancheria sporca perché gli faccia il bucato!
Non credo che gli uomini italiani **siano cambiati**, né che cambieranno mai!

Comprehension 3   **1** She tried to guarantee a certain level of income so as to be able to do the things she was used to and at the same time keep alive and well her relationship with her daughters. She thinks, looking back, that she did succeed.
2 She herself made many sacrifices; and she regrets now that perhaps she should have forgone certain material things in favour of an hour or two more with her daughters. But she wonders whether, if they had forgone certain possessions, their relationship would have been as beautiful as it has been. She doesn't know.
3 She thinks the important thing is not necessarily feeding the children, catering to their physical needs, but the time spent with them. But she thinks being with your children all the time is not necessarily best. What is important is to be completely available to respond to their needs for a certain amount of time each day, and this may only be for three hours. Not all mothers can be with their children 24 hours a day and remain patient, available ... **4** They have the same problems as she had. For nine hours a day they don't see their children. **5** Being separated from the children's father. She felt guilty about this. **6** She thinks she was the sort who was a better mother for being with her children less, but available to them fully at certain times. She doesn't think she would have been able to be patient etc. had she been at home all the time.

Activity 9   **1** le donne riescano più degli uomini. **2** su 1000 femmine con la licenza media, 160 arrivino alla laurea contro appena 107 maschi. **3** la presenza femminile sia davvero ridotta nei luoghi in cui si decide. **4** nell'università le donne raggiungano l'11,1 per cento dei professori ordinari. **5** il tasso di disoccupazione femminile oscilli ....

Activity 10   1 Le chiavi di casa, ce le ho? Sì, ce le ho. 2 Gli appunti per il convegno, ce li ho? Sì, ce li ho. 3 L'indirizzo dell'albergo, ce l'ho? Sì, ce l'ho. 4 Il telefonino, ce l'ho? Sì, ce l'ho. 5 La patente, ce l'ho? Sì, ce l'ho. 6 Gli occhiali, ce li ho? Sì, ce li ho. 7 L'agendina, ce l'ho? Sì, ce l'ho. 8 Le pastiglie per il mal di testa, ce le ho? Sì, ce le ho.

Comprehension 4   1 At the fairs where he worked there was an organization promoting rice. He was able to get a good supply of rice at promotional prices and by eating rice at all meals, he was able to make ends meet. 2 He sees himself as having been lucky in two ways: he has always worked in easy markets and he has always succeeded people who were either incompetent or not very hardworking, a bit lazy. 3 He was a manager by the age of 28 and he points out that in those days this was important, quite something! 4 He thought the firm would exploit him for what they could get from him and then jettison him. 5 Because he learned an enormous amount: to be tough, to do demeaning jobs when necessary, to face up to responsibility. **Sporcarsi le mani** means *to do things beneath one's status*. 6 It was his first experience as an entrepreneur – we learn later that he enjoys that, when he implies that he got less enjoyment from his work when Cinzano was bought out by a multinational. And he obviously enjoyed being in an area where there were many Italian and German immigrants, and where good wine was produced; perhaps the vineyards were planted by the immigrants. 7 He was running a company and was able to expand it at quite a remarkable rate: from 50 employees to 180 in about a year, with three new products which he also exported. 8 They didn't particularly enjoy the 'rich man's' lifestyle. And they obviously worried about their children coming to take it for granted. 9 Because he took over from someone who was all show, not a reliable worker; and also because it was a time when he could easily expand his company's market, with a number of events in Spain drawing visitors from over the world. (Cinzano produces and sells alcoholic drinks. Its fame rests on vermouth: wine with a high alcohol content, infused with herbs. A speciality of Piemonte, Carlo's home region.) 10 Because they have given him very clear instructions; and probably too because these instructions leave all the responsibility in his hands. If he succeeds, fine; if he fails, he is out! 11 Stock is the first company he has worked for which was not prospering. By the time the present owners took over, it was in serious difficulties and his first task for them was to restructure, which meant reducing the labour force. The restructuring was not covered in the interview but we know that he is proud of the way he did it, in collaboration with the unions, trying to make sure that each worker made redundant was in a position to go forward in his/her life. This was helped by a generous financial allowance from the German shareholders to make that possible. He was at the time of the interview embarking on more restructuring, but this time by deals with multinationals to share products and markets – if we understood correctly; it was not entirely clear! 12 Our impression during the interview was of a man who enjoys his work; who is very competitive

– or at least certainly was as a young man; who is modest about his successes, saying they came easily; who knows how to seize opportunities; who tends to turn everything positively, an optimist who gets the most out of situations; who enjoys a challenge – for instance he is clearly pleased to be given a free hand to try to turn his company round. He gives the impression of being at peace with himself, a confident man, in charge of his life. He is also a 'family man'. His family means a lot to him, witness his decision to leave a very comfortable position rather than allow his children to be spoilt by having life too easy.

Unit 8

Comprehension: Readings 1 and 2   1 It seems to lie in the fact that the first article counted not only Italians currently active in voluntary work but also those who had done such work in the past. This gave a figure of nearly 9 million, 18.1% of the population over the age of 15. The second figure in the first article is of those who had done some sort of voluntary work in the previous 12 months, presumably up to June 1998. This gave a figure of 3,900,000 people. In the second article on the other hand, the figure was for 1997. And the second paragraph implies that those who were counted were those who had given at least 5½ hours of their time a week. The figure given was 5,397,000. **2 Sociale** would probably mean helping the less fortunate; **civile** is more likely to be environmental work or help in natural disasters. They would inevitably overlap. 3 It would seem not. The second article concludes by saying the statistic falls within the European average: **un dato nella media con i paesi europei.**

Activity 1   1 fossi 2 avesse 3 dicessi 4 chiedesse 5 scoprisse 6 passasse 7 fossi, avessi, scoprissi 8 fossero, stesse 9 desse 10 avessimo, dovessimo

Comprehension: Interview 1   1 They helped the old people with various bureaucratic procedures, went with them to the optician to buy glasses, the orthopaedic doctor, etc. 2 They did it largely for fun, to be together. 3 She met her husband in this group.

Activity 2   1 a. sediona b. sedia c. sediolina 2 a. ciotolona b. ciotola c. ciotolina *or* ciotoletta 3 a. lettone b. letto c. lettino. It is usual to use -**ona**, rather than -**one**, with the feminine words above. We said the whole business was difficult for non-Italians. Don't worry! You'll be understood.

Activity 3   (a) <u>Not modified by suffixes</u> (some of these, e.g. cassetto, probably originated as a modified word but are not viewed as such nowadays): 1 *drawer* (the diminutive is **cassettino** *small drawer*) 2 *turkey*, the large edible bird (the diminutive of **tacco** *heel* is **tacchetto**). 4 *fillet*, as in fillet steak, a fillet of sole. 6 *hood*, as worn by some monks, for instance. Sometimes barmen call a cappuccino **cappuccio**, possibly making the assumption **cappuccino** is a diminutive of cappuccio, whereas it is more likely the name comes from the colour of the milky coffee which is the same as that of the habits of Capuchin monks. 7 a type of bread. (b) <u>Modified by suffixes</u>: 3 *really dreadful day* (giornata + -accia.) 5 *puppy, dear little dog* (cane + -olino) 8 *a little house* (casa + etta).

Comprehension: Interview 2

1 The Gruppo Mio was formed when some friends spent a retreat day together and decided not just to meet as a group of friends but to do something for others, for those in need, both in the locality where they live and beyond, wherever help was most needed. 2 They do a number of things: (a) they are part of a missionary group and help support the work of a leprosy hospital in Brazil. They do this in two ways: largely by raising funds and collecting medicines to send; the funds are raised by collecting waste paper, metal and rags; by selling handicraft work and talking to schools about the work; by holding charity events (the interview was conducted in a room off the new, main church in Moriondo, while in the background were the sounds of a spirited rehearsal in the church of a musical, *Joseph and his Amazing Multicoloured Dreamcoat*, to be performed to raise funds); and also some members of the group have gone out to Brazil to help personally in the work of the hospital. (b) they help in strictly church activities such as providing music at mass; (c) they run the Sunday School and more recently have also started a Saturday club for local children; (d) they run a two week summer activity programme for local children; (e) they run a summer camp for local children in the mountains; (f) they visit an old people's home on Saturday afternoons and spend time with the old people, trying to cheer up those who are sad and lonely. 3 Their motivation lies partly in their religious faith, but they also enjoy the friendship of the group – perhaps that was the first motivator. They also seem aware of the way they have been helped by the group, the enjoyment and fulfilment it has given them and they want the younger generations to share this too.

Activity 4

Riccardo: the use of <u>questo</u> when really the definite article would do; **hanno avuto <u>un po'</u> questa proposta …; questa voglia dentro ognuno <u>così</u> di noi …;** perhaps the use of <u>quindi</u>; certainly his repetitions or rephrasing of the same or a similar idea. There is much 'redundancy' in what he says, a feature of spoken language, saying more than is strictly necessary, which actually helps the listener get the general gist without too much effort. Antonella: <u>diciamo che</u> **il nostro gruppo è un gruppo un po' strano, <u>no</u>?** The no? at the end of a phrase is frequent in certain people's speech. There is much redundancy in what Antonella says, too. Monica: **Noi ci raduniamo lunedì sera <u>appunto</u> intorno alle nove <u>così e, niente</u>, programmiamo <u>un pochino</u> l'attività …:** così e, niente, has really no meaning (we have already drawn attention to this frequent use of **niente** in speech); **appunto** and **un pochino** add little to the meaning and are all part of the redundancy. Monica also adds **no?** to phrases.

Activity 5

1 siano; 2 sembri; possano; 3 abbia; 4 esistano; 5 giochi; 6 risultino.

Comprehension: Interview 3   1 Because she was moved by the desperate conditions of the lives of Kurdish refugees in Switzerland. 2 Murder. 3 A Turk, another immigrant. We assume readers will be aware of the relations between the Turks and the Kurds in Turkey and also know that the death sentence (question 4) may well have been imposed for actions which elsewhere would not be considered worthy of punishment, let alone such punishment. 4 He was under sentence of death in Turkey. Moreover he had a young wife and a baby daughter. 5 He provided a chauffeur and a car to go and collect the man from the prison where he was being held, and a psychologist to go to help cope with any problems the man might be facing as a result of what he had been through. 6 She had to look after the man since the city of Bologna could not take on that responsibility. 7 A convent, where the nuns had never before had a man as a guest. As a result, the nuns started to support the cause of the Kurds.

Activity 6   You should have changed all the perfects to the past definite. The imperfects should have remained unchanged. Both the perfect and the past definite are for events. The imperfect does its jobs (see Unit 4) alongside both. 1 splendeva; 2 tornarono; 3 decisero; 4 era; 5 combattevano; 6 sapevano; 7 dovevano; 8 erano; 9 pascolavano; 10 giocavano; 11 sentirono; 12 si buttarono; 13 arrivarono; 14 avevano; 15 volevano; 16 disse; 17 sparavano; 18 sparavano; 19 erano; 20 presero; 21 finì; 22 andarono; 23 era; 24 uscirono; 25 erano; 26 tornarono; 27 decisero.

Comprehension: Reading 3   1 They freed from water, mud and oil the streets, the books in the National Library, paintings, the objects on display in the Archaeological Museum, the monuments of the city. Once the immediate emergency was past, they worked on the restoration of the works of art damaged by the mud. 2 To commit oneself personally to voluntary work, particularly, one imagines, to work for the environment. 3 In the first paragraph he refers to the **dissesto idrogeologico che tuttora, in misura sempre maggiore, interessa l'intero bacino dell'Arno e non solo quello.** *The hydrogeological mess which even now still threatens the Arno basin and not only that!* He sees flooding almost as a fact of life, although he implies it need not be so if only more were done to prevent it. At the end of the passage he says a number of things (neglect, uncontrolled building) make the art and natural treasures of Italy very fragile: (this flood and the many which have followed it) **hanno dimostrato come l'incuria, la cementificazione selvaggia e spesso abusiva del territorio, il conseguente dissesto idrogeologico rendano estremamente fragile il tesoro d'arte e natura che possediamo.**

Italian–English glossary

This glossary is selective. The meaning given is the one relevant to the texts in this book. Words easily guessable (e.g. **descrizione**) are not included nor are words which are almost certain to be known from basic courses. Gender is indicated for nouns not ending in -**o** or -**a**; the feminine of adjectives is given where is it different from the masculine. Where a verb has an irregular past participle, it is given.

Abbreviations: n = noun; v = verb, adj = adjective, adv = adverb, m = masculine, f = feminine, s = singular, pl = plural. (These are indicated only to avoid ambiguity.) A vowel underlined indicates that the syllable is stressed, either because the stress is irregular or because the student might be unsure about stress (e.g. in nouns ending in -**io**).

abbacchio *roast lamb*
a mio agio *at (my) ease*
abbastanza *fairly*
abbinare *to combine*
abusivo/a *illegal*
accendere (acceso) *to turn on (appliance); to light (fire)*
accingersi a (accinto) *to get ready to*
accogliere (accolto) *to receive, to welcome*
accorgersi (accorto) to realize
accorrere (accorso) *to run to help*
aconfessionale *not linked to a church*
acquisti (m.pl) *purchases*
adatto/a *suitable*
addirittura *downright, frankly*

addormentarsi *to fall asleep*
adeguato/a *right, fitting*
adoperare *to use*
affari (m.pl) (s: affare) *business*
affidabile *to be trusted*
affinché *so that*
affittare *to rent*
affrontare *face up to*
aggiornato/a *brought up to date*
aggirarsi *to be approximately*
aggiungere (aggiunto) *to add*
aggraziato/a *graceful*
aggregarsi *to get together*
agguerrito/a *ready for war*
ahimè! *alas!*
aiuto *help*
al di là di *beyond, on the other side of*
allegria *happiness*

allegro/a *happy*
allestimento *preparation*
alloggio *lodging*
alluvione (f) *flood*
almeno *at least*
alto/a *tall, high*
altro/a *other*
alzarsi *to get up*
ambiente *environment*
(nell') ambito di *in the confines/compass of*
amicizia *friendship*
ampliamento *enlargement, expansion*
andare in giro *to go around and about*
anelito *strong desire*
anguilla *eel*
annoiarsi *to be bored*
anzi *indeed, on the contrary, or rather*
anzi che, anziché *rather than*
anziano/a (n or adj) *elderly person; elderly*
appartenenza *ownership*
appartenere a *to belong to*
appena *scarcely, only just*
appendere (appeso) *to hang*
appunto *precisely*
aprire (aperto) *to open*
aquila *eagle*
argine (m) *bank (of river)*
arrangiarsi *to get by, to manage*
arredo *furnishing*
arretrato/a *backward*
arrossire *to turn red, to blush*
artigianale *belonging to/produced by a craftsman*
ascensore *lift, elevator*
ascoltare *to listen to*
asilo nido *day nursery*
aspettare *to wait for*
aspettarsi *to expect*
aspirapolvere (m) *vacuum cleaner, hoover*
assegno *cheque*
assolvere (assolto) *to find not guilty*
assomigliare a *to resemble, to take after*

assumere (assunto) *to take on, to appoint (staff)*
attaccapanni (m) *coat-hanger*
attaccare discorso *to strike up a conversation*
atteggiamento *attitude*
attenersi a *to abide by*
attirare *to attract*
aula *classroom*
autista *chauffeur, driver*
avvenire (m) *future*
avvicinare *to come close to*
azienda *company, firm*
azionista (m or f) *shareholder*

bacino *basin (of river)*
ballare *to dance*
banchetto *stall*
barattare *to barter, to exchange, to trade*
battere uno scontrino *to key a sum into the till to generate the receipt*
benché *although*
benedizione (f) *benediction (a church service)*
biblioteca *library*
bisnonno/a *great grandfather/mother*
bolletta *bill (for utilities, items consumed before payment)*
bonaccione *easy-going, goodnatured*
bottega *workshop (of craftsman)*
(a) braccetto *arm in arm*
braccio *arm*
bravura *skill, ability*
bruscamente *suddenly*
brutto/a *ugly, nasty*
buffone *joker, jester*
bugia; dire bugie *lie, fib; to lie*
buttare *to throw*
buttarsi *to throw oneself*

calcio *football, soccer*
calo (in) *declining*
camerino *dressing room (theatre)*
camicetta *blouse*
camicia da notte *nightdress*

camminare *to walk*

campagna *country (as opposed to town)*, *countryside*

campana *bell (of church, for instance)*

campanello *doorbell*

campo *field*

cantante (m or f) *singer*

cantina *cellar*

canzone (f) *song*

capo *boss, person in charge*; also: *item of clothing, garment*

Capodanno *New Year*

capoluogo *main town, capital*

cappotto *overcoat*

carica *office*

carne (f) *meat*

carrello *supermarket trolley*

carta *paper*

castani (m.pl form) *chestnut (of hair)*; *hazel (of eyes)*

catena *chain*

cattiveria *nastiness*

cattivo/a *bad, naughty*

cena *supper*

cera *wax, wax polish*

cercare *to seek, to look for, to try*

cerniera *zip fastener*

chiacchierare *to chat, chatter*

chiarezza *clarity*

chiedere (chiesto) *to ask*

chiesa *church*

chiudere (chiuso) *to close*

ciascuno/a *each, each one*

cibo *food*

cieco/a *blind*

cifra *figure*

ciliegia *cherry*

cintura *belt*

circa *about*

circo *circus*

clima (m) *climate*

coda *queue*

coetaneo/a *of the same age*

cognato/a *brother/sister-in-law*

cognome (m) *surname*

coinvolgere (coinvolto) *to involve*

colazione (f) *breakfast*

collettino *little collar*

colpa *fault, blame*

commettere (commesso) *to commit*

commistione (f) (unusual) *mixture*

commuovere (commosso) *to move (emotionally)*

comodità *'mod. cons.', convenience*

compagno/a (n) *partner*

comperare, comprare *to buy*

compiere gli anni *to have a birthday*

compleanno *birthday*

comportarsi *to behave*

comprare *to buy*

comprendere *to comprise, to take in*

comunque *however*

concorrenza *competition*

condividere (condiviso) *to share*

condurre (condotto) *to lead*

confezione (f) *tailoring, dressmaking*

confine (m) *frontier*

coniglio *rabbit*

coniuge (m or f) *spouse (husband or wife)*

conoscere *to know, to be acquainted with (person or place)*

consegnare *to hand over, to deliver*

contadino *peasant farmer*

contanti (m.pl) *cash*

controllare *to check*

convegno *conference*

coprire (coperto) *to cover*

correre (corso) *to run, to race*

corriera *country bus, mail bus*

corriere *carrier (of goods)*

cosa *thing*

così *so, thus*

cosiddetto/a *so-called*

cospargere (cosparso) *to sprinkle, to strew*

costeggiare *to be alongside*

costruire (costruito) *to build, to construct*

crescere *to grow*
crescita *growth*
cucinare *to cook*
cucito *sewing*
cuciture (f.pl) *stitches, seams*
cuoco *cook*
cuoio *leather*
cuore (m) *heart*

danneggiare *to damage, to cause harm to*
dappertutto *everywhere*
datore (m) di lavoro *employer*
decidere (deciso) *to decide*
deficiente *stupid*
degno/a *worthy*
dente (m) *tooth*
dentro *inside*
destinatario *addressee, recipient*
diapositiva *colour slide*
difetto *defect*
diffuso/a *widespread*
dimagrire *to lose weight*
dimenticarsi *to forget*
diminuire *to decrease*
(i) dintorni *the surrounding area*
dipendente (m or f) *employee*
dipingere (dipinto) *to paint*
direttore generale *general manager*
dirigere (diretto) *to direct, to manage, to be in charge of*
(a) disagio *not at ease, uncomfortable*
disatteso/a *not heeded*
discapito *detriment*
discutere (discusso) *to discuss*
disegnare *to draw*
disegno *drawing*
disponibile *available*
ditta *firm*
divario *variation, discrepancy, difference*
divenire (divenuto) *to become*
diventare *to become*
diverso/a *different*
dolce (m) *pudding, sweet*
domare *to control*
domatore (m) *tamer*

dote (f) *gift, natural quality*
dovere (n.m) *duty*
dovere (v) *to have to*

economie (f.pl) *savings*
edilizia *building trade/industry*
ente (f.) *organisation, bureau (usually public)*
entrarci; non c'entra *to come into it, to be relevant; it is nothing to do with …*
entro; entro sabato *by (with expression of time); by Saturday*
equo/a *fair, equitable*
esempio *example*
esercito *army*
esigenza *demand, necessity, need*
esilio *exile*
esplicitezza *explicitness*
estate (f) *summer*
(all') estero *abroad*
estivo/a *summer, summery*
estraneo/a *outsider, who does not belong*
età (f) *age*

fabbrica *factory*
facile *easy*
facoltativo/a *optional*
fango *mud*
fantasia *imagination*
fare finta di *to pretend to*
fare parte di *to belong to, to be a member of*
farmaci *pharmaceuticals*
fatica *effort*
faticare *to have difficulty, to work hard to*
faticoso/a *needing a lot of effort, tiring*
fattoria *farm*
felice *happy*
ferie (f.pl) *paid holidays*
ferire *to wound*
ferito/a *wounded, hurt*
ferro *iron*
festa *party*
festeggiare *to celebrate*

fianchi (m.pl) *hips*
fiera *trade fair, market, show*
filiale (f) *branch (of business)*
fiore (m) *flower*
fiume (m) *river*
fonte (f) *source*
forse *perhaps*
fosso *ditch*
fotomodella *the model
(photographed wearing the
designer's clothes)*
frainteso/a *misunderstood,
misinterpreted*
francese *French*
(nel) frattempo *(in the)
meanwhile*
fresco/a *cool*
frittata *omelette*
funzionare *to work*
fuori *outside*

gatto *cat*
gemma *gem, jewel*
genere (m) *kind, sort*
(in) genere *generally*
genero/nuora *son/daughter-in-law*
genitore *father or mother*
gente (f.s) *people*
gergo *jargon*
gestione (f) *management*
gestire *to manage*
giardinaggio *gardening*
giardino *garden*
ginocchio *knee*
giocare *to play*
giocattolo *toy*
giocoliere (m) *juggler*
giornale (m) *newspaper*
giovane *young*
(nel) giro di poco tempo *in a
short time*
gonna *skirt*
gradino *step, rung (of ladder)*
grana *irritation, problem*
(non) granché *not very*
guadagnare *to earn*
guadagni (m.pl) *earnings*
guardare *to look (at)*
guarire *to get better (from an

illness)*
guasto/a *out of order, broken*
guerra *war*
guidare *to drive*

idraulico *plumber*
igiene (f) *hygiene, public health*
imbastire *to tack*
imbustare *to put into a (plastic)
bag/into an envelope)*
impallidire *to turn pale*
imparare *to learn*
impegno *commitment,
engagement*
impiegato/a *office worker,
employee*
impresa *enterprise*
(all') improvviso *suddenly*
in attesa di *waiting to/for*
in fondo a *in the depths of, at
the bottom of*
incentivare *to stimulate*
incubo *nightmare*
incuria *carelessness, indifference*
indossare *to wear, to put on
(clothing)*
indumento *garment, clothing*
infatti *indeed*
ingrandire *to enlarge*
ingrassare *to get fat, to put on
weight*
iniziare *to begin*
inizio *beginning*
innanzitutto *first of all*
insediamento *establishment,
setting up*
insegnante (m or f) *teacher*
insegnare *to teach*
insieme, insieme a *together,
together with*
insomma *in short, in conclusion*
instancabilmente *tirelessly*
intendere (inteso) *to understand*
intreccio *interlacing*
introdurre (introdotto) *to
introduce*
inutile *useless, pointless*
invecchiare *to grow old, to age*
invece *on the other hand, instead*

inverno *winter*
istituire *to set up*
istruito/a *educated*

laboratorio *workshop*
lamentarsi *to complain*
lasciare *to leave, to let*
latte (m) *milk*
lebbrosario *a leper hospital*
legare *to tie, to tie up*
legge (f) *law*
leggere *to read*
leggero/a *flighty*
legno *wood*
lento/a *slow*
letto *bed*
lettore (m), lettrice (f) *reader*
libero/a *free*
libreria *bookshop*
libro *book*
licenziare *to dismiss, to sack, to fire*
ligio/a *loyal, true*
lingua *language*
lirico/a; teatro lirico *opera; opera house*
litigioso/a *quarrelsome*
locale (m) *premises*
lucidare *to polish*
luna *moon*
lutto *mourning*

macchia *spot*
macchina *car*
magari *maybe, perhaps*
magazzino *warehouse*
magistero *teaching*
(lavorare a) maglia *to knit*
maglieria *knitware factory*
maglietta *lightweight sweater, jumper*
mai *never*
mal di schiena *backache*
mal di testa *headache*
malattia *illness*
mancare *to be missing, to pass away*
marito *husband*
materia *(school) subject*

media (n) *average*
medio/a; scuola media *average; middle school*
medioevo *Middle Ages*
meno *less, minus*
meridionale *southern*
messa *mass*
mestiere *skill*
metà (n.f); metà agosto *half; mid August, half way through August*
mettere (messo) *to put*
mettersi a *to begin to*
mezzo *half*
migliorare *to get better*
modelli *patterns*
modo; a modo mio; modo giusto *way; (in) my way; right way*
moglie (f) *wife*
molla *spring, trigger*
molto (adv) *very, a lot*
molto/a/i/e *much, a lot of*
mondo *world*
morire (morto) *to die*
morte (f) *death*
mostra *exhibition*
motivo *reason*
motorino *motor scooter*
mungere (munto) *to milk (animal)*
muoversi (mosso) *to move*
mura (f.pl) *walls (outer, defensive walls)*
museo *art gallery, museum*
mutevole *changeable*

nascere (nato) *to be born*
nascita *birth*
neanche *not even*
negozio *shop*
nemico *enemy*
neve (f) *snow*
nido *nest*
niente *nothing*
nonno/a *grandfather/mother*
nonostante *in spite of the fact that*
noto/a *known, well-known*
nubile *unmarried woman*

nulla *nothing*
nuotare *to swim*

obbligo *obligation*
oca *goose*
occasione (f) *opportunity*
occuparsi di *to take care of, to look after*
odiare *to hate*
ogni *each, every*
oltre *beyond, more than*
onda di piena *wave of flood water*
opera *work*
oppure *or*
ordine (m) *order*
orgoglioso/a *proud*
ormai *now*
ospitare *to give hospitality to*
ospite (m or f) *guest*
ospizio *old people's home*
ottenere *to obtain*
ovunque *everywhere, anywhere*

paese (m) *village; country, nation*
pagare *to pay*
palestra *gym*
pallottola *bullet*
panchina *bench*
pantaloni (m.pl) *trousers*
parametro *parameter*
parecchio/a *quite a lot*
parecchi/ie *several*
parente (m or f) *relation*
parere (parso) *to seem*
parete (f) *wall (of house)*
parola *word*
parole incrociate *crossword puzzle*
parrocchia *parish*
partigiano/a *partisan*
partire *to depart, to leave*
partita *match (e.g. soccer match)*
pascolare *to graze*
passaggio *a lift (in a car)*
passeggiata *walk*
pasto *meal*
patria *homeland, fatherland, mother country*

pausa pranzo *lunch break*
pavimento *floor*
pecora *sheep*
peggiorare *to get worse*
pendolare (m or f) *commuter*
per via di *on account of*
perché + indicative *because; why*
perché + subjunctive *so that*
perciò *therefore*
perdere (perduto or perso) *to lose; (of tap) to leak*
perfino *even*
perlustrare *to search (a place)*
permesso di soggiorno *residence permit*
permettere (permesso) *to allow*
però *however*
perseguitare *to persecute*
pesare *to weigh*
pescare *to fish*
pesce (m) *fish*
piacere (n.m) *pleasure*
piacere (v) *to be pleasing*
piacevole *pleasant*
pigliare *to catch, to take*
pilastro *pillar, core product*
piovere *to rain, to be raining*
pittura *painting*
più *more, plus*
piuttosto *rather, fairly*
politica *politics; policy*
porre (posto) *to place*
portafoglio (m) *wallet*
posato/a *poised, sedate*
posto *place*
posto di lavoro *job; also: workplace*
potenza *power, capacity*
potere (n.m) *power*
potere (v) *to be able to*
pranzo *dinner, main meal*
pratica – fare pratica *to practise*
precipitarsi *to rush*
preferire *to prefer*
pregio *a good point, quality*
premio *prize*
prendere (preso) *to take*
prendere in giro *to tease*
presentare *to introduce*

presso *at the premises of*
prestare *to lend*
prestarsi *to lend itself*
presto *early*
pretendere (preteso) *to expect, to demand*
prevedere (previsto) *to foresee, to make provision for*
preventivo *estimate*
prima che *before*
(il) primo *the first course of an Italian meal is the pasta/risotto course; meat comes in the second course*
problematiche (f.pl) *range of problems*
prodigarsi *to devote oneself to*
prodotto *product*
promuovere (promosso) *to promote*
pronto/a *ready*
propenso/a a *inclined to/towards*
proporre (proposto) *to propose*
proprio (adv) *really*
proseguire *to continue*
prova *trial*
provare *to try*
pulire *to clean*
pulizia *cleaning*
purtroppo *unfortunately*

(a) quadri *checked*
qualcheduno, qualcuno *someone*
qualcosa *something*
qualora *if, in case*
qualsiasi *any, no matter which*
qualunque *any, any whatever*
quasi *almost*
quotidiano/a *daily*

raccolta *collection*
raccontare *to tell (a story)*
radunarsi *to meet, to get together*
(a) ragione *rightly*
(avere) ragione *to be right*
ragioniere *book-keeper, accountant*
rallentare *to slow down*
rapporto *relationship*

rassegnarsi *to resign oneself*
reddito *income*
registrato/a *recorded*
reperto *object in a collection*
resistere *to hold out, to endure*
restare *to remain*
restituire *to hand back*
retribuire *to remunerate, to recompense*
ricavato *proceeds*
riconoscere *to recognize*
ricordarsi *to remember*
ridere (riso) *to laugh*
rientrare *to be within*
rifiutare *to refuse*
rimanere (rimasto) *to remain*
rimetterci (rimesso) *to lose*
rimpianto *regret*
rincarare *to get expensive*
rincorsa *run-up*
rintracciare *trace*
riprendere (ripreso) *to take up again*
risparmiare *to save*
rispetto a *compared with*
rispondere (risposto) *to answer*
ristrettezza *poverty*
ristrutturare *to modernize, to rebuild*
ristrutturazione (f) *re-building*
ritenere *to consider, to maintain*
ritenersi *to consider oneself*
ritmo *rhythm*
riunione (f) *meeting*
riuscire a *to succeed in, to manage to*
riva *bank (of river)*
rivista *magazine*
romanico/a *romanesque*
romanzo *novel*
rompere (rotto) *to break*
ronzare *to hum*
rotolo *roll*
rovinare *to ruin*
rubacchiare *to pilfer*
rubinetto *tap*
ruscello *stream*

sacerdote (m) *priest*

saggio *essay*
sala da ballo *dance hall*
salvaguardare *to safeguard*
sangue (m) *blood*
sanità *health*, (colloquially)
  health service
sapere *to know (a fact)*
saponetta *bar of soap*
sbagliare *to make a mistake*
sbocco *outlet, opening*
scappare *to run away*
scattare *to go off (of an alarm)*
scavare *to dig out, to excavate*
scegliere (scelto) *to choose*
scelta *choice*
scemo/a *silly, stupid, half-witted*
scherzare *to make jokes*
scherzo *joke*
schiacciare *to press, to squash*
sciagurato/a *wretched*
sciolto/a *fluent*
scomodare *to make
  uncomfortable*
sconosciuto/a *unknown*
scontentare *to make unhappy*
scontrino *receipt*
scontro *clash*
scopo *aim, purpose*
senza scopo di lucro *not for
  profit, charitable*
scoppiare *to explode; (war) to
  break out*
scoprire (scoperto) *to uncover, to
  discover*
scorso/a *last (i.e. one just
  finished)*
scrittore (m), scrittrice (f) *writer*
scrivere (scritto) *to write*
sebbene *although*
secondo *according to*
sede (f) *head office*
sedere, sedersi *to sit*
seggio, seggiolino *seat, little seat*
seguire *to follow*
selvaggio/a *uncivilized, ferocious*
seminare *to sow (seed)*
sentire *to hear, to feel*
senz'altro *without a doubt, of
  course*

servire *to be helpful, to be useful*
settentrionale *northern*
settimana *week*
sforzo *effort*
sfruttare *to exploit*
sgraziato/a *ungainly*
siccome *since, for the reason that*
sicuramente *undoubtedly,
  certainly*
sicuro/a; di sicuro *sure,
  confident; definitely, certainly*
sigla *acronym*
sindacale *related to trades unions*
sinteticamente *in outline, briefly*
sistema (m) *system*
smarrire *to lose, to mislay*
smascherare *to unmask*
smettere (smesso) *to stop, to cease*
soccorrere (soccorso) *to help,
  particularly the sick and
  wounded*
società *company*
soddisfazione (f) *satisfaction*
soffiare *to blow out*
soffitto *ceiling*
soffrire (sofferto) *to suffer*
sogno *dream*
soldi (m.pl) *money*
solito/a; di solito *usual; usually*
(lettera di) sollecito *letter urging
  prompt action*
solo (adv) *only*
solo/a *alone*
sondaggio *survey*
sopralluogo *on-site meeting*
soprattutto *above all*
sopravvivere (sopravvissuto) *to
  survive*
sordo/a *deaf*
sorridere (sorriso) *to smile*
sostenitore (m), sostenitrice (f)
  supporter
spagnolo/a *Spanish*
sparare *to shoot*
sparatoria *burst of gunfire*
sparo *gunshot*
spasso; andare a spasso
  *enjoyment, pleasurable activity;
  to go for a walk*

spaziare *to range*
spedizione (f) *despatch*
spensierato/a *carefree, thoughtless*
sperimentare *to experiment*
spesso *often*
spettacolo *show*
spiacevole *unpleasant*
spingere (spinto) *to push*
splendere *to shine*
sporcare *to dirty*
sposarsi *to get married*
sposo/a *bridegroom/bride*
sputo *spit*
squadra *team*
squattrinato/a *penniless*
stabilire *to establish*
stampa *press*
stanco/a *tired*
stenografia *shorthand*
stentare a *to find it hard to*
stesso/a *same*
stipendio *wage, salary*
stirare *to iron*
stoffa *fabric*
stracci *rags*
straniero/a *foreign*
strapieno/a *very full*
stravincere (stravinto) *more than win* (stra: suffix meaning *extra, over*)
stringere (stretto) *to squeeze*
stufa *stove*
stufo/a *fed up*
stupido/a *stupid*
succedere (successo) *to happen*
suocero/a *father/mother-in-law*
suonare *to play (musical instrument)*
superare *to overcome, to get over, to exceed*
sussidio *subsidy; teaching aid*
svago *amusement, recreation*
svantaggio *disadvantage*
sviluppo *development*
svolgere (svolto) *to carry out*

tacco *heel*
tagliare *to cut*

taglio *cutting, cut*
tailleur *(ladies') suit*
tanto *so much*
tappeto *carpet*
tardi *late*
tartufo *truffle*
tasso *rate*
tedesco/a *German*
tela *canvas*
tema (m) *theme*
temere *to fear*
tempo *time; weather*
tenere *to hold*
tentare *to attempt, to try*
tesoro *treasure; darling*
tessuto *material, fabric*
testimoniare *to bear witness*
tifoso *fan (e.g. soccer fan)*
tirare su *to pull up*
titolare (m or f) *owner*
togliere (tolto) *to take out*
tornare *to go back, to return*
torneo *tournament*
torta *cake*
tra l'altro *by the by*
tradurre (tradotto) *to translate*
traduzione (f) *translation*
tramonto *sunset*
trascorrere (trascorso) *to spend (time)*
trasferirsi *to move (house)*
trattare con *to deal with, to negotiate with*
trattarsi di *to be a question of*
travolgere (travolto) *to sweep away, to overwhelm*
troppo (adv) *too*
troppo/a *too much*
trovare *to find*
truffare *to cheat, swindle*
tuffarsi *to dive in*
turno *session, sitting*
tuttavia *nevertheless, all the same, however*
tuttora *still now*

uscire *to go out, to come out*
utile (adj) *useful*
utile (m) *profit*

utilizzare *to use*
valere (valso/valuto) *to be worth,
  to be valid for, to apply to*
valere la pena *to be worth it*
valigia *suitcase*
vecchiotto/a *aging*
veloce *fast*
verifica *check, inspection*
vespa *wasp*
vestaglia *dressing gown*
vestito *dress; (men's) suit*
vestito/a da *dressed as*
viaggiare *to travel*
vicenda *happening, event*
vicino *near*

vincere (vinto) *to win*
vincolo *chain, fetter*
viso *face*
vistoso/a *showy, very visible*
vita *waist; life*
vivere (vissuto) *to live*
voce (f); ad alta voce *voice; out
  loud*
volere *to want*
volere bene a *to be fond of, to love*
volontà *will*
volta *time, occasion*

zio, zia *uncle, aunt*

index of language points

teach
yourself

world cultures: italy
derek aust & mike zollo

- Are you interested in the story of italy and the Italians?
- Do you want to understand how the country works today?
- Are you planning a visit to Italy or learning Italian?

World Cultures: Italy will give you a basic overview of Italy –
the country, its language, its people and its culture – and will
enrich any visit or course of study. Vocabulary lists and 'Taking
it Further' sections at the end of every unit will equip you to talk
and write confidently about all aspects of Italian life.

Afrikaans
Arabic
Arabic Script, Beginner's
Bengali
Brazilian Portuguese
Bulgarian
Cantonese
Catalan
Chinese
Chinese, Beginner's
Chinese Script, Beginner's
Croatian
Czech
Danish
Dutch
Dutch, Beginner's
Dutch Dictionary
Dutch Grammar
English, American (EFL)
English as a Foreign Language
English, Correct
English Grammar
English Grammar (EFL)
English for International Business
English Vocabulary
Finnish
French
French, Beginner's
French Grammar
French Grammar, Quick Fix
French, Instant
French, Improve your
French Starter Kit
French Verbs
French Vocabulary
Gaelic
Gaelic Dictionary
German
German, Beginner's
German Grammar
German Grammar, Quick Fix
German, Instant

German, Improve your
German Verbs
German Vocabulary
Greek
Greek, Ancient
Greek, Beginner's
Greek, Instant
Greek, New Testament
Greek Script, Beginner's
Gulf Arabic
Hebrew, Biblical
Hindi
Hindi, Beginner's
Hindi Script, Beginner's
Hungarian
Icelandic
Indonesian
Irish
Italian
Italian, Beginner's
Italian Grammar
Italian Grammar, Quick Fix
Italian, Instant
Italian, Improve your
Italian Verbs
Italian Vocabulary
Japanese
Japanese, Beginner's
Japanese, Instant
Japanese Script, Beginner's
Korean
Latin
Latin American Spanish
Latin, Beginner's
Latin Dictionary
Latin Grammar
Nepali
Norwegian
Panjabi
Persian, Modern
Polish
Portuguese

Portuguese, Beginner's
Portuguese Grammar
Portuguese, Instant
Romanian
Russian
Russian, Beginner's
Russian Grammar
Russian, Instant
Russian Script, Beginner's
Sanskrit
Serbian
Spanish
Spanish, Beginner's
Spanish Grammar
Spanish Grammar, Quick Fix
Spanish, Instant
Spanish, Improve your
Spanish Starter Kit
Spanish Verbs
Spanish Vocabulary
Swahili
Swahili Dictionary
Swedish
Tagalog
Teaching English as a Foreign Language
Teaching English One to One
Thai
Turkish
Turkish, Beginner's
Ukrainian
Urdu
Urdu Script, Beginner's
Vietnamese
Welsh
Welsh Dictionary
World Cultures:
  China
  England
  France
  Germany
  Italy
  Japan
  Portugal
  Russia
  Spain
  Wales
Xhosa
Zulu

the A-Z of teach yourself language titles

available from bookshops and on-line retailers